A10

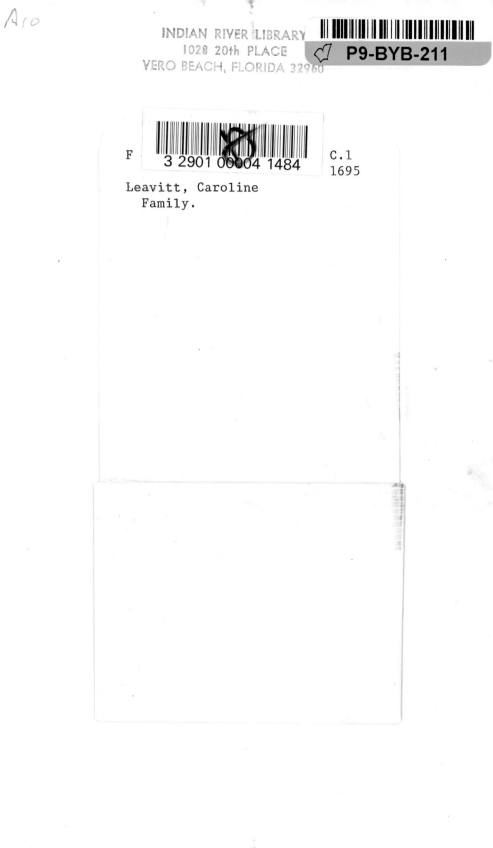

FAMILY

FAMILY

CAROLINE LEAVITT

ARBOR HOUSE ❦ NEW YORK

Manufactured in the United States of America

10 9 8 7 6 5 4 3 2 1

Library of Congress Cataloging-in-Publication Data

Leavitt, Caroline.
  Family.

  I. Title
PS3562.E2617F3 1987 813'.54 87-1817
ISBN 0-87795-904-8

BOH 1H8H

For Steven Zamrin, with love

PREFACE

D
ore told Robin the earliest stories about Nick, starting way before anything Robin's mother had ever revealed. They were stories like confessions, spilling over, stopping only when Dore realized just whom it was she was telling her whole life to. It was all still a puzzle made up of other people's memory, blurred outlines Robin needed to decipher, and when the final pieces came, the heart, they came much later, almost after everything else had happened, but they came from Nick himself. They were given to her like a gift, when she was lying sick across his couch up in Madison, listening only to the mad flutter of the bats trapped in the attic room above her, their crazy bangs and shufflings amplified in the stubborn stillness of the house. But by that time, she had no more reason to disbelieve anything he might say to her, and he . . . well, he had no more reason to lie.

ONE

• • •

In the Fifties, Nick still had family. His father worked steadily in the mills, making enough to go down to South Street every Friday night and get himself good and blitzed and play some back-room poker. There were always guys he knew who were more than willing to take his money, to accept the makeshift IOUs he scribbled on the greasy napkins. He almost always lost everything. Money. His black cowboy boots with the red lizard dappling the sides, the watch his wife had engraved for him for their wedding day, "Helen loves Tom." He stayed in the games until he was kicked out, and then he would slowly wind his way home, feverish, drunkenly roaring out all the geographic songs he could think of, singing to all the places that called to him. Ok-la-ho-ma. San Francisco had his heart, Georgia throbbed in his mind. By the time he flopped back into the heady warmth of his house, his head was reeling.

Helen, waiting up for him, was always angry. He'd scoop her up, making her do a clumsy kind of waltz step with him across the kitchen floor. He'd murmur stories about France to her, how the three of them could live on bread and cheese and all those lights, how they'd have wine with every meal, even Nick. "No wine," Helen said, but he dipped her down low, making her hair flicker under the cheap lamp, and when she tugged away, her face still stubborn, he eased her back, kissing her. "I know you," he said. "You want the ocean. Orange groves. My California baby." He whispered into her hair. "You're drunk, Tom Austen," she said, and he rubbed

1

her back, soothing her until she gave in, resting her head against his shoulder. "You'll wake Nick," she said.

But Nick was almost always awake, standing silently in the hall, his parents dancing so close to him they could almost have touched him. Apart, they paid attention to him. His father taught him how to find the Big Dipper, how to read a Texas road map and find north by the smell in the air. His mother took him to the movies and read his fortune from the tea leaves in a cup. She bought him the Davy Crockett hat he wore everywhere. But when his parents were together, they seemed to see no one else, their hearts became finite. He'd interrupt them sometimes, courting them with his own songs, but Helen just laughed, and Tom continued to sway her against him.

Once, when Nick was really young, when he was feeling most lonely, he had walked into the kitchen the way he had sometimes seen Tom come home, his body jelly-limbed, his mouth open. Tom's face had twisted. Helen had stopped what she was doing, all right, her wood stir spoon lifted, and then she'd taken two swift steps toward him and slapped his face. He pulled back, wounded. He went outside and sat in the high grasses where the grasshoppers bred and buzzed, and when he came back indoors, miserable, they both acted as if nothing were wrong.

They didn't treat him the way his friends' parents treated them. He wasn't called angrily in to supper. He could come in when he wanted. If dinner was too cold, he could make himself peanut butter and marshmallow sandwiches, he could eat the rest of the eggs. He decided what he wanted to eat, and if it was in the house, then he could have it. They didn't worry. He was ten. He was responsible. Tom had made sure Nick could recite his name and address and phone number from the time he could talk. There wasn't much money in the family for choices, but what choices there were, Tom made sure Nick took advantage of. He was always allowed to pick out his own clothing. He favored orange pants in kindergarten, so bright, the other children stared; he went through a phase of bowling shirts; and once, for two months, he wore a baseball uniform he and Helen found at a resale store. He also decided on his punishments: When he drew on the walls, Nick denied himself the snowy picture of the TV; when he was caught ringing doorbells and running, he wouldn't let himself read any of the library books he had taken out. It made him feel strong and proud; it made him adore his parents.

He had one friend, Chuck Raymond, who loved to hang out at Nick's because of the way the house was run. He could go into the bread box for day-old doughnuts the same way Nick did; he could lie on any of the beds and just read. "In my house, every man is king," Tom told him solemnly. "In my house, it's my father," Chuck said.

Chuck lived right across the street. His father was convinced the cold war was about to escalate any second. He didn't trust Eisenhower; president or not, he was sure Ike was just another Communist, many of which, he hinted, were right in the neighborhood. He spent every free moment methodically digging up his driveway, trying to turn it into a fallout shelter. He showed Nick the plans he had drawn up, where the bedrooms would be, how the steel door would be so heavy that no one from the neighborhood would even think of breaking in. Nick and Chuck helped him dig sometimes, and all the while Nick dug, he searched for dinosaur fossils, for evidence of alien spacecraft, but he kept his opinions against his chest, he nodded when Chuck's father waved and pointed at the blueprints.

Chuck's father didn't approve of Nick's parents, and he kept telling Nick that he ought to persuade them to work on a shelter of their own. "I know you're Chuck's pal, but there's just so much room in the shelter," he said apologetically. "And Pittsburgh . . . well, we got your steel, we got your iron—we'll be the first place blasted."

When Nick told that to Tom one evening, when the two of them were watching the sky, Tom laughed. "I can't think of a place more deserving," he said. He hated Pittsburgh. He was always talking about getting out, winning enough money to go someplace quiet and green and pretty. The Pittsburgh Plan, he called it.

When Helen had been pregnant with Nick, she'd stayed cooped up in their hotbox of a house because she had it in her head that the Pittsburgh air would hurt her baby. She had paced the rooms, prowling the house until Tom came home, and then her mouth would wobble and go all runny, and she'd be crying.

"You ought to get out," he said. "Ten minutes never hurt anyone."

But she was a coward. She waited, and then, one cool day, she went out and bought herself a surgical mask. She still stayed inside. She said she was too embarrassed to go outside looking like a scrub nurse, and anyway, who knew what a mask really kept out? When Nick was born, she used the mask on him, covering his bright little face, letting him toddle about in the scrubby backyard. She took him on the bus with her like that, ignoring the frank stares of the other people. But she always took the mask off when Tom came in. He'd tell her she was just giving credence to the bad air; that if she didn't think so hard about it, it wouldn't exist. And then, of course, Nick was old enough to tug the mask off himself, to be hot and embarrassed by it. Even then he had a mind of his own. A mind like Tom's.

It was something Tom had planned. Nick had grown up on Tom's stories. His first books were the colorful travel brochures Tom used to filch from the agencies. Nick would stand up in front of his class, just a small boy with uncombable black hair, in clothing too big for him, the colors mismatched, and tell the class when the best time to go to the beaches in France was, why the summer festivals in Venice were better than those in Spain. He had no idea who Humpty-Dumpty was; he had never read Peter Rabbit, not when Tom was giving him dimes for every foreign fact he could recite, nickels for every capital he could pick out on the frayed map they kept in the kitchen.

And the stars—oh, the stars. Tom would wake Nick up sometimes just to show him Jupiter. He'd walk him about the neighborhood at three in the morning, when it was so clear and cold you could see your breath, and he'd do it just to remind him that everyone else may be sleeping behind locked doors, alarms carefully set, but they two were *alive*. It intoxicated Nick. He'd be so wired, he wouldn't be able to go back to sleep. He'd hear Tom snoring and then he'd get up and get his jacket and he'd walk around the neighborhood himself, just once, before he came back inside to lie down in his bed, to listen to his heart, how hard and fast it was beating, a Morse code he somehow understood.

Every Sunday, Tom went to the library to read the help wanteds in the California papers and the *New York Times*. He applied for everything—clericals, messengers, once even as an animal groomer in San Jose. He made up references, he lied about experience. But for the one position he actually thought he had a shot at—as a foreman in an automotive plant in California—he didn't lie at all.

He wanted that job so badly he couldn't talk about it, not even to Helen, who shared all his secrets. Guilty, he bought her chocolates. For Nick, he found a stray yellow cat. Nick was eleven then, and although he really wanted a dog, any pet was something, and this one, being a stray, had a certain wild romance to it. But when he tried to hug it, the cat swiped at him with needled paws. He had pinprick scratches on both arms, but he thought they looked kind of like tattoos, and he rolled up his sleeves to show them off. He named the cat immediately, trying to make it more his. Shelter, he called it, after the driveway shelter Chuck's father had abruptly abandoned, leaving it inexplicably in rubble for the boys to play war in.

The cat kept out of everyone's way at first. Nick kept trying to make it sleep on his bed, but the only person in the family the cat liked was Tom. Nights, when Tom would sit out on the front porch, watching the stars and worrying, the cat would suddenly settle into his lap. At dinner, it was Tom the cat sat by, washing itself and purring, spreading out to sleep. Nick mashed up his food against the sides of his plate; he thrust pieces of chicken at the cat, who, uninterested, pulled away.

It was a strange animal. It was really more like the dog Nick had wanted. Now, when Tom got up to walk, the cat followed, and when he stopped, the cat stopped, too. He'd test it, walking farther and farther away every night, seeing just when the cat would turn and skulk away. The cat was with him the night he picked up the letter from California, asking him to come out and interview for the foreman position, his expenses paid.

He was delirious. He ran back to the house, the cat lagging behind him, and when he told Helen he had an interview, she started to cry. "California!" he shouted. "Grass! Beaches! A whole brand-new sky!" He looked over at Nick, who was standing, amazed, by the kitchen stove. "I'll show you stars like you've never seen in your whole life."

He worried, though. He was convinced the right suit would get him the job, the right haircut. He spent hours prowling the cut-rate stores, making Nick come with him to pick out something right.

Man to man, he said. He got superstitious. He kept thinking, if only he could win a little money, he could take his family with him for the interview. It would be like a vote of confidence in the future he had to have, and then maybe things would work out—he'd get the job and they'd never have to come back to Pittsburgh ever again. He could get someone from the plant to pack up the stuff here. Or they could just leave it for vandals, for anyone. What did he care?

He began gambling more and more, losing what money he had saved for another haircut, for a new pair of shoes, getting more and more frustrated. One night, he was starting off for Wobbly Joe's when the cat started following him. He was sure it would turn back, but it came all the way to the bar, and when he went inside, why, the cat came in, too, prowling about the corners, disdaining the hands that reached down to stroke his fur. Tom went to the back for the poker game, the cat beside him, and while he played, the cat twitched and fished through his legs.

He liked having the cat there—it relaxed him, made him play bold. And that night, Tom had his first win. Two hundred and eighty dollars. Enough to take his family with him for the interview. He scooped up the money in one hand, the cat in the other, and the two of them went home.

He didn't say anything to Helen or Nick when he and the cat came in, his face all lit up and secretive. He poured the cat some milk into a blue dish. "Hey, that's my good dish," Helen said, but he stopped her, digging into his pockets, bringing up all that cash, crumpled, as green as sprouted grass. "The cat brought me luck," he said. "We're all getting out of here, we're all going. Like a vacation that won't ever end on us." He looked down at the cat. "You, too," he said, and the cat licked at the edge of the bowl, toppling it, empty.

Chuck's father was retarring the driveway because neighbors had complained, sure the kids would pick up pieces of rubble and put one another's eyes out with it. Nick sat with Chuck on his front steps.

"You'll forget me," Chuck said. "I just know it."

"Will not," Nick said, but even then he felt himself moving away. He couldn't stop thinking about California. He could be doing perfectly normal things—brushing his teeth, pulling on a striped blue jersey that was too big for him—and he'd think, I could be doing this in California, and suddenly every motion would seem charged, somehow different and wonderful. He practiced what it might be like. He filled the bathtub with cold water and salted it with Morton's, and then got in with his underwear, because he didn't have a bathing suit. He shut his eyes and imagined he heard gulls. When he came out of the tub, his skin flushed, his eyes glittering, he stared at himself in Helen's mirror, imagining that even his features were miraculously changing. He put on all the lights in his room, sitting under his desk lamp as close as he could, imagining he was tanning, until Helen came in and scolded him about wasting electricity.

Oh, she was caught up in the trip, too. He saw how she put a big map of California on the kitchen door, how she stared at it while she fished the soapy dishes out of the sink, while she patted hamburger meat into a loaf for supper, giving generous pinches of it to the cat. She couldn't stop talking about the sun there. She had always been the sort who ticked off the months on the kitchen calendar until summer. In December she would go through Tom's travel folders until she found the ones for the tropics, and those she would tack up on all the cabinets. She never minded not being able to afford fans for the house. She said there were loads of cool breezes and she would just open up her house to encourage them in. Pulling open the windows, the doors, letting the sweltering heat enter, clamp down, and stick. Nick got used to swatting June bugs in the house, to seeing a bumblebee angrily circling in his bedroom, popping against the glass panes. He stepped on the garden ants that scouted kitchen sugar; he picked up the frogs and shooed them outside.

In summer, Helen always seemed in a trance. There was really never enough money, but in winter she managed to stretch out the cheap cuts of meat, adding flour to fill things out. Summers were different. Who could eat in this weather? she said. She insisted it was healthier to eat less. She stashed away the money she would have spent for milk, for bread, and on nights when Tom was gambling, she took Nick over to one of the dance halls. She sat him down in a corner and he watched while she wound her way from stranger to stranger, dipping and swooning on the music, laughing. He liked how she became. He felt as if she were letting him in on some secret. She left with her hair damp, her dress pasted along her back. There would be this patina of dream about her that wouldn't fade. She'd smile at Tom when he came in, his money gone, maybe his socks, too, but she wouldn't grouse at him, she wouldn't tell him about her evening, either. And when she looked at Nick, she winked.

It was snowing the day they were leaving, just two days after Nick's twelfth birthday. They had packed more than they needed because Tom said they weren't coming back. Nick had a pile of books, some schoolwork Tom had promised Nick's teachers he would do, work Nick already planned to flutter out the window onto the highway. The only thing the school knew about the trip was that it was some kind of family emergency, and when Helen fussed, Tom said that it really wasn't a lie.

"It's your fault," Tom said to Nick. Meaning the cat, the careless way Nick hadn't slammed the door shut, hadn't felt the cat slip out through his legs. Tom wouldn't think of leaving without the cat. As far as he was concerned, the whole trip was the cat's doing, and to leave without it would be folly. He insisted that Helen climb into the car with him and drive around and around the neighborhood, calling out cat siren songs. Helen laughed. She had on dime store sunglasses so dark that you couldn't see she hadn't slept, that her eyes were shadowed, restless with excitement.

"You stay here and watch for Shelter," Tom told Nick. "You call him every once in a while." He rubbed at his eyes until Helen pulled his hand free. "You want to get wrinkles?" she said. She buttoned up her coat, bundled a scarf about her hair. "Let's get this show on the road," she said.

Nick watched the car leave. Helen had the window rolled down an inch or two and was blowing on her hands. Nick stayed by the front door until the car was out of sight, then went into the kitchen to get himself something to eat. There was peanut butter, and he took the jar and a butter knife and sat down in front of the television and avidly watched some cowboy movie about a rustler and his partner, who happened to be a woman. It was pretty good. Every few minutes he got up and checked the door. He left it open so he could hear the cat, and, more important, so he could hear his parents' car,

so he could dash back out and pretend he had been watching all the time.

He fell asleep in the middle of the movie, waking only when he heard someone rapping against the glass of the front door. He jerked up. He had a funny metallic taste in his mouth from the peanut butter; his eyes felt itchy and red. He scrambled to his feet. He had been in the bathroom—he could always say that. He had had a stomachache. Helen was always sympathetic to ailments; Tom's certain fury would fade. He walked into the living room, rubbing at his belly, his head down, and when he looked up, he saw the two policemen, waiting, watching him steadily through the glass.

It was just a kid. Sixteen years old, driving his brother's jeep, speeding. He didn't know how fast. Not that fast, not murderous. He was blasting the radio, bebopping the tune on the steering wheel. Then he saw a dog, he thought, or maybe a cat, dancing right into the path of his car, and when he swerved to avoid hitting it, he lost control. He was skidding, careening crazily straight for the other side of the road, right where Nick's parents were standing. They were thrown. They might have made it if they had hit the soft bank of snow, but their own car was so close, the metal so relentlessly impassable.

It kept playing in Nick's mind as he moved through a paralyzed haze, as he let the cops lead him right into the back seat of his car. They didn't rush him; they let him go into the bathroom first, where he locked the door and sat on the tub, thinking, This is my bathroom, that green toothbrush is my father's, the red one belongs to my mother. There was the heater where the cat used to love to sleep nights. Sometimes he'd step on it by mistake, the cat tensing beneath him. He heard the sudden sharp drone of a bee and he looked around, half expecting to see it buzzing by the sink, and then he realized that it was just the heater kicking on, and he thought how unnatural it all seemed, how everything was suddenly not quite right.

"Do you have family?" the cops asked. "An aunt, an uncle you can stay with?"

Nick, speechless, stared at them.

"Friends?" one cop said. "What about friends?" And then, sighing, he patted Nick on the back. He started to lift Nick's California suitcase, to get it out of the way, and Nick flinched back, as if he had been struck.

Later, he'd remember only outlines. There was Miss Harry, the caseworker assigned to him, a rabbity-looking woman who kept asking him about his family, about his friends, who later told him she had found Helen's address book in the house and had taken it upon herself to call each and every number to see if Nick could be taken in. "They all had such wonderful things to say about you," she said, while Nick sat there, shamed. "But these times . . ." She lifted her hands helplessly.

He remembered two silent days at a youth shelter, where he lay stiffly across his bed, not eating, not washing his face, his hair grown so tangled he couldn't even get his fingers through it. He wouldn't unlace his shoes. He refused to sleep under the blanket. When Miss Harry came to take him to the funeral, he refused to go. He heard her talking outside in the corridor, saying, well, he was just a boy, she wasn't so sure it was smart to force him; it had been . . . and then both voices softened, pulling away from him.

He would never go to the cemetery, he would never think about it. He told himself his parents weren't dead. He hadn't seen any bodies, and even if he went to the funeral, there was no reason why someone couldn't have just buried a box. His parents had amnesia, knocked into a kind of sleep by the blow from the car. They were living in a totally different city by now, working, wondering what it was they were missing. Soon, suddenly, he would prickle back into their memory and they would come and get him. Maybe they would go on Walter Cronkite and hold up his picture, not knowing where he was, not remembering the city they had both wanted to forget. "Do you know this boy?" He rolled over onto his back, watching the ceiling, pinching his own flesh, running his hands over his legs, his belly, cupping his hands over his face so he could feel his own breath. His parents would find him.

He remembered his court appearance, in a jacket, his hair slicked back with oil because Miss Harry had insisted. The judge, a man no older than his father, kept watching him, frowning, kept asking him

why he didn't want a foster home, why he kept insisting he had a home, had parents. And when the judge told him he was a ward of the state, and as such would be put into the care of the Pittsburgh Home for Boys, Nick suddenly couldn't breathe, couldn't move his hand to tell anyone he was dying. Everything shimmered, floating by him. Miss Harry touched him then, and he folded right over, almost falling, until his head was against the cool wood of the table, and then fiercely, for the first time, he cried.

His last memory was of driving with Miss Harry, on the way to the home. She kept the radio on low—"Easy Listening"—and when she drove past his neighborhood, he asked her to stop. She didn't say anything, but stopped where he had asked and didn't try to keep him from going up the chipped flagstone walk to his house. He tried the door, but it was locked. He wrenched at it, he kicked. It was his house. There was his room inside. He knew where the burns were in the rug from Tom's cigars, he knew where Helen kept her pictures of beaches, stashed under the cards in the den, hidden under a kitchen towel, little fixes that warmed the chill of the long winter months. He tugged at the door and then started pounding at the glass, over and over, and then Miss Harry was racing up the flagstone, her heels clicking, grabbing hold of him and forcing him toward her. He had let her touch him then. He had felt her hands moving over his hair, along his spine, but then, when he had felt her heart, he had panicked, pulling himself free. She had said something to him, her face earnest, pleading, but he hadn't heard any of the words; he had felt only her voice washing over him like a wave, when he was already drowning.

It was funny. All his life he had lived in Pittsburgh, but he had never been this far east, this near the edge of town. He couldn't remember seeing this big red brick building, the gated scrubby yard.

The director of the home was a tall, bony man named Mr. Rice. He spoke privately with Miss Harry for a while, and then Miss Harry spoke with Nick. She told him she would come to see him, she'd make sure he was all right. There were bills, she explained, but the sale of the house should cover them, and if there was money left over, she'd put it in trust for him; he could get it when he turned eighteen.

"Come on, I'll show you the dorm," Mr. Rice said. He took Nick up two flights to a large white room. Twelve beds in a row, the same brown wood dresser beside each one. There were a few posters hanging up over each bed. Rock stars. Movie stars. A few calendars with days X'd off. "Ah, here we go," said Mr. Rice. "Yours."

Nick settled tentatively on the bed.

"Oh, don't look like that," Mr. Rice said. "This isn't a prison. We think of ourselves as a kind of extended family, I suppose, with rewards and punishments like everywhere else. Demerits, you know— no radio at night, no going out nights, things like that. I have a little booklet I can give you. Come on, cheer up. You'll see how it is. You're going to be just fine."

Just fine. Nick pinched himself, bright spotty bruises, trying to jolt things right. He wasn't sleeping. When he did, he dreamed of his parents. Tom pulling the stars out of the sky and juggling them; Helen dancing, a white transistor clapped against one ear. The alarm would wake him, and he'd burrow into the sheets, waiting for the familiar smell of Helen's perfume as she bent to shake him awake, waiting for the heavy dark odor of Tom's coffee. And then, after a while, other smells would filter in. Ammonia. Urine. Dirty socks. And then he'd hear strange voices, and he'd open his eyes. He'd see the room, the other boys watching him, waiting. What was happening to his life? He'd feel himself falling, falling, and then he'd jerk up and race to the bathroom, turning on the shower as hot as it would go, standing under it so the sting of the water would burn away his terror.

He saw how it was. Everything was firmly scheduled. You had to get to breakfast by eight if you wanted the gluey oatmeal, the plate of soggy toast. You had to sit at the row table and eat whatever they had that morning or go hungry until lunch. You had to be at the home's school until four, and you had to sign up for at least one activity—a sport, a club. There was even a therapist on staff who called you in once a month to talk, who always wanted to discuss some comment a teacher made about you. Weekends were your own; so was the time between classes and after dinner until eleven, when you had to be in bed with the lights clicked dark. They didn't care what you did as long as you signed in and out, and if you did chores, if you swept the front stoop or washed a floor, you could earn more time.

He kept to himself. A few boys approached him, impressed that he had actually had parents, wanting to know what it was like. "It's like nothing," Nick said. He wouldn't socialize with any of them; he wouldn't for one moment let himself think this life was real. And when, rebuffed enough times, the other boys kept their distance, when he overheard one tell another that he was weird, he felt a hard, raw flush of satisfaction, and then a yearning despair.

He told himself he would run away; he plotted where he would go, places Tom had told him about. When he was outside on free time, he'd start walking and walking, and then he would panic a little. Where could he go with two dollars in his back pocket? What kind of work could he get? How would he live? He'd come back to the home furious with himself. He'd try to go to sleep, half-certain that if he slept deeply enough, he'd wake up from the dream, back in his parents' home.

The other kids thought about escape, too, but it was always adoption. The babies always left almost as quickly as they arrived, and the smaller boys could usually find homes. But the older you got, the more difficult it became, and everyone knew it. As soon as a couple walked in, boys would be spitting into their palms, slicking back their hair, straightening up and smiling, but the couple almost always left promised a newborn.

The home tried to help. Every month they put someone's picture into the Sunday *Press*, with a small blurb detailing how smart that particular boy was, how well behaved, and why you should think seriously about adopting him. The paper never said how a boy burned tattoos into his arm, how a boy wet his bed so many times a night he had to keep clean linen on a chair next to the bed. It was all vaguely humiliating, and only one boy in three years had ever been adopted because of the picture. But always, always, when it came time for volunteers, there were all these restless hands shooting up, uncontrollable as weeds.

A few boys got foster homes, sending postcards back to the home that were tacked up on the bulletin board in the dining room. "Have my own room," the cards said. "Have my own dog." One or two of the boys always came back, stiff and silent, curled about their time outside as if it were a wound.

Nick wrote postcards, too, and letters. Every trip outside the home, he stopped at a pay phone and tried to find the address of someone who had known his family, someone who had known and liked him. There weren't many names. His parents hadn't really made room for anyone in their lives except each other and him. Still, he kept thinking, maybe people didn't realize what had happened to him; maybe they had just assumed he had aunts and uncles like everyone else. He'd do it right, he thought. He wouldn't just show up on someone's doorstep, embarrassing them. He'd write a letter that showed how intelligent he was, how well bred.

He wrote to Tom's boss, promising to work in the mills for free if he was taken in. He wrote to Helen's one friend, telling her that he knew how to cook macaroni and cheese, that he could scrub a kitchen floor so shiny you could see yourself reflected in the gloss. He wrote to his last teacher because she had taken him aside one day and told him what promise she thought he had. And then he wrote to Chuck, a simple plea.

He mailed his letters and then he waited. No one at the home ever got any mail. All letters went right to Mr. Rice, and so every time Nick passed him, he looked at the director anxiously. When he passed a phone, he thought about nonchalantly calling some of the people, asking casually. "Oh, did you get my letter?" His fear, small and dark within him, took hold.

It took another week, and then a few responses trickled in. Mr. Rice gave him five envelopes, smiling, not asking him one question, and Nick raced with them into the bathroom, leaning along the tiled wall, his hands shaking as he ripped open the letters.

There was a note from Helen's friend, polite and sad, telling him how much she missed Helen, how she knew Nick would grow up to be a credit, and then her signature. There were listless responses from neighbors who said that if Nick was in the neighborhood he should call—he was welcome to potluck dinner anytime. And there was a letter from Chuck. Chuck said his father had left as soon as the driveway had been repaved, without a word of explanation. They thought he had gone someplace south, because he had taken only his summer shirts. His mother was waiting tables over at Tiffany's, and he himself was thinking of going over to Giant Eagle supermarket and trying to get work as a boxboy, to earn at least some of his keep. "If anyone needs rescue, it's me," Chuck wrote.

Nick stopped writing letters, stopped thinking about taking the bus to his side of town to look for familiar faces. When he walked, he hunched over, keeping his face in shadows. Once, when he was outside reading, he looked up and saw an old gambling buddy of Tom's. He was walking, a paper trapped under one arm, and he whistled. He wasn't even one of the people Nick had written to. Nick felt his breath chip. He got his hand up in a kind of frantic half-salute, and then he remembered all those letters, how they had come back to him, and he jerked his hand down, furious, burning with need.

Nick would turn fifteen in the home. He kept trying to keep himself as apart from the home as he could. He wouldn't wear the clothing the home provided—the hand-me-downs from churches and Goodwill, the donations from the Girl Scout groups and ladies' clubs that came to the home on holidays, grinning, carrying themselves like saints. He wouldn't go when Mr. Rice herded ten boys over to the cut-rate stores to shop. He knew how it must look, one man with all those boys politely calling him mister, fingering the chinos everyone wanted, but Mr. Rice said were too faddy. The kids all got the same kinds of stuff, cheaply made, with colors that bled in the wash, pinking your underwear and your socks.

Nick began doing chores, taking what money he could earn and saving it for clothing. He also got permission to work two afternoons a week at the Cluck-a-Buck, a chicken place in Shadyside, where he served family after family, mopping up the messes they made, getting them extra fries, extra water, extra everything for the meager tips they doled out. He had to wear a yellow hat shaped like a big chicken comb, a yellow shirt that said "Cluck" across it, but he didn't care. It all had a purpose. After a month, he walked right onto the main floor of Kaufmann's and bought himself chinos and loafers and a pale blue shirt. Every night he carefully swabbed out the bathroom sink and handwashed his shirt, hanging it in the shower to dry.

He paid for his own haircuts. He hated the crew cuts the home

provided, and although the barber promised to do whatever Nick
wanted, Nick didn't think he could give a cut that didn't have an
institutional look to it. He began taking two buses over to the
Wilfred Beauty School, where for only two dollars one of the students would cut your hair. The only catch was that you had to give
them carte blanche—you had to trust them. Nick didn't mind. The
students were friendly girls, in white uniforms and nurses' shoes,
their names on blue name tags. Dot. Amy. And they talked to him
while they fussed with his hair; they treated him as if he were just an
ordinary kid coming to get his hair cut.

He had startling cuts. Ducktails, bangs, once something called a
Whiffle Ball, a cut that bristled up about his head. He couldn't recognize himself in the mirror.

"You hate it," the girl working on him said. She kept rubbing her
hands along her uniform, as if they were wet. She glanced toward
the supervisor, who was shouting at another student for having left
some peroxide on far too long.

"No, no, it's great," Nick said, and then, as soon as he left, he
went to the five-and-dime and bought himself a golf hat to tug over
it. The other kids in the home made fun of him, but he didn't care.
He studied his reflection in the mirror, and he thought no one would
ever mistake him for an orphan.

When he was sixteen, Miss Harry suddenly stopped coming. He
had a new social worker, a thin young woman, fresh out of school,
who took him out for burgers and fries, who said she wanted to be
his friend and kept glancing at her watch. She told him Miss Harry
had gotten fed up with the pressure and had moved to Florida.

Florida. It made Nick think about travel. It rekindled memories of
Tom and his brochures, his road maps. Nick began to hang around
the travel agencies in town. Like father, like son, he thought, and it
was a kind of comfort. He crammed brochures into his jacket when
no one was looking. He stared so long at the posters that once an
agent gave him one, telling him to come back again when he was
with his parents, and she would give them a deal. At night he lay
across his bed, the brochures spread about him, waiting for it to be
nine, the time he had overheard that the Pan Am flight took off for
Spain.

He hung his poster—a brilliant African sunset over the veld—over his bed. He began to plan what he would do when he got out. He knew a lot of the kids here stayed in town. Fine for them, he thought. They could wake up to the pollution reports; they could wash their hair every day because it was so grimy. But he—he was going to be different.

He began to study a little harder in classes, trying to get better grades so he could get a scholarship to some college. Because of his hard work, he was given more free time away from the home. He fed his loneliness at the cafeterias, at the cafés that were just springing up. He nursed the bitter espressos, tried to look cool and important, and talked to whoever would listen to him. At first it was simply housewives, older women who were always comparing him to their sons, inviting him over to their houses, and almost always thinking he was a few years younger than he really was, because he was so small and skinny. He liked talking to the women, but he didn't want them pitying him, so he made things up about himself. He was Teddy, he was Bill, and once, for a week or so, he was Simpson, Jr., the son of a famous surgeon. Some of the women got to recognize him and he liked that, although it was awkward when they called him by last week's name. He had to pretend to have two names then, a middle and a first.

He began to look for kids his own age. He wandered around, trying to figure out where the high-school hangouts were, the places outsiders might go. Musicians. Poets. And girls. He wanted to meet girls. Their hair clean and long, wearing velvet or suede, looking at him like he was some secret they had to discover.

He found one place after a while, a café called Marks, owned by two University of Pittsburgh students who weren't even there half the time. You could get a huge platter of blueberry pancakes for a dollar. Or you could sit at one of the splintered wood tables for hours and not order one thing and no one would care, no one would slap down a menu unless you were impatient enough to ask. It was rumored that the café would close down any second, that there were all these shady matters of unpaid taxes and unpaid bills.

Nick believed it. The lights flickered on and off, the heat never worked, and no one ever counted the money Nick gave them for his bills. Sometimes no one even gave him a bill at all, and when he asked for it, he was told to do the tally himself; he was trusted. Most everyone in the place was his age or a little older. He saw sleeping bags shoved into corners, he saw girls helping themselves to muffins and coffee, and he saw a few guys getting up to wash a dish or two before they sat down again.

Nick loved Marks. He would go there and sit at one of the tables and fool with the chessboard until someone would sit down beside him and want to play. He became a decent enough player because of all the people offering to teach; and it was at Marks, too, that he learned to smoke cigarettes.

He thought it looked really cool—that long, easy drag on a cigarette, the tapping ashes dusting onto the floor as you leaned toward some girl, talking to her in a low, soothing kind of voice, getting her to lean just a bit closer. He'd wanted to try smoking, but was too proud to admit he didn't know how, too ashamed to let anyone see him fumble. So he waited until it was time for him to rush out for the last bus back to the home, and then he casually bummed a cigarette, shaking his head at the proffered light, saying he'd use his lighter, and then dashing out before someone could ask to use it, too. Outside, instead of asking a stranger for a light, he went into a cheap diner and filched a pack of matches. Then he made his way onto a deserted side street and huddled in the darkness.

He let the cigarette hang between his fingers. He took slow, careful draws at first, doubling into his coughs, forcing himself past the nausea. He goaded himself into puff after puff, trying to smooth it out, to gain a little finesse. He reeled home, greenish, swaying a little, and curled up into a tight ball on his bed, trying not to look at anything. Above his head, the poster of the African veld spun.

The finer points of smoking he took care of in the early morning, an hour before anyone else was up. He stood in front of the bathroom mirror, a pencil stub between his fingers, practicing different methods of holding the cigarette. It took him weeks to get really proficient, and by then, smoking had become a craving. He had to sneak his packs of Luckies into the home, and in the middle of the night he'd go into one of the toilet stalls and surreptitiously smoke. He thought of his addiction as a kind of victory.

He smoked at Marks constantly, watching the couples, hiding his yearnings behind a veil of smoke. There was always some guy with a crummy Sears guitar, strumming "Five Hundred Miles" or "If I Had a Hammer," trying to get everyone to sing along. Some people did, but Nick, who couldn't carry a tune, looked away. Someone else was reciting from a book of beat poets, pounding the table as if it were a bongo drum.

Everybody seemed to know everybody else, but they were still friendly enough to Nick. They bummed smokes and borrowed chairs from his table, and then conversations would start. Nick kept up an air of mystery. He wouldn't talk about his school or his parents, and when prodded, he'd get up and go for more coffee, waiting for the conversation to turn before he came back. It just made them all the more curious about him. Finally, he said he went to a special place for gifted kids. He said his parents might just as well not exist. He said this darkly, with his lids lowered.

He studied the girls, anxious, afraid. He didn't want to catch any girl's eye, because he was terrified of seeing disapproval or, worse, amusement. He was suddenly hypersensitive about his looks. When he sat, he cupped his hands about his ears so they wouldn't look too big. He tried to sit most of the time so you couldn't tell he was small. He began wearing his hair longer because he saw the girls gravitated to shaggy-headed boys.

He lay awake nights, twisting in the sweaty sheets, listening to the helpless syncopation of his heart. How could he ask a girl out when he had a curfew? How could he compare with guys who had cars and records and homes? If he dared to tell a girl the truth, she'd tell the others, wouldn't she? And that would infect his mystery with pity, make everyone polite and distant to him.

There was this one girl, though, who actually seemed to like him. Her name was Desmond Dickens. She was sixteen and she went to Allegheny High with most of the others. She was small and had red curly hair, and when she was beside Nick, he felt his breath clamping up inside of him. He couldn't concentrate on what she was saying; he had to hunch his body forward to hide his desire. She wanted him to come to some party she was having. She smiled at him, and he suddenly stood up. "I can't make it," he said. He never gave explanations—no one at Marks ever expected one. But still, when he saw how her face was folding up, how it was losing some of its light, he felt ruined.

He began lying. He started idly telling everyone about his girl, Betty, who lived in a big white beach house in Florida and was always begging him to visit. When he talked to Desmond, he asked her what kind of a gift he should get Betty for her birthday. "Oh," Desmond said, picking at a nail, and he hated himself, he wanted to lean across the table and grab her and smash her against him. "I like bracelets," she said. He looked at her wrist, thin and cool and white, and thought of encircling it with his fingers, and then she stood up, excusing herself, and went to another table, leaving him helpless and confused.

He worried her in his mind, he played out scenarios, and then one day she waltzed into Marks on the arm of Freddy Johansen, a guitar player with a local band. They sat at a table and held hands, they nuzzled while Nick sat there, queasy, and when Desmond came over to say hello, he was curt. The whole bus ride back to the home, he thought about her hair. Her eyes. The heat from her body. The way her voice was. And when he was finally dropped off in front of the home, he felt as if something important had been taken from him.

By Nick's last year at the home, he was one of Marks' regulars. He knew everyone by name, although he had never been to anyone's home, had never really socialized. It was a year when everyone was applying to colleges, talking about Harvard or Yale or the University of Texas. Nick slunk off by himself those uneasy nights. He walked the streets, miserable, unsure.

He had applied to twenty different schools, all for scholarships, and although he had been accepted at Berkeley, there was no money, and he hadn't saved enough to buy books for one year, let alone tuition. He told himself it didn't matter. He'd go to New York—he had money enough to get there—and he'd find a job, take classes at night.

He swaggered into Marks, almost defying anyone to tell him good news. And then he felt a hand on his shoulder and he whipped around. Desmond.

"Say hey," she said, smiling. She sat down, pushing at the sleeves of her sweater. "So guess what?" she said.

"I don't know," Nick said, tapping cigarette ash on the floor. "What?"

"I was accepted at Oberlin."

He stubbed out his cigarette and lighted another. "Great," he said.

"Um, yeah, it is," she said. She started fiddling with her sweater cuff. "So, if you get out that way, I hope you'll come and visit."

He looked over at her.

"Well, will you?' she said. She rummaged in her purse until she fished out a pen, a scrap of paper, and then she scribbled out her address and handed it to him. "I don't know what dorm I'll be in yet or anything, but that's my school address." She laughed, her nose bunched up so that all he could think about was what it would be like to kiss it. "My school!" she said. She leaned toward him. "Would you come out that way, do you think? I know it's Ohio and all"—she made a face—"but really, it's the coolest school. Big in the arts and stuff."

"Sure," he said. "Sure, I'll come out."

He took her address and put it into his back pocket and then he looked at her again.

"Well," she said, "is the offer reciprocal?"

"Reciprocal?"

"Yeah, I mean, am I invited to come and visit you?"

He hesitated, and then he took the paper and pen and wrote out Nick Borden, 141 West 22nd Street, New York, New York. He had no idea what the zip was, so he scribbled in 14772, hoping it was at least close, hoping she wouldn't really know either. He handed it back to her.

"God, New York," she said, impressed. "You're going to school there, you lucky duck."

He shrugged.

"You know Donald Ditwild? He's going to Columbia."

"NYU," said Nick.

"You'd show me around if I came up that way? I've always wanted to see New York."

"Sure. Sure I would."

She shook her head. She said she couldn't get over it. New York. She said she might have known he wouldn't be living in a dorm like everyone else, not the way he was about his privacy and everything, but how did he ever find a place he could afford?

"Oh," he said, "you know. . . ." And he suddenly began worrying about just how much a place might cost him, just how much it might be to live in a city like New York for even six months. He had his savings, the little he put aside every month in a local bank; and, too, he would find a job.

She grinned. "I knew you wouldn't tell me." She suddenly reached over and took his cigarette, taking a slow, easy drag from it before passing it back to him. His fingers felt charged when he touched the cigarette. He was afraid to put it back to his mouth, and when he looked at her, she flushed.

"Listen," she said. She looked at her hands, at the glimmery rings across her fingers. "Listen, the thing is, I've . . . I've always kind of loved you."

She stood up, not looking at him. "I'm not seeing Freddy anymore," she said, and then someone called her name, and she turned, just long enough for his panic to propel him outside.

He didn't know what to do. He stuttered back and forth in front of the door. He could see her still in there, leaning across a table, talking to some girl in a red bandanna. She was laughing, and when she glanced up toward the table where he had been, he sprinted ahead.

He was sweating. He'd call her, he'd make some apology. He'd wait a month or so. No. He wouldn't. She'd think he had been making fun of her. She'd think he was pathetic. He looked back at the café. "Baby, I Need You." That was the song the five-hundred-miles guy had been singing before. He turned away, and then he started the long, lonely walk home.

He never went back to Marks. He did write Desmond one letter, telling her the truth, pouring it across the pages, but he couldn't quite seal the envelope; he kept reopening it to stare in abject terror and mortification at his words. In the end, the stamp wore off the envelope, the address smeared in the rain, and he threw it out.

He concocted scenarios. How she'd write and write to the address he had given her, her letters bouncing back, stamped "addressee unknown." Frustrated, she might write to that jerk she knew at Columbia; she might sweetly plead with him to hand-deliver her letter, promising to take him to dinner, maybe even hinting that she might

take him to bed. Her friend might take a subway over to the address,
the whole time thinking about the white flash of her legs, the swell
of her breasts. He might buzz the number, might wake some poor old
man who might buzz him up thinking he was the grocery boy. Desmond's friend might puff his way up five flights just to find out there
was no Nick there—had never been a Nick.

Or maybe there wasn't even an apartment at that address, maybe
there was a Chicken-a-Go-Go, an establishment the owner would
hotly insist had been there a good forty years. Desmond would hear
the news by phone. She'd gently get out of her promise of a movie, a
dinner, a night that already had him itching, and when she hung up,
she would take the letter she had been writing to Nick and carefully
fold it into a drawer. He'd be in her blood then, a mystery she had
never solved.

And Nick . . . well, he'd remember her. He wished he had a
photo of her, something he could look at and think about, a reminder that a girl had loved him, that she had wanted the connection.

Nick took care of the details. He put what money he had managed
to save into traveler's checks; he spent ten minutes making the bank
teller reexplain how to use them. He reserved a room at the "Y" in
New York City, then went to the library and wrote to colleges for
their schedules of evening classes.

Everyone knew he was leaving the home, but no one made any
fuss about it. Boys left as soon as they were eighteen. No one told
him to write, no one said they would miss what they never really had
known. Some boys had parties thrown for them when they left; everyone herded into the rec room for cake and vanilla ice cream, the
one flavor Nick hated. Some boys left with jobs, with schools to go
to. Some left with nothing—and always returned to the home a
month or so later. Just to visit, they said, but they never wanted to
leave. The cook had once been one of the home's boys, and he joked
about it, admitted he couldn't leave. He was thirty-six and he had a
girl who came to pick him up evenings, a skinny blonde with a
gummy smile.

On Nick's last day, one of the boys came over to him, Denny

Chernoff, a boy who had more friends than anyone. He said he bet Nick was scared shitless.

"No way," Nick said.

"They think I'm fifteen," Denny said. "They don't know shit. My aunt wasn't real swift with dates, and luckily there wasn't any birth certificate."

He squinted at Nick. "You think I'm fifteen? I'm sixteen. Maybe eighteen. I can't be sure. What am I going to do outside? I'm not that smart. But I don't like working with my hands, and there aren't any girls with money lusting to take care of me. What am I going to do, commit some crime so I can get put into jail?"

He saw suddenly how Nick was watching him, dumbfounded. "You tell and you die," Denny said.

"What did you tell me for, then?" Nick said.

Denny shrugged. "I had to tell someone," he said. "And I knew you'd keep your mouth shut about it."

Nick nodded. "I want to leave here," he said.

"Sure," Denny said. "You would. You could get your birth certificate forged—you could say the other was a fake. You could get sick. They aren't about to make someone sick leave."

Nick laughed. Denny grinned, but his eyes were serious. "I'll see you," he said, and, turning, he fanned his fingers in a wave. One, two, three, fist closed.

Mr. Rice called Nick into his office to shake his hand and give him a twenty-five-dollar savings bond. He couldn't understand why Nick wanted to leave Pittsburgh; he said there wasn't one place worldwide that was prettier. Not with Point State Park, not with the fountains and Squirrel Hill. "Well, I hope you'll always think of us as family," Mr. Rice said.

"You think of me as your son?" Nick asked.

Startled, Mr. Rice laughed. "Don't you?" he said, opening the door for Nick, patting him goodbye on the back.

At first, Nick was so busy in New York, he didn't have time to be lonely. He had his room at the "Y," he had a string of terrible part-time jobs—washing dishes, cleaning out other people's cramped, gritty apartments—and in his spare time he took classes at Queens

College. He watched the women in his classes, but he didn't have the time or money to flirt. He couldn't buy himself a pretzel on the street, let alone treat someone else—and anyway, he was always mad-dashing from job to job to school to job. He had to stay up half the night nursing black coffee he warmed up on a contraband hot plate, popping Stop Sleep tablets, just so he could get his studying done.

New York astounded him. It was hard to stay inside and crouch over his books, hard to soap up greasy dishes in the steamy back room of a restaurant, when he knew there were marvels going on outside. He tried to walk everywhere because every street seemed dappled with miracles, with vendors selling books and jewelry and strange foods, with girls in lots of beads and high leather boots, with dogs in beaver coats. He saw a man walking a llama one day, and Nick seemed to be the only person turning around to gawk.

Sometimes, he looked for Desmond. He imagined her up here visiting her friend at Columbia. He tried to study in the places he thought she might go to—the coffeehouses in the Village, the grassy parts of Washington Square Park, where there were always people playing folk music on their guitars. He didn't start to feel lonely until it was time to get up, time to go back home.

It would take Nick over five years to get his degree. The whole time, he knew he should have been studying something more practical, something he might make some money with. He sat in on a few business classes, some prelaw, but he was restless, he couldn't concentrate, and in the end he took class after class in literature and anthropology, in zoology and botany. It didn't matter. He was less than one month out of school when he found a job. A salesman for a children's book company. Brooksider Books.

He couldn't explain it, but he somehow began feeling real. He had this job. He had this tiny studio apartment over on Thirtieth Street and Tenth Avenue. He had had to bribe the super for it. It was a six-flight walk-up with a slanting, rotted floor and a dark, dangerous shower that he sometimes entered with rubbers flapping on his feet. The neighborhod wasn't so great either; he had to pick his way over the winos and around the steady, insinuating hiss of the dealers. But he had three big windows and lots of light; he had so few roaches he never even bothered to buy boric acid, let alone sprinkle it in the corners; and he could walk everywhere.

He loved coming home. He'd open his door and just beam because the place was his, because he didn't have to share it or clean it or hide one thing in it. At first he didn't want anyone stepping into his place except him. He didn't mind talking to the other tenants as he passed them in the hall—the young mother on four, the old Spanish lady who had three parrots that could swear in Chinese. He liked the sense of community.

But it was different when the old woman knocked on his door and wanted to come inside just to visit; or when the young mother asked to borrow sugar and ended up spending an hour and a half sitting on his sofa bed asking him over and over if he thought the landlord was going to start evicting people. He felt itchy having people in his place. He felt as though they had somehow taken hold of something that was his, as if they were taking that part away with them, away from him. He began creeping up the stairs when he came in, rushing his key in the lock. He played his radio loudly enough so he wouldn't hear the knocks, and even when he did, he ignored them.

He wasn't home that much. He had his job, which he loved because it let him travel. Oh, not to anyplace exotic, but he did get to Boston, he did get to Washington, D.C., and at every place he bought postcards and T-shirts, he bought processed snapshots of the city sights. The clients loved him because he was so enthusiastic about their cities, because he actually wanted to see what sights there were. And, too, he was honest, he was an unpushy salesman.

He liked to walk around their shops first. He'd pick up the books and see which ones had jam stains on the pages, which ones had the spines starting to crack, because those were the books the kids loved—he didn't care what the sales said. Sales were what grandmothers thought their grandkids should want. The whole trick was to promote the books the kids themselves loved, to set them right out front, to lie and say they were the best-sellers if that was the only way to get them into a kid's hands. He had personal opinions on every book that he showed them; and despite what his company told him about "creative" selling, he had read every one.

His clients began to know him by name. He had a boss who shared an occasional beer or two with him. And in hotels, it didn't matter that he was alone, that he had one glass of wine in the bar alone, that he went upstairs early, because it was all part of working, all part of who he was now.

The only snags in Nick's life were the holidays, the times when he was most reminded that he had no family. The city seemed to empty out. He'd go buy himself Thanksgiving dinner in a restaurant filled with old people and loners, with gay couples who preferred love to family confrontation. He went to all-night movies on Forty-second Street, and he got up at six in the morning to go to the Macy's Thanksgiving Day Parade, just so he could be a part of the crowd. It was bone-chillingly cold that day, and by noon it was snowing, white confetti on the black tarry street, but he stayed until the parade was over, taking his leave with the last of the stragglers.

When he came back to his apartment building, he knocked on the Spanish woman's door. She wasn't so terrible. He thought he'd take her out for coffee, maybe treat her to a dessert. But when the door opened, he was startled to see two women in there, two single beds jammed into the corner spaces. "Ah, the stranger," she said, smiling. She told him her sister was living with her now, but she didn't introduce him, she didn't invite him in, and neither she nor her sister seemed the least bit interested in how he would spend his night.

He walked around the city. He tried to flirt with some of the women, but he must have looked too needy, he must have been sending out the wrong kind of radar, because no one even smiled. He decided to be more aggressive. On subsequent outings, he began talking to women in movie lines, at the poetry readings he went to in the Village where everyone was in black sweaters and boots.

He had a few dates, but none of the relationships lasted. He told himself, okay, okay, it was all experience and he would keep on trying. He went back home and pulled out his sofa bed and stretched out across it and then he imagined that there was another body next to his. He shut his eyes—he swore he could hear another heart beating, yearning toward his own.

TWO

• • •

Dore was thirty miles away from Nick's apartment, in the New Jersey high school where she taught. She had a headache so blinding she could hardly move. It was G block, her last class to teach, and her least favorite. It was an odd assortment of kids, the ones bounced from class to class because they still couldn't read, still couldn't write a sentence that made one whit of sense. She would write "food on the table" across the dusty blackboard, and half her class would stubbornly assure her that it was a perfectly good sentence, and that the only thing wrong with it was the messy slant of Dore's handwriting.

Debby Brown in the first row told Dore that *food* was the subject, *table* the verb, because verbs showed action, right? Wasn't that what Dore had told them? You ate at a table, and anyone who said eating wasn't action was just plain dumb.

Dore was stupefied.

Donald Steiner stood up and scornfully told Debby she was a moron. "Where are you from, outer space?" he said. He said *table* was the adjective because adjectives described, and he himself could rattle off five different kinds right now: pine, maple, cherry, oak, and Formica.

Worse though, and more chilling, was Timmy Mathews, who cleared his throat and then told her that really he couldn't give a flying hoot what a verb was, because he was going to hire himself a pretty secretary to take care of all that gunk for him. He'd pay her plenty to know that kind of thing, because he was going to be an executive, he was going to attend to the really important junk.

Dore got more and more tired, but she tried. She never used the textbooks, hating them even more than the kids did. She made up her own sentences, trying to shock them into a little attention, putting up their names, the names of the rock stars she thought they liked. "Elvis Presley took his guitar to the store." Find the verb. Find the subject. She got startled looks, but only a moment or two of attention. "You look more like the Wayne Newton type to me," Debby said, squinting.

Dore made them write, calling it "senior essay" to give it some importance. She scribbled "hunger" across the board and gave them the whole period to write about it, anything they wanted—a story, a description. She loved senior essay. It gave her a whole forty minutes to relax her headache away, and she felt she deserved such breaks. Look at her class.

Ronnie Dazen. Big and dirty blond, hulking over his front-row seat and mooning at her so she wanted to smack the expression right off his face. His eyes followed her. When she went to the board, she felt uneasy. She kept touching the hem of her skirt to make sure it wasn't riding up. She fingered her buttons to make sure they were fastened good and tight.

Ronnie had called her at her apartment once. He was very polite. He told her he had forgotten what the homework was, and could she please refresh his memory? She told him to call a friend. "But I am," he said. He breathed in the silence. He wouldn't hang up, so she had to do it. One time, he even walked his dog on her block, a whole two miles away from where he lived. He must have packed the dog in the car and driven it over. He teased and tormented the dog until it whined and carried on so much that she came to her window to see what the commotion was. He was soothing the dog down, blinking up at her, innocent. She hadn't been able to concentrate, knowing he was out there with his dog, knowing he knew just where she lived.

In the back was Ricky Hall, the boy the others dubbed the Quaalude Kid. He shimmied in his seat; he talked and laughed to himself. He was skinny and small, swimming out of the T-shirts he marked up with Magic Marker, "Eat me" bleeding in a murky black drool across his chest. He strode past her, defiant, turning a little so she could see, but she just told him how pleased she was to see his spelling improve, and that she expected a passing grade from him on his next word test. His grin deflated.

Ricky was smart enough never to carry any drugs on his person, and the one time she had sent him home on suspicion, his father had called up, threatening her, threatening the school, demanding proof that his boy wasn't as clean and innocent as a fresh sheet of paper. The principal had taken the boy's side; she had been reprimanded, reminded what a lawsuit might cost, and she had walked back into her classroom, defeated.

Beside him now, two boys were surreptitiously chewing tobacco, spitting it into a blue Dixie cup. It was forbidden, and at least once a month Dore had to collect the cups, sickened. When the boys saw her coming, one of them handed the cup to Rick. "Pepsi," he whispered. Rick was tilting the cup to his mouth when Dore said sharply, "That's *enough*," startling him, making him drop the cup, creating a slide of brown stain across the pale wood floor.

She sent a boy off to get a wet paper towel, half expecting him not to return. She went back to her desk, removing her glasses, rubbing her eyes. Someone wolf-whistled and she looked up, trying to look menacing. Without her glasses, she couldn't see six inches past her face, but she didn't think her students knew that. She hadn't thought it was such a good thing for them to know, a weapon they might use against her. She sometimes took off her glasses at her desk, looking out across them, just so they'd think she could do without them.

She had been just about legally blind since birth, although to this day her mother insisted it wasn't so much physical as plain old stubbornness on Dore's part. A lack of vision. A refusal to see things the way they really were.

Her mother could point back through time, pulling out Dore's baby pictures. Oh, such a sweet baby face; such frilly dresses that Dore consistently muddied up in the backyard; the smooth, buttery hair that had to be clipped short so it would curl, that wouldn't stay in place no matter how much sugar water was drenched into it. And the glasses. Oh, Lord, the glasses. Candy-striped frames, tipped at

the corners like a smile and tied in back with a blue ribbon, because
where could you get glasses small enough to stay on a baby?

No one in her family had bad eyes. But there was Dore, creeping
into walls, grabbing for her mush and missing. Her father had
bundled her up and taken her to the doctor, had bought her her first
pair of glasses.

Dore had hated them at first. She wouldn't wear them unless she
was watched. She lost them in the grass and insisted she could see
perfectly fine. It gave her mother a perfect reason to blame: Dore's
poor vision and her refusal to correct it were clearly why she wore
too much makeup at fifteen, why she couldn't dress with a little
ladylike reserve. And of course there was the time when Dore was
seventeen, when she had fallen in love with the neighborhood
butcher.

His name was Franky Hart. He was a high-school dropout who
had inherited his father's business, and he was twenty-five when
Dore knew him. He knew absolutely everything there was to know
about tenderloin and rib roast. He could tell you how to bring out
the flavor in chicken, how to dress up liver so that even the kids
would be clamoring for seconds. He charmed women. He noticed
their dresses, their hair, and ignored their protests that they were
certainly too old to be called "pretty." He kept the air sweetly sugared, and even Dore's mother fell under his spell. She took special
pains with what she wore when she went in there, but really, no
more than the other women—and anyway, having a harmless crush
yourself was a hell of a lot different from having a daughter actually
go out with the object of your affections.

Dore started going out with Franky the first and only time she ever
stopped at the store, to pick up some hamburger meat for her
mother, who was shivering out a summer cold, bundled up in bed.
Franky hooked Dore with his smile, and persuaded her to let him
drive her home on his motorcycle. When he showed up one Friday
to take Dore to the movies, his hair slicked back, his jacket pressed,
Dore's mother was livid. She felt betrayed. She stood watch at the
window; she saw how Dore hitched up her skirts to get on his motorcycle, how she looped her arms about his waist, pressing herself in
close.

"I don't care for that class of boy," she sniped to Dore when Dore came home, out of breath, rumpled, her glasses stashed in her purse or lost. "Don't you see what you're doing?"

"I see just fine," Dore said.

She sneaked around seeing Franky for over a year. Her mother began going to a different butcher, and the family sat at dinner after dinner picking at fatty roasts, pushing away stringy gray lamb. Dore never wore her glasses when she was with Franky. He didn't like them. He'd take them off if she didn't, stashing them in his own shirt pocket so that she sometimes forgot to get them before she went back into the house. She got used to seeing her world in a blur, got used to the headaches that sent her to her room nights with the lights off, a towel stuffed under her door to muffle sound.

In the end, she had gone off to college. She had seen him for a while. He had come to visit, but he was ill at ease and out of place. He stayed overnight with her in her dorm room, chipping in ten dollars to get her roommate to stay someplace else, but the lovemaking wasn't what Dore had expected. He was impatient. He preened and he said he'd known it would be this good. He tried to joke. "It takes a sexual man to make a chicken sensual," he said. But she didn't laugh; she sat up in bed, reaching for her glasses, and when he tried to stay her hand, she brushed it away.

He took up with another girl, a tall redhead with big green eyes and perfect vision. It had mattered once, but it didn't anymore. Dore was through with him, suddenly through with school and Chicago, and she graduated and moved out to her new job in New Jersey. She thought about getting contact lenses, but her eyes wouldn't adjust, and now she just wore her glasses all the time.

"Jeepers creepers, look at teach's gorgeous peepers," Ronnie sang. "You ought to ditch those dumbo glasses for good."

"Finished your essay, have you?" she said, and he took up his pen again. She twisted round to the file cabinet, just for a second, to get a Kleenex to clean her glasses, and when she turned back around, her glasses were gone.

"Ha-ha," she said. "Very funny. Okay, Ronnie, let's have them."

He looked up. "You said we had until the end of class to finish."

She told him what she meant, and, insulted, he stood up and emptied his pockets. He dumped out his knapsack on the floor, spilling packs of gum, cigarettes, some stray papers, and a packet of rubbers. Defiantly, he sat down again. She was close enough to make out the objects on the floor, to know her glasses weren't in that jumble. "A joke is a joke," she said. "Now let's have them."

No one knew a thing. Debby said she hadn't seen anyone do anything. Rick said he bet the glasses were in Dore's top drawer. "I want those glasses on my desk by the bell or you all get F's." Dore felt like a fool. She couldn't read what was playing in their faces, but they knew her well enough to know what a softy she was, how unlikely her threat.

"First good grade I'd have all year," Tim muttered.

The bell rang, and then her class was spilling past her, dusting her desk with papers, calling out hopes that she'd find those glasses, voices friendly, uninvolved. "Ronnie," she called, thinking he'd surely help her if it meant a little extra flirting time, but he was whisking out the door, waving his blurry hand at her in goodbye.

She patted her way along the corridor to the office. She could see well enough to know where she was going, but she'd never be able to drive home. She trailed her fingers up against a big sticky wad of gum and recoiled. She had this sudden image of all the students she had ever flunked emerging from the corridors, coming in for the kill when they realized how helpless she was. Things like that happened here. Cherry bombs under the French teacher's skirt. A gym teacher getting knifed because he had made a boy do one too many squat thrusts.

She told herself she was different, she was invincible. Two years of teaching and not one bad thing had happened to her. She had confiscated whiskey bottles and knives, and no one had threatened her, much less retaliated. She'd even had students come back to visit her after they had dropped out of school because she had failed them for yet another term. Students gave her gifts on her birthday. She remembered one boy had written her a poem. She had begged him to try to publish it, and had brought him the addresses of small literary magazines. She couldn't understand his moody refusal—until a month later, when she had been in the Thrift-T-Mart, buying grapes, and had heard the words of his poem woozily crooned out by Frank Sinatra over the loudspeakers.

She suddenly felt someone in the corridor with her, and she squinted. Up ahead. A muddied image. A man, leaning against the wall, silently watching her. She wasn't sure what to do. She knew every teacher here by shape as well as sound; she knew the colors and clothing they wore. This man was small and lean and in a suit, something the other men avoided. It could be a parent, she thought, except he didn't seem lost, and he didn't seem angry about his kid making him trek all the way out here. He was just leaning, just waiting for her.

She felt foolish trailing her hand along the wall. She took it down and started striding blindly down the hall to the main office. The principal's secretary lived near Dore; she'd give her a lift. Dore was almost to the man when she stumbled on something, and then she felt his hand on her arm.

"Are you all right?"

"Yes . . . No," she said, letting him help her stand, moving a step or two from him. She squinted at him. He didn't look dangerous.

"Listen," she said, "a kid took my glasses. I'm afraid I can't see very well. If you could just help me to the office, I can get a ride home. There," she said, pointing.

"I can drive you," he said.

"I'm sorry, I don't know you," she said. "I can't take a ride with someone I don't know."

"I just sold two dozen books to your school librarian," he said. "I'll take you to her and you can ask her—she can identify me. I've got a business card, too, if you think you can read it. And a number you can call to check up on me."

Dore squinted at him.

"Really. I was just leaving anyway," he said.

He had stepped back from her. He was too far away for her to really make out his features. She was curious about them, though. Curious, too, about why he had been just standing out there in the hall, what he had been waiting for. "Okay," she said. "I'll take the ride."

The whole time he was driving her home, she kept wondering what he might really look like. She wasn't so blind she couldn't see his black hair, cut a little wild and funny, a nose a little prominent, a rumpled dark suit that seemed a bit big. The details, though, were missing, and she couldn't just move up close to stare, to read his face like braille.

She made him wait outside her door; she told him she just had to grab her extra glasses and then she wanted to get a catalog from him—maybe she'd be interested in ordering some of his books for her class.

She went into the bedroom and rummaged around in a drawer for her glasses. They were old frames, out of style, and she didn't think she looked so good in them. Still, she stopped to fluff up her shortish hair, to smooth her blouse, and then she stepped out into the foyer.

"Well, teacher," he said, smiling. "Do I pass?"

"Do I?" she said.

They began seeing each other. He lived a half-hour's drive away and he'd come out to see her or bring her back with him to the city, and when he was on the road, he called her, every night, with stories. She liked him. He was different from the other men she had been with, boyfriends who were always jaunting off mornings to be with their buddies, leaving her with a messy bed, with a breakfast table littered with toast crumbs and cigarettes, with spilled black coffee working its way right into a stain. She had had men who would make love to her, and then, a minute later, would casually wipe off their gummy penises with her lace underwear, would reach for her phone to schedule a tennis game, joking privately to someone whose sex she wasn't even sure of.

She felt happier with Nick, who wouldn't leave her alone, who told her that he didn't know what it was about her, only that there was something that kept drawing him, that wouldn't let go. He said that when he had first seen her, feeling her way along the wall, he was certain all the time that she was feeling her way toward him, that he had been her destination right from the start, and that all he had to do was wait for her, holding his breath, mesmerized.

There was no one else laying claim to him except her. He didn't even have any real friends to speak of, let alone family. She had to pull all those orphan stories out of him; he seemed vaguely shamed, reluctant, and when she told him that she loved those stories, that they made him more lovable, more charming, he looked at her stupefied. "You do?" he said. "They do?"

She didn't tell him that it made him seem more hers, made him seem more vulnerable. She said only that she had never known anyone who had grown up that way, and it made him special. He touched her face when she said that. He couldn't stop looking at her, almost as if he were searching for something.

He was interested in everything about her. He pored through her yearbooks, her family albums; he held up face after face for her to identify. Her mother. Her father. Herself, a sulky seventeen, perched on Franky's motorbike. He made her tell her own growing-up stories, over and over, until he said he felt like they were his. He couldn't understand why she didn't get back to Chicago more often to see her parents, why she had moved away from them. He offered to go with her on a visit, but she turned him down. "If you had parents, you'd understand," she said. "It has nothing to do with love."

He charmed her. He didn't care about her glasses. When she took them off, he just brought himself in close, so near he could see the gold flecks in her pupils; he swore he could feel the boundaries of their skins.

She felt funny, she felt different with so much attention. She let the kids carry on in class. She ignored it when Ronnie dropped his pen, stooping so he could try to look up her skirt. She daydreamed about Nick while three boys in back threw spitballs, while the girls traded blush and eye shadows, layering it on over their grammar papers, returning the papers to Dore with soft dustings of blue or rose.

She began wearing more interesting clothing. Softer shirts, silkier dresses, earrings made of cut glass that caught and refracted the light into millions of tiny suns across her desk. She grew her bangs and then went into Woolworth's and sat for four photos, which she shyly gave to Nick.

She told him not to, but Nick always called her at school. Teachers weren't supposed to get personal calls. There were only two phones in the whole school—the one the secretary used and the one in the principal's office. If you had anything at all personal to say, the secretary was always right there, leaning toward you, fashioning gossip and juice out of whatever words you let slip. When Nick called, a monitor came into Dore's room to get her. Her students whistled as she left to take the call. "I missed you," Nick said. He promised he wouldn't call again, he said he had just ten minutes, and then two hours later he'd call again.

They ate dinners together. Nick made huge spreads of food for her, so much that she could only stare blankly at it. She never ate a quarter of what he put before her, but Nick kept starting and stopping. He tossed most of the food out, and when she said she'd take some home with her, he laughed. He said he had grown up with leftovers, that he had done more than his fair share of penance and didn't think either one of them should do more. He was always hungry, always eating, and always lean.

He slept with his arms about her, sometimes one leg trapping her hip so she couldn't move. If she rolled away, he rolled with her. It used to annoy her a little, but then she noticed how on the nights he was away, she wouldn't be able to sleep until she had twisted the sheets about her, until she had the pillow pushed up against her, so close she was nearly off the side of the bed.

Nick had her pictures all over his place, in his wallet, in his pockets—once, inside his sneaker. He didn't mind coming home to an empty apartment, because really, it wasn't empty anymore. No place was. Everywhere seemed flooded with Dore, with her voice, her face, the heady possibility he felt when he was with her. She was suddenly everyplace he had ever wanted to be, she was the road he felt destined to travel.

Dore was his first love.

THREE

                                                      • • •

T hey began living together in the spring. They couldn't afford very much. A client of Nick's had called up a rental-agent friend in New York, but the places the agent had shown them were all dark and roachy, with cracking plaster and drippy sinks, and they had cost so much money that Dore would have had to work nights and weekends just to pay her share of the gas bill. The places they saw in New Jersey weren't much better. It was Nick who thought of the trailer courts. He remembered driving past them on his trips selling books. They looked like real communities to him, like places where you couldn't possibly be lonely—and best of all, they were so ridiculously cheap, you could own one for less than $10,000. "Think of it," he kept telling Dore. "It could be ours. No one could take it away from us. We'd own something real."

Dore wasn't so sure about living in such a place, but she went with Nick to scout them out because he was so taken with the whole idea. She went inside a few of the trailers, which were actually pretty spacious, clean and light. They weren't the kind of trailers you just hooked up to the back of your car; they seemed more like homes to her, with foundations and backyards and driveways, and in the end, they bought one on the spot.

Flybird Court was the name of the trailer court they moved into. It was in New Jersey, close enough to Dore's school that she could take a bus to work if she wanted. Nick loved having a place they actually owned. Every time he jiggered the key in the lock and

walked in, he felt flooded with light. He'd stand in the center of the
trailer, grinning like a fool. He'd go and find Dore and make her just
sit with him in the living room, holding hands because he was so
happy.

The first night they moved in, struggling to unpack, trying to
spread their meager furniture around so it looked like more, three
families from down the street came over with a pot of coffee, a
home-baked cake. One of the women had brought a sack of sugar
and some salt: She said the sugar was for sweetness in the new home;
the salt, to give their life bite. Dore was delighted, but when she
started talking about her teaching, when it became clear that she
and Nick didn't have kids, that they didn't even seem to want them,
and—worse—probably weren't even married, the friendliness evapo-
rated a little. "They just need to get used to us, that's all," Nick told
Dore that night as they lay together in bed. "We'll be a part of things
soon enough."

They didn't worry about it at first. There was the trailer to get
used to. Dore couldn't sleep nights. She'd bolt awake, hearing steps
in the kitchen, murmuring voices she swore came from the living
room. She got up with Nick to investigate. They stood still and
silent until Nick heard a familiar sound. A toilet flushing noisily. A
door. He recognized a voice, heard the name of the man down the
street, and a kid being scolded for not turning off the lights. Some
nights, it wasn't voices. The wind would crash against the flimsy
window, shaking the trailer so the dishes rattled in the cupboard.
Breaking glass next door reverberated in their living room. Nick
found himself talking to Dore in a low voice, pulling her close so he
could whisper, so he could protect his thoughts.

Things happened in the trailer. Winters, the pipes froze. Dore
would step into the shower and nothing would come out of the
spigot. The toilet froze up. Dore would have to go next door to the
Rivers' place and, shamed, ask if she could use the bathroom. They
were friendly enough, but she was mortified, coming into a stranger's
home while they were eating their dinner, clinking their silver and
staring at her. She worried about stomachaches, about getting sick.
She wouldn't leave school until the very last minute, then always
visited the bathroom whether she had to go or not, and she wouldn't
drink a thing.

One night she woke up at four, her bladder swollen. Desperate, she went into the kitchen. She was ready to hoist herself up and pee into the sink the way she knew Nick did when the toilet wasn't working. She thought about going outside, but there was no privacy, there were still lights from all the other trailers. She finally took a jar of grape juice out of the refrigerator and dumped it out; she peed into that.

Sometimes they'd pile into the car and drive to a gas station, to the cheap eateries along the highway, ignoring the signs that said rest rooms were for patrons only. Well, they became patrons. They slid into the cheap plastic seats and ordered the least expensive thing on the menu, ignoring the gloomy frowns of the waitress. Tea. Coffee black. One piece of toast, no butter. They'd wait until the waitress left and then they'd get up and use the rest rooms, washing up with a whole sinkful of hot water, brushing their teeth, coming back just to slap a dollar or two on the table and leave.

But the worst thing about the trailers was that they were firetraps. In fact, it was impossible to get any insurance. Dore was sleeping one night when she felt restless, suddenly hot. She kicked the covers off, and then felt a shimmer of sweat moving over her. She woke Nick, and it was he who noticed the yellow curl of fire through the window.

They bundled into sweaters and went outside. The trailer down the block was blazing, making the sky blurry with smoke. The whole court seemed to be outside, huddled together, everyone talking and whispering as the fire trucks whined steadily toward them. Dore recognized the woman next to her; she was the one who had brought Dore the sugar, the salt for bite.

When Dore leaned toward her, the woman gave a weary smile. "Flora," she reminded Dore. She nodded to Nick. She told them how dangerous a thing like this was, how easy it was for sparks to blow and strike like flint against another trailer. "This fire belongs to everyone here," she said. "The whole court. The trailer next to the one burning is already so hot you couldn't get near it if you wanted to." She pointed to the fireman who was hosing it down, cooling it so it wouldn't flame. "It happened once," Flora said.

"What did?" asked Nick, mesmerized by the fire.

"A whole community," Flora said. "Two kids just pranking around with matches because their mother didn't have sense enough to watch them, and then thirty trailers burned right up, falling like they were dominoes."

Dore wrapped her sweater about her, but Nick abruptly walked away, his face averted, unreadable. He walked toward the burning trailer. "Excuse me," Dore said, tilting her head toward Nick. Flora just nodded, stepping back a bit. Dore went over to Nick, but at first he didn't even seem to see her. She was about to tap his shoulder when, without even turning, he reached for her hand, he held it.

"I never saw anything go so fast," he said.

The fire lasted another half-hour before the trailer collapsed to the ground. The trailer next to it was badly scorched but still standing, needing only minor repairs, a fresh coat of paint. No one talked much walking away from the fire. The people who had lost their trailer, a family with a two-month-old baby boy, were taken in by another family, and in the eerie stillness you could hear the woman softly crying. That night, Nick stayed up, staring out the front window at the ruin down the street, and when Dore touched his shoulder, for the first time since she had known him, he seemed not to see her.

The people who had owned the trailer moved out of state. They sent only one postcard, a week or so later, addressed to the whole court. It was tacked up on the community bulletin board, the front of it showing a garish white southern mansion, the back spider-webbed with print. "This is our grand new digs. Ha ha. We've been staying with Betty's folks in Virginia, hope to have our own place quick. Love to all from June, Henry, and Little Bill." There was no return address.

Nick kept walking past the burned-out lot where the trailer used to be. Some nights he just stood in front of it, uneasily surveying the court. For a while, there was some talk about the court finally setting up its own volunteer fire patrol, and there were even a few fire-prevention meetings in the community center. Nick went to every one of them, but nothing ever got accomplished. Harry Corcoran, who lived two trailers down from Nick, got up and showed diagrams of commonsense measures, things like throwing out oily rags, not leaving the iron on, never smoking in bed. Another woman, Ellie

Lambros, suggested everyone watch out for everyone else. Several people wanted smoke detectors installed.

Fewer and fewer people showed up at the meetings, and gradually the talk died down. No one really wanted to talk about another fire. The ground where the trailer had burned was going to be all dug up and reseeded. The company who managed the court was already planning to put a new, bigger trailer in there. And the people whose trailer had been scorched were busy sanding it down, planning on painting it a nice cheerful blue.

Nick, though, couldn't forget. He brought the fire up in so many casual conversations with other people that they began crossing the street when they saw him, waving a hand and then moving on. Flora cornered Dore and asked her if she couldn't do something about that alarmist husband of hers because he was scaring the kids.

Nick came home one night with a small fire extinguisher. He set it up in the kitchen, taught Dore how to use it, and then tacked up the number of the fire department right by the phone, where they could see it. This was his home, the first he'd had in a very long time, and he had no intention of losing it again.

Nick waited for the community to take them in. The other men kept watching him suspiciously. They didn't like the way he was changing the trailer, putting on a small cement porch in back so he and Dore could sit out on cool evenings. He never went down to the grassy field to play ball with the other men after supper, he never sat with them listening to the radio droning out baseball games and pop music, and he never once shared the beer getting warmer in the dizzy heat. Instead, he ran every night he was home, round and round the trailer court, six times by Flora's own count, his black sneakers attracting all the court dogs like iron to a magnet. He had appeared at the field only once, and then with Dore, the only woman there, holding her hand, bending her to him for kisses, bold as a looking glass, clearly more interested in her than in friendship with any of the men. The men all felt it, and they carried resentment like an itch they weren't sure how to scratch.

Dore, too, was carefully watched and considered. The other women all kept house, they all watched over the husbands they had married fresh out of high school. They cooked and shopped and traded recipes, sitting out cool evenings on nylon chairs, watching the kids banging a ball around, playing freeze tag until they had to be pulled inside and calmed down enough for bed. Everyone got up early, but it was to fix the kids pancakes and cereal, to make sure their husbands had their coffee. No one was rushing off to work themselves at 6:30 in the morning unless they had to; no one worked for the pleasure of it. And no one came home with a box of shoes from Saks, leather sandals that cost more money than any one of them would spend on the whole family put together.

Dore and Nick were inseparable. They would take walks at night holding hands, nipping kisses back and forth like hungry teenagers. They'd go for drives and come back sharing the same pint of ice cream, using their fingers to feed each other. The few parties they went to at the community center, they never split up into the husband and wife groups the others made. Nick swooned Dore in his arms, romanced her with whispers, acted as though he saw no one else in that room. It prickled up feelings in the others—so that Flora strode purposefully across the floor and took her surprised husband's hand; so that Harry Werner, the center manager, watching his wife smoking, her eyes irritated slants, went outside to stand helplessly under the stars.

They made it so clear that they missed each other sometimes. When Nick was at home, he'd walk to the entrance of the court to wait for Dore to get home from school, a bouquet of dandelions in his hand for her. And when Nick was away on business, Dore seemed faded, a little lost. She'd work on the tomatoes she was planting in the back, laughing when someone suggested that all those plants would just bring bees. She'd sit on the cement porch that Nick had built and read, or correct papers, stopping to look out across the sky. When the phone rang, she'd drop the papers, not caring that they scattered in the yard for the court dogs to fetch and rip wildly, and then she'd be inside on the phone for an hour before she came out again, cheerfully shooing the dogs.

They both tried to be friendly. The first few months Nick and Dore must have smiled at every face they saw. They both tried to strike up conversations, but nothing seemed to take. Dore even walked next door to ask Flora if she wanted to have coffee with her, but at that time Flora had her hands full making dinner for her kids; she couldn't stop to get all caffeined up with a neighbor she wasn't so sure about knowing in the first place.

Nick began bringing home samples of the kids' books he sold, thinking he could give some out since a lot of the families in the court didn't have extra money for things like books. But when he gave a few to some of the fathers, they looked at him like he was from another planet, they flipped the books over and over in their hands before grudgingly accepting. When Nick passed by the women, he tried to small-talk and tease a smile from them, but they dismissed him with curt nods. Yet for all their seeming disinterest, he couldn't help noticing that every time he got into his car, a shade would flutter; that every time he came home after a few days on the road, the women talking in one of the front yards would go silent for a minute—they'd listen to how he greeted Dore, how she greeted him. It was as if they were piecing together his life for him, making it into a drama he wasn't to participate in.

The lack of community really bothered Nick. He bound tighter to Dore and he concentrated on his work. Although he missed her when he was away—although every bookshop and library he walked into reminded him that she was elsewhere—sometimes, too, he'd feel this odd stab of relief when he got into his car and pulled out of the court, when he saw the whole block quietly receding into his rearview mirror.

And then, just six months after they had moved into the court, Dore got pregnant, and everything changed.

The stories Dore would later tell Robin always started at this time, when she was the happiest, living in the trailer court with Nick and newly pregnant, basking in a time when love seemed as much an unending miracle as the baby within her. Nick got her a great doctor in New York City and watched her as if she were breakable. She felt smooth and calm and absolutely anchored to her life with him.

She remembered it all—how her pregnancy had changed things, how it had made all the women in the court suddenly friendly to her. Flora had come over first, balancing a home-baked ginger cake in one hand, a spool of new white thread fisted in her spare. She told Dore she knew how to tell the sex of a child before it was born just by the way a section of thread swayed over your belly; it was something her own mother had handed down to her. It didn't matter how early a pregnancy was, it didn't even matter if you knew you were pregnant, the thread would sway rightside for a girl, list left for boy. Flora's own mother used to put the thread over Flora's belly every Friday night when she came home from a date, checking, making sure all those kisses Flora was collecting weren't so sugared up they were causing danger.

Dore didn't believe one thing about the thread, but Flora had hardly spoken to her since she and Nick had moved in. Dore placed the cake on the kitchen counter and followed Flora over to one of the sunny benches by the community center. She sat beside Flora and watched her lazily unwind the thread, testing its flutter in the wind. It was silly business, but even so, Dore closed her eyes, letting Flora's features fade. She found herself taking a breath and holding on to it. She felt the long, loose drift of Flora's sleeve moving across her, and then nothing. And it was the nothing—the clear emptiness of the moment—that made her jerk her eyes open. Flora was rewinding the thread, carefully wrapping it tight, her face lowered. "Flora," Dore said, and Flora looked up, smiling. "You got yourself the best," she said generously. "You got one of your own kind."

Dore told Nick, who laughed. Flora told the other women, who began trickling over Saturdays, when Dore didn't teach. They sat on the floor pillows, eating the pies they had brought over, and they gave Dore advice. They told her to quit her job, that even an unborn child could use some tending. "I never understood why you worked anyhow," Flora said. "You sure don't look like it's a need or anything."

"I like to," Dore said.

Flora looked at the other women, blinking.

Dore found she liked the trailer women coming over. She looked forward to their visits. She was nervous sometimes about being pregnant, and they offered support, they opened up their lives to her like training manuals she could keep referring to. They brought over old baby books, the pages turned back and underlined, mottled with formula, and Dore would touch the stains with one finger and think: I'm tracing a life. The women brought her their kids' old baby clothing, the toys their kids no longer had any use for. They told her how wonderful children were, how there was nothing in the whole wide world nearly so special as being a mother. Ruby Tyler, Flora's best friend, told Dore that childbirth pain was like a blink. You forgot it as soon as you had the baby; it erased itself into the strong new life of a child that loved you before its eyes were even opened.

Ruby had five girls of her own, and she kept bringing Dore bags and bags of her old maternity clothing. Ruby was a big woman, with heavy black hair she cropped short. She favored lace and ruffles, the kind of cheap synthetics that felt spongy and dead in Dore's fingers. There were sweet prints Dore wouldn't be caught dead in, fluorescent plaids that made her ill just looking at them.

Ruby insisted on showing Dore every item, fishing in the bags, plucking out dresses and pants and smoothing them flat across her body so Dore could see. She kept up an energetic commentary the whole time she was modeling the clothing. All Dore would have to do was hem a few things, maybe take them in a bit. Later, after she had the baby, she could still wear the dresses just by investing in a few belts or using a bright scarf or two to cinch back a waist.

Dore was politely grateful. She cared more for the company, for the advice, than for the clothing, and she needed to keep Ruby as her friend. She waited until Ruby had gone before she stuffed the clothes back into the bags, into her closet.

She never wore any of Ruby's dresses, even when she was swelling up with baby, but Ruby kept bringing her things. Shoes with the toes cut away because Ruby said your feet swelled during pregnancy. Stained robes she claimed were perfect for feeding a messy baby. What did you have to look good for? Who would see you? Babies didn't care a hoot, and you didn't want to be attracting any male attention; when you needed all your energy for caring for a baby, you didn't want to be starting up another. Dore was amused, but she said nothing.

The bags of clothing began taking up all the closet space they had. She didn't want to hurt Ruby's feelings, so she waited until night to pack up the car, and then she dropped everything into the Goodwill box by the market.

Every time Nick came home, there were women in the place, talking, laughing with Dore, glancing up at him when he passed. No one stayed long after Nick came home, and when he asked Dore what they had been talking about, she just laughed at him, told him it was just woman talk.

Woman talk. But he was involved, too. This was his son, his daughter. These were his cells bonding up with Dore's in a connection so permanent it never ceased to amaze him. Every time he reached for her at night, he thought about it. He kept tracing his hands over her belly, resting his head gently on the swelling, and whispering down to the fetus.

Dore laughed. "Hey, what's going on down there?"· she asked, soothing his hair with her fingers.

"Top secret," Nick said. "Strictly between me and my baby."

He whispered stories to the fetus, having read somewhere that life always recognized life; that even a fetus might respond and remember. He told the baby who he was, how he felt, how he was going to be the most spectacular father the world had ever seen. There would be stories written about him in *Time* and *Newsweek*; there'd be other kids clamoring for him to be their father, but he'd have eyes only for his own. He told the baby he'd never leave it, never let it feel unloved or lost or lonely or set apart—no, not for one second. And then he drew himself up and looked at Dore's smiling face and he began tenderly stroking her breasts, her face, the curve of her back. He rolled her into lovemaking, all the time feeling that he was somehow making love to his child as well, and that it was all right this way, it was just the three of them all connecting at once.

He wanted to talk to everyone about his baby, but the trailer women withdrew when he sat with them, and the men didn't do more than offer congratulations. Except for Flora's husband, Bill, who told him where he might find some innocent pleasures when Dore got too big with baby—girls, he said, who were clean and would do whatever you wanted without stitching up their faces and making you feel guilty about even asking.

So Nick went further—he began confiding in his clients, courting their advice. The men handed him birth books put out by various women's groups; the women all told him they swore by Dr. Spock. He liked it better when they told him about their own experiences: when the men talked about their wives giving birth quickly, without pain, and said how wonderful their babies had been, how much fun. His women clients pulled out photo after photo of their kids and, prompted by Nick's giddy pleasure, asked to see Dore's. "Oh, such a lovely wife!" they said.

It made him think, it made him unsure. He and Dore had never really thought about marriage. At least, she had never pressed him, and he had felt so bonded to her, it seemed unnecessary. Besides, the paperwork made him think of all the social workers he had had back at the home, made him think about the whole trapped way the place had made him feel, and he got suddenly uneasy and restless, sud-denly almost angry with Dore, as if she had brought that feeling back to life.

He told himself to forget it, that what a baby needed was love and parents, not paper, and he roamed the stores for baby things, for toys and sweaters. It was only when he was leaving that he passed the jewelry counter, and he stopped, looking down at the shimmery gold bands. One set was very cheap, and when he bought them, he told himself it was just as a token, that it didn't have to mean anything. He brought them home and hid them in Dore's top drawer, under the cucumber cream she smoothed on her belly at night because she was worried about stretch marks. When she was finally ready for bed, when she saw the rings, her face went funny. She sat down on the bed.

"It's because of the baby, isn't it?" she said. "I can't have you marrying me just because of the baby."

"That's not it," he said, but she shook her head.

"No," she said. "I couldn't be sure of that."

"I could," he said, but she wouldn't listen to him. She carefully wrapped the rings back up in the tissue and put them back in the drawer, and then she curled up around him.

"I'll take them back," he said, but she shook her head again.

"We'll keep them," she said. "For when I'm ready."

"Okay," he said, dipping to kiss her, suddenly light with relief.

She taught until her eighth month. Her class grew less restless, more polite as she increasingly swelled. The boys began opening doors for her, getting her a chair; the girls shyly approached her after class, wanting to touch her belly, to feel a kick if they could. The whole class gave her a going-away party, a week before her maternity leave began. Ronnie spiked the cherry Kool-Aid with whiskey, but he wouldn't let Dore have one sip. He insisted she drink the bottle of ginger beer he had bought especially for her; he said he had heard somewhere, maybe even on the news, that carbonation was good for pregnancy. He watched her, his face solemn, as she drank. They even gave her presents. Stuffed baby toys, tiny blue T-shirts, a cut-glass rose with a note that said, "From all of us with love." Dore felt like crying. "Come back," Debby told her. "Don't you dare let that baby make you forget us."

"If you do, we'll find you and we'll kill you," Ronnie said. "I'll walk my dog right in front of your trailer every night at three in the morning, and I'll make him bark his head off, too."

"Oh, don't do that," Dore said, but she laughed, pleased.

The baby was born in March. Nick was in the delivery room, holding Dore's shivering hands, moving around so much that the doctor snapped at him: If he couldn't keep out of the way, he would have to leave. Nick breathed when Dore did; the contortions in his face matched hers. He swabbed her forehead with a cool cloth, he bent to kiss her, and all the time he felt his body getting lighter and lighter. When the baby was born, Dore gave a small cry and Nick reached for the child, but they were putting drops into its eyes, they were gently washing it, and when they turned, they walked past Nick; a nurse gently placed the baby on Dore's sweat-soaked chest. "Girl," the doctor said, grinning, slapping Nick on the back. "Got yourself a hell of a daughter."

They called the baby Susan, and right from the start, Nick fell in love with her. He couldn't get over the dusting of hair she had, as black as his own, how such tiny eyes could mirror Dore's. It never stopped astounding him that there was this whole new person in the world, someone so irrevocably his. She made him feel he had a right to be on the earth, if only to take care of her. She gave him his passage.

The whole first week when Dore was in bed, exhausted, a little dazed, Nick stayed home with her. Flora had given them a white crib as a present, but he liked bringing the baby right into bed with them, where he could sit with the two of them, just beaming and beaming because he was part of a family. He wanted Dore all the time now, but she kept having to wave him away. She reminded him that she had just had a baby, and he told her that that fact was exactly what was moving his desire, heating him up like a Roman candle. She laughed at him, she nuzzled the baby, and then she drifted to sleep. She slept a great deal, in vague fits and starts, and even when she was awake, she seemed tired, content to let Nick take care of things.

The women in the court never stopped coming over. It was Flora who noticed the curiously shaped birthmark on Susan's shoulder, who said the baby was marked. When she saw Dore's startled face, she softened a bit. She said it could be a good sign; that after all, only a fool would be positive about anything. The other women were more polite. Ruby pointed out the baby's dimples, exclaimed over the blue eyes. The women brought over ready-made suppers in covered casseroles. They brought mops and cleaners and diaper pails.

At first, Nick was a little unnerved. He wanted time alone with his family. He appreciated the suppers, but he didn't see why the women couldn't just leave them on the table and then go. And he didn't like the way Flora kept studying him, the way she followed when he went into the baby's room. He shut the door on her a few times just so he could rock his own daughter in peace.

He whispered stories to her. He made up lullabies so sweet and gentle that the one time Dore heard one, she had to catch her breath to keep from calling out to him. He lost track of everything but the slow rise and fall of Susan's chest, and as soon as he stepped out of the room, he yearned to go back inside, to pick her up and feel her in his arms once again.

"What's going on in there?" Flora said, but he refused to tell her; he said it was between him and his daughter, a family matter.

He would have booted all of the trailer women out if it weren't for Dore. While she had been calm and strong during her pregnancy, being a mother made her nervous and unsure. At first she kept calling her parents, begging advice, but her mother seemed strangely uninterested. Although Dore was certainly full-grown and responsible, her mother considered being an unmarried mother and living in a trailer court as much a lack of vision as falling in love with the family butcher. Her father was silent and disappointed. They acted as though it were another phase that would pass soon enough. They had no interest at all in speaking to Nick, which bothered Dore so much, she finally stopped calling. "It's okay," Nick said, trying to soothe her. He told her her parents would come around, to just forget about it, and in the meantime she could lose herself in him and the baby.

But it was the other women Dore turned to. They relaxed her. They told her how to diaper and feed Susan, they coaxed her out of bed and into the sun so she could get some color on her. She could ask the women anything and they would reassure her. Everyone had been nervous with a brand-new baby; everyone had felt less than perfect; no one had known what was the perfect way to raise a child. Flora told Dore to call her anytime, even in the middle of the night, and she'd come over. Dore liked the women coming over; she was more than willing to let Flora hold Susan all afternoon, more than happy to let Ruby feed her her bottle. Although she loved the baby, she wasn't quite sure what to do with her, how to behave; and although it made her feel guilty, she was happiest when Susan just slept.

It was difficult for Nick to go back on the road. The trailer women made it a little easier for him because of the way they took care of Dore. But still, he'd be all ready to leave, and then he'd find reasons to go back into Susan's room. He'd lift her up for a moment, and then place her back in her crib, and then he'd be frozen at the door, unable to tear his eyes off her.

When he traveled, he called in to talk to the baby as well as to Dore. He made Dore hold the phone up against Susan's ear so he could sing to her. He figured the baby would recognize the sound of his voice, the baby would know she had a father who was alive in the world and thinking of nothing but her.

When he was home, he told Susan stories. Dore would watch him from outside the darkened room, giving him his time alone with his daughter, and the stories he told made her fall in love with him even more. He made up wild things—places where all the cats were psychic and had the power of speech and could tell you your future in soft, insinuating purrs. He told stories about people in Brazil who changed themselves into dogs and horses at will, who could fly from one end of the globe to another in less time than it took a puppy to sneeze. And, too, he told the stories Tom had told him; and as he told them, he remembered his own wonder, and he thought of himself as reconnecting to his father, as passing him down like a heritage.

Dore waited until Nick was finished, and then it was her turn to tiptoe into the room and gently take Susan. She would sit in the rocker and tell stories of her own. "Peter Rabbit." "Little Red Riding Hood." The stories any mother would tell any daughter.

Nick would never less than adore Susan, but for Dore it was something else. She could never quite relax into being a mother. She was tired all the time; she wanted to sleep through a lazy afternoon instead of getting up to change her daughter or coax her out of a crying fit. She'd watch Nick doting and feel tight twinges of guilt. She kept telling herself it would pass.

And then, abruptly, Susan began having bad dreams. She screamed and twisted in her sleep, and Dore, thinking she was just hungry, just wet, would go into her room with a bottle and a dry diaper. Susan wasn't even damp, and she flinched from the bottle Dore offered; she flailed her arms and pushed away from her mother. Dore, terrified, would watch Susan struggling in her crib, and would finally grab her up and pace, singing bits of songs, trying to hush Susan a little. But the baby wouldn't be pacified. Her face got so red and contorted, Dore feared she was strangling. She called up Flora, who told Dore she had been on her way anyway, that you could hear the baby halfway across the court.

Flora took the baby from Dore and set her, still screaming, into her crib. She took Dore firmly by the arm and shut the door. "Let her cry it out," Flora said. "It's just bad dreams."

"Bad dreams?" Dore said. "What could a baby possibly have a bad dream about?"

Flora shook her head. "I don't know. It could be just indigestion. Or then again, it could be a sign of something. You might want to take her to a doctor."

Dore sat up. "What sign?" she said. She remembered the birthmark on Susan's shoulder. She had rubbed it with mineral oil until Nick had caught her hands and stopped her, telling her the mark was part of who Susan was, and shouldn't be tampered with.

"I don't know," Flora said. "That's something you'll just have to figure out yourself, because sure as all hell, this little one isn't going to tell you." She rubbed Dore's back. "Don't worry," she said. "Listen. You hear that? She's sleeping now."

Dore, in the silence, suddenly wanted to sleep herself. She started to get up, but Flora stopped her. "You might start her up again."

Dore worried. She took the baby to a doctor, who looked at Dore as though she had three heads when she started talking about signs and nightmares. He told her it sounded like a virus, and gave her a prescription for drops she was to put in the baby's milk, three times a day. The prescription cost twenty dollars, and when she gave it to Susan, it just made Susan get sleepy faster, and the nightmares occurred that much sooner.

Dore got tense waiting for the screams to start. Flora was good about coming over—she'd bring her knitting, the kids' jeans to mend—but all she could really do was offer Dore support.

Nick was home one afternoon when Susan had a nightmare. He hadn't really believed Dore's stories, he had been sure she was exaggerating, but then he heard Susan's terror for himself and saw what happened to her face. Dore gave him a hopeless look of fear, but he went and picked up Susan and walked her back and forth in the trailer, singing, bouncing her, doing whatever he could think of to soothe, while Dore stood in the hallway, pale and exhausted. Susan didn't seem to cry as long when Nick was carrying her, and she finally fell asleep right in his arms. He put her back in her crib and she slept through the night.

Whenever he was home, then, Nick began walking the baby's terrors away, calming her, taking less and less time to do it. And then the nightmares stopped, as abruptly as they had begun. There was one quiet afternoon, with both Nick and Dore tense, and then another, and then things eased back to normal. "I wonder what that was all about," Nick said. But Dore, remembering how the baby stiffened in her arms, remembering Nick turning to her with Susan sleeping in his arms, averted her face, taking it all as blame.

FOUR

· · ·

Susan was barely six months old when Dore began to feel guilty. Sometimes she thought it was because of Nick, because of her anger at him. He seemed more in love with his child than with her. He couldn't go down to the supermarket for a box of Kleenex without taking the baby with him. He had to take her to museums; to drive-ins, where he'd make a soft bed for her in the back seat; to restaurants and shopping malls. He just wouldn't go anywhere unless the baby went along as well. As soon as he stepped into the trailer, before he even saw Dore waiting for him, waiting for the kisses that should be hers, he was in the baby's room, teasing her, singing and nuzzling, riling Susan up so she wouldn't sleep later.

Dore tried to pull Nick back to her. She put on sheer black night-gowns, she dusted herself with perfumed powder, and then she started seducing him—unbuttoning his shirt, tugging him down on the living-room rug if she had to. She felt it, though, how he some-how wasn't there, how he kept listening for a voice that wasn't hers, for sounds she wasn't making.

"I'll just be one minute," he'd say, bending to kiss her breasts before rising up away from her.

She'd wait one minute, then two, before storming to her feet. She didn't have to guess where he was, she knew his face was softened in wonder, that he was leaning over Susan's crib. But she couldn't yell at him. How could she? A man had the right to adore his daughter. And it was more than most of the men in the trailer court were capable of. None of them took his kids to the park the way Nick did; not one of them would be willing to spend a whole Sunday just sitting on a blanket with a baby. The children here all belonged to the women who bore them.

The trailer women saw how Nick doted on Susan, but even so, they gave their advice to Dore. They didn't discuss children with men. Dore saw the pictures Ruby's girls drew, taped up on the kitchen cabinets. Ruby was always drawn big and bright, taking up the page with her outstretched hands, her mass of hair, and her smile. But her husband, Danny, who was even larger than she was in real life, was dwarfed on the paper. He had no arms, and in some of the pictures it looked like he was wearing a skirt.

The first time Dore saw those drawings, she had to sneeze to keep from laughing. She waltzed home and curled about Nick in gratitude. She used to think she knew what Susan's drawings would look like, but lately she feared that she would be the person dwarfed and disappearing in a drawing. She thought the baby preferred Nick. Susan quieted right down when it was Nick who picked her up. She didn't stiffen in feeding the way she sometimes did with Dore. Susan would let Nick change her without a fight, and when Nick was away on the road, the baby seemed to know. She'd get cranky, spit up in her crib, and refuse her bottle. She perked up only when she saw Nick again, when he asked how his girl was. "Oh, we're both dandy," Dore said.

The whole thing vaguely shamed her so that she couldn't talk about it, not even with Flora. She told herself she wasn't a bad mother, there wasn't one thing defective about her. If there had been, the other women would have picked up on it, they would have noticed it and scolded her. She watched the way they were with their babies. She didn't think they showed any more love than she showed Susan.

No, she took good care of her baby. She rocked her and told her stories. She took Susan into the bathtub with her and filled it with bubbles. She'd look at her baby and feel half-dizzy with love. She didn't know. It was just that whole nightmare period, the way Susan was somehow different with Nick. Dore thought maybe she just needed to get out alone with Nick, without the baby. Maybe when Susan got used to that, Dore could even think about going back to work again. Nick, after all, still had his job. They could hire a girl, just for half the day, just until she got home. Dore remembered Ronnie Dazen's eyes suddenly, how they had followed her, had seen no one else but her—and despite herself, she blushed with pleasure.

Nick was uneasy about getting a sitter, but he agreed to it when he saw how unhappy Dore was, how much she wanted to get out alone with him. He wouldn't hire anyone from the trailer court, though there was certainly a wealth of baby-sitting material there. The girls scribbled advertisements for themselves on colored index cards they tacked up on the bulletin board by the pool. The names blurred from the splash of the water, the slogans ("Leave the baby with someone you know, then what a treat to get up and go"; "Hire me, I'm great, you see!") grew smeared and inky. Nick didn't trust any of them. They were too young, too silly. They whispered every time he walked by them.

So Nick called up one of those services, and there were a few interviews, and finally they hired a high-school girl named Monique Lelac, who came with two references. Monique was tall and pale and thin, studying to be a painter. She was from France, finishing her basic schooling before returning. Nick thought she was great. The first time she came over, he saw how she moved right toward the baby, how she pulled two soft cotton blocks out of her bag and handed them to Susan.

Nick insisted on giving Monique a detailed lesson on how to use the fire extinguisher. He showed her the numbers of the police and fire departments tacked up right by the phone, and he showed her how to light the stove, making her do it while he watched. Dore told him he was being silly; that if they wanted to make the movie, they should go now.

Their first few times out alone, Nick called Monique from the theater, from the restaurant. He didn't relax until they were back in the trailer and he saw for himself how Susan was sleeping. "You see?" Monique said. "Everything is fine."

They hired Monique every week. Nick began trusting her enough not to call her at all, and Dore finally relaxed. She found she liked her daughter much better when she didn't have to spend every minute of the day with her, when she could have Nick to herself for a whole evening. It felt like they were courting again. They held hands in the dark of the movies. At restaurants, she would lean over and nip him on the neck. One evening he surprised her by driving out to one of the lakes and parking with her. There were other cars scattered about, just teenagers, fumbling in the back seats, passing Thunderbird wine back and forth. But Nick had brought champagne and he spread out a soft plaid blanket across the back seat, and when the two of them came home, they were both flushed, their eyes glittering like mica. "Have a nice time?" Monique asked.

No one in the trailer court went out as often as they did. No one could afford to, or maybe no one wanted to. Sometimes, when Nick was away for a week, Dore would call Monique just so she could get out and go to a movie by herself or go shopping. It was too hard being without Nick and having to stay in the trailer all day. "A baby needs attention," Flora said. "She gets it," Dore said, balancing Susan in her lap.

Her guilt made her try harder. She'd put Susan into the backpack Nick had bought and take her to the park. "What a good girl," she crooned. "My little plum." She'd turn and look at Susan with rare delight. She'd start to feel wonderful. And then her back would begin to hurt so she'd have to unbuckle the backpack and carry Susan in her arms. By the time she got home, exhausted, hot, Susan burbling and happy, she'd need to curl up around the heating pad to uncramp her muscles. She tried to talk to Susan, saying, "Listen, I'm your mother and I love you, I do." She told her stories about mothers who loved their babies so much they created whole magic kingdoms for them. And then she'd lie back in bed and remember how complete she had felt carrying Susan, how content and whole, and she'd try to figure out just why that feeling had left her, just where it had gone, and why love wasn't enough.

Dore felt the women watching her when she went out nights with Nick. She sensed eyes behind the curtains studying Nick when he walked Monique out to the car to drive her home, her long white legs flashing in the moonlight. The trailer girls who baby-sat resented this usurper. They snubbed Monique every chance they got, deliberately gathering in front of Dore's to talk, becoming sulky and silent when Monique walked past. Girls who had once come out of now-where to help Dore carry groceries from her car, to help with the stroller, seemed suddenly to evaporate.

Ruby, whose girls baby-sat more than anyone, came to visit Dore less and less, and when she did come, she was critical. She noticed the baby's wet diaper before Dore did; she commented on the brand of baby food Dore used, telling her stories about glass being found in the jars. She judged everything, but she never once came out and asked why Dore hadn't hired one of Ruby's own girls to tend her baby. Monique even made the mistake of putting her own index card up on the bulletin board for baby-sitting. It was ripped down every time she tacked it up, and of course no one ever called her.

The thing about Monique was that she didn't even like kids. She needed occasional work that paid decently, and baby-sitting was the one thing she knew she could get. People were morons. All she had to do was say two words with her French accent and suddenly she was in hot demand. It was all such baloney. No one ever bothered to check her references, which were coaxed from old beaux, written in false hands.

She didn't do much with Susan. She set her into her playpen and then studied for an hour or so before she got on the phone. She would have invited her American boyfriend over if it weren't so far out of the way, and if the people in the court didn't watch her so. Instead, she phoned him. She knew how to time things, how to gauge when Nick would call, irritating her with a million stupid questions, reminding her over and over about the damned fire extinguisher. He didn't even keep ashtrays around, at least not that she could find. He had babyproofed the place so well it once took her a half-hour just to find a sharp knife to cut some cheese. But at least after he had called, she knew she was free for the night. An hour before they were to return, she'd tend Susan, changing her, giving her a bottle. She put Susan to bed briskly, with no stories, with only a snap of a kiss. She was a good enough baby. She didn't cry that much, and despite herself, Monique was actually beginning to like her.

They were dancing, moving among the kids and the bright lights, when Nick decided to call Monique again. He was gone for only a moment, and when he came back he was vaguely irritated. "She's been on that damned phone for hours," he said.

"Well, she's a kid," Dore said. "What do you want?"

They left early, though, and when they walked into the trailer, Monique was curled on the couch, reading a botany textbook. The place was so quiet, you could hear the ticking of the clock. "You're home early," she said.

Dore brushed by the baby's room and peeked inside. Susan was under a light yellow blanket, her soft white toy lamb beside her. When Dore walked back to Nick, she said, "She's perfectly fine," and then she went into the kitchen for some water.

"And no more phone calls that take two days," Nick said to Monique, handing her her money.

"What two days?" Monique said. She stretched, waiting to be driven home.

Probably no one would have noticed anything for a while if Nick hadn't decided to go and check on his daughter himself, if he hadn't taken Dore's peek one step farther, bending down to kiss Susan, to stroke back a soft wisp of hair, the same inky black as his own.

The name for it was crib death. A simple catch in the breath, a death so soundless you could stand right over a baby and never even notice that one moment there was an intake of breath, and the next, nothing. It was a mystery unprotected by fire extinguishers and phone calls, by rope-tied drawers and covered wall sockets.

Monique had insisted on coming to the hospital, terrified that she had done something she shouldn't have. Even after she knew it was crib death, she still couldn't meet anyone's eyes, and when she left, she left alone, hailing a cab in the darkness.

Nick and Dore were sleepwalkers. They rode home not speaking, not touching. It wasn't until they reached the entrance of the court that Dore got hysterical, that Nick remembered, almost as if waking from a dream, that Susan wasn't going to be there. His hands started shaking; he violently swerved the car around, careening, driving like a crazy person to the Holiday Inn at the next exit.

He felt safer in the hotel. He kept telling himself it was somehow a mistake, that none of it was really happening. He'd wake up in the morning and realize his error and then he'd owe Monique all this money for spending a whole night watching over his daughter, his girl. He tried to breathe normally. He sat on one of the beds in the room, beside Dore, but her eyes were glassy with pain, and when he touched her, she flinched.

Dore eventually cried herself into a restless sleep, but Nick stayed up, one hand on her belly where it rose and fell with her breath, the other hand moving on his own knee, the way a stranger's hand would in comforting. Don't think, he told himself. Don't think.

They stayed at the hotel until after the funeral, and when they drove home, they drove with people from the trailer court and Dore's parents. No one knew what to say to Nick. The men patted his arm, stiff, uncomfortable; a few muttered vague sorrow. But all the women concentrated their energies on their own kind, on Dore. Flora wouldn't let Dore alone for one moment. She even offered to move the two of them into her trailer for a while; she said she wasn't so sure that being alone right now was such a hot idea. "She's not alone," said Nick, but Flora paid him no mind.

Nick sealed up the baby's room, but Dore kept walking by, jerking the door open, straining to hear anything, a cry, a breath. She couldn't believe she wouldn't open the door Nick kept shutting and find Susan laughing in her crib. It wasn't true.

Dore's parents left, and the women from the court began coming over with plates of cold cuts. They all let Dore be. No one thought of blaming her for hiring a sitter outside the court, for going out so often; no one even mentioned the mother's intuition they all depended on. The only person doing any blaming was Dore herself.

She told them what a terrible mother she had been. She'd get so wrought up she'd have to go into the bathroom. They'd all hear the water rushing into the sink, masking her crying, and when she came back out, no one said anything about her red eyes, no one looked at anything but the tangle of needlework in their hands, the plates on the table. Dore told them she was responsible, that she was an unnatural mother, that she had ignored her own baby.

"Oh, hush, you did not," said Ruby.

"The baby had nightmares," Dore said suddenly. "She wouldn't stop crying." She looked at Flora. "You knew. Everyone knew. You said you could hear it halfway down the court. I don't know, maybe she knew what was going to happen. Babies are so close to their beginnings, maybe they can see their own ends, too. And—and—she was marked." She touched Flora. "You said so."

"Dore," said Flora. "That was just a birthmark, nothing more than a daub of extra color. And I never in my whole life saw one single baby who didn't wail his lungs out once in a while. You're just tormenting yourself, and for no good reason at all."

"Listen," Dore said. "I did nothing. I could have wheeled her in the park more. I could have taken her to the baby pool. I went out by myself, leaving her with the sitter. I could have taken her, I could have."

"You could have been the first man on the moon, too," Flora said. She took Dore's hand. "There's no one to blame," she said.

Dore said nothing, but she kept looking. She went to the library and got medical texts and turned to the pages on crib death, writing down statistics, details, on small scraps of paper that she'd jam back into her purse. She bought medical paperbacks in the drugstores and read them in the trailer. She hid the books from Nick; she never discussed what she read with him, and when she came home one day to find him reading one of the books, his face steel, she averted her eyes. Neither of them said anything about anything. Dore sprawled across the bed, watching the ceiling, listening to the steady turn of the pages Nick was reading, waiting for him to come across the one sentence in the book that would, once and for all, irrevocably blame her.

Dore needed Flora more and more. She needed the women in ways she didn't need Nick. She almost couldn't bear to be with Nick. Every time she saw his face, she remembered just who had prodded and prodded for a sitter, just who had insisted on making those nights under the stars last and last because she couldn't let go of any of the sweetness. When he tried to touch her, she flinched. She kept going over to Flora's, walking into the other woman's kitchen as if it were her own. She'd start washing Flora's dishes in the sink, she'd shell the peas for Flora's dinner, keeping her back straight, her eyes unfocused, and Flora, knowing mindless work was just what Dore needed, said nothing.

* * *

Nick couldn't believe it. He felt that he was precariously floating through life, unattached to anyone or anything. Dore talked only to the women, and the women ignored him. He walked toward the men, but they were embarrassed by his grief. They'd pat his back and avert their eyes; they'd mutter what a tough break it was and then excuse themselves, leaving Nick standing in the middle of the street, alone.

At night he reached for Dore. He wanted to make love to her, to be inside of her, as deep as he could, so that he'd know he was a part of someone, but she stiffened, she pushed him aside. "I can't," she said.

He knew she blamed herself, but as far as he was concerned, he was the one at fault. How could he have agreed to a sitter? How could he have allowed himself all those times away from his daughter, away from his life?

He saw the baby everywhere. At first, just glimpses. Under the bed, a gurgle by the back door. Sometimes, too, he simply smelled her. Milk scent heavy in the sheets, so elusive, so strange, he'd tear the covers from the bed trying to find her. Only once did he see her whole. He was stepping from the shower, and there she was, just under the steam by the door, crawling toward him.

He quickly crouched, reaching out his hands, his heart slamming against his chest. He shut his eyes, grabbing for her. All he had to do was just touch her, fingertip on skin, and she'd be real, she'd be alive. He knew it, and then his hand trembled, and he grasped for her, and instead of her downy dark hair, her peachy skin, he felt the sudden rough terry towel on the floor, the smooth side of the shampoo bottle, and he opened his eyes and she was gone. His baby, his girl. He slumped to the damp tiled floor and put his hands up to his face and wept into them. He wished he were holding his daughter— and, oh, God, he wished he were holding Dore.

He began working. At first, to forget. Later, because it became such a simple pleasure, walking into a room, finding a face that seemed glad to see him. He would never have left Dore for a moment if she had seemed to need him, even a little, if she weren't so wrapped up in her cocoon of women. He was nervous about seeing his clients at first. He was used to treating them all like friends, telling them all about Dore, all about his daughter. Before he even started pulling out the new crop of book jackets, pitching his books, he'd be pulling out snapshots of Susan, showing her off. But now he didn't want to talk about anything; he didn't want to have to say the words, to remind himself all over again what had happened, freshening his pain until it was all he could do to breathe. He didn't want anything more than the warmth of a welcome.

He had nothing to worry about. He didn't have to tell his clients anything, because somehow they already seemed to know. No one said anything, but clients had hot coffee ready for him as soon as he stepped in the door. There were crullers and chocolates set on a plate. He was taken to lunch, to dinner, made to have a cocktail or two. And clients bought more books from him than he knew they could sell, and when he pointed that out, he was waved aside. He couldn't bring himself to ask any of the old questions about how their families were doing, and no one volunteered information; they seemed to be waiting, poised on his words.

Nick finally broke down at the Stonewall Bookshop in Philadelphia. The book buyer there, a friendly young woman named Felice, led him to the back room and made him sit on a box of books and talk to her. She listened while he spilled out his grief; she kept her hand lightly on his shoulder and she never once took her eyes from him. When he was finished talking, she didn't say anything. She didn't tell him it would get better with time, she didn't say she understood, but she kept her hand right where it was so he could feel her pulse moving through her fingers, and she sat so close, he could hear her breathing.

She made him go with her to a movie, right that moment, and she kept talking to him through the film, ignoring the angry hushings of the people around them, not letting him brood, and it wasn't until afterward, over coffee, that she told him she had heard the news a week ago, from another salesman. "News like that spreads," she said, and then she waved at the waitress, tilting up her coffee cup to show it was empty.

Nick worked long hours. He liked being busy, out on the road, his mind filled with schedules and billing sheets. His hours were so crowded, he could fall into bed and sleep from exhaustion, deep and dreamless; he could wake up and the million things he had to do that day would push into his mind, leaving no room for Susan, for Dore.

When there were lulls, when he did call Dore, she usually wasn't even home. He'd have to call over at Flora's. "She's sleeping," Flora told him. "She's out back in the sun." The times he could persuade Flora to get Dore to come on the line, Dore sounded distracted and very far away from him.

"I hate to leave you alone," he said.

"I'm not alone," Dore said. "I sleep at Flora's."

She didn't want to talk. There were long silences that he kept trying to fill, and as soon as he hung up the phone, he wanted to dial her again right away.

It was funny, too, that now, for the first time in his life, when he climbed back into his car for the drive back to Dore, he felt a sudden unwillingness, a raging yearning to stay where he was, moving from bookstore to bookstore, collecting smiles like medals.

He began thinking they should move. It was too hard to drive into the court, to have every single trailer remind him of what he wanted to forget, to see his past in every face. And, too, he had this strange feeling that the trailer court was gradually taking Dore away from him, transforming her, and that the longer they stayed, the more he would lose. He wasn't quite sure where they should go or how to approach it, until he saw a notice on the company bulletin board. They needed a salesman in the Boston area. He started to think. He remembered a brochure Tom had about Boston; he could almost see the picture of the skyline. He remembered Helen saying a city like that didn't interest her, because a place that got so cold in the winter wouldn't allow a proper summer to get anywhere near it.

He talked to his boss, and then he went to Dore. He told her it was a great career move, and he told her that they needed to get away from their past, needed to be in a place where every single thing they encountered wasn't a memory.

"I don't want to leave here," Dore said.

"Yes, you do," he said.

She didn't say anything, and when he prodded, she sighed. She said she would think about it, and then she went back into the kitchen and he heard the slap of the door, her slow, careful steps on their way to Flora's.

She wasn't lying. She did give it some thought. She thought about how much easier it was for Nick, how his loss was less total than hers because, after all, he could still sense the baby around him; he sometimes even saw her, she was sure of that. Oh, she knew, she knew. She had seen him sniffing at his shirts, she had seen him turn toward Susan's room, startled, listening, and when she asked him what was he listening to, he had become flustered. He had told her it was nothing, but he hadn't been able to meet her eyes. She never once managed to feel Susan around her, no matter how she strained with her eyes clamped shut, no matter how she sniffed and sniffed until people started asking her if she was catching cold. She thought it all must be part of her punishment for not having loved Susan enough, for not having been a good enough mother.

Sometimes she thought Nick was right about leaving. It wasn't always enough to spend the afternoon at Ruby's, the slow, steady evenings with Flora. Ruby suddenly didn't like it when Dore did her dishes; Flora told her to leave the meat loaf alone because she had her own secret recipe she liked. The women let Dore stay as long as she wanted. No one ever told her to leave, but they were reclaiming their old lives, leaving her with nothing more to do than sit with her hands in her lap. She had time to think then, time to know that all she had to do was get up and look outside and she would see Nick crouched down among the flowers she had planted, parting the petals in his search. She knew what he was looking for. She knew, too, what she would never find.

She woke up one night and Nick wasn't there and she suddenly started remembering how it was with them when they were first courting, how just the sight of him had made her heart helpless. She missed him, she suddenly wanted him there beside her. She got up and went to the window and saw him, standing out in the middle of the street, fully dressed. He was rocking on his heels, his hands in his pockets, and she went outside in her white T-shirt and panties, and when she got close enough to him, she saw he was crying. She rested her head against his back, felt how warm his body was, and then, without turning, he looped his arms about her, he rocked her in his rhythm, and then she said it was all right, they would leave.

They moved to Sommerville, to a large, sunny, one-bedroom apartment right on the trolley line, just fifteen minutes from Boston. At first Dore didn't even bother to leave the apartment. She spent a lot of time on the phone talking to Flora or Ruby, trying to keep up the connection. She missed the trailer, she missed the whole layout of the court. The week they had left, the place had thrown them a going-away party at the community center. Someone made fried chicken, someone else brought cole slaw and hot dogs. The trailer kids ran around and threw chips at one another, the babies got cranky, and the men idly flirted with their buddies' wives. Nick had brought the young couple he'd sold the trailer to, and he moved them through the crowd for introductions, becoming more a part of the trailer court in his departure than he had ever been while he lived there.

Now, though, Dore felt that part of her life receding, telescoping away. After a while, Flora on the phone didn't feel as familiar as she used to. Ruby, on the phone, was rushed. She had kids pulling at her skirts; she had the woman who had moved into Dore's old trailer coming by for coffee. Dore, no longer part of the community, felt pushed out on her own.

She moved tentatively. She walked two blocks to the supermarket. She took the trolley to Boston and wandered through Filene's basement, but everything she picked up was pulled from her hands by another, more ambitious shopper, and in the end she just gave up and came home with nothing.

Nick watched her. A simple thing like buying herself a new belt would make him smile at her, treat her like everything was going to be just fine. She'd wake nights burning, wanting him, but then she'd turn and see him already awake, leaning on one elbow staring at her, and it made her so angry that she'd get up and go to sleep on the living-room couch.

She found a teaching job at a private high school to keep herself busy, but she couldn't get excited about it, or care even slightly about what might happen. Her teaching was subdued, reflective. Her students imagined there was something dangerously aloof and mysterious about her, and they adored her for it. They smiled. They treated her as if she were alive and worth knowing. Dore began finding love notes slid into the pages of her grade book. She got essay after essay from young girls about their stormy love affairs. She got comically inaccurate descriptions of abortions. She got suicide tales told by someone who was burning away in hell, looking sorrowfully back on a damaged life. She graded every paper without comment. She wouldn't meet the disappointed stares of her students when she passed their papers back into their hands.

She came home evenings and made dinner. She graded papers. She saw Nick watching the corners of the rooms, cocking his head at the sounds she never heard, and then, in the stillness of the night, she, too, tried to feel her daughter. She listened for her. Come home, she thought, come home.

Nick had thought the move would change Dore, and it had, but not in any of the ways he had hoped. Sometimes she slept pressed tightly against him, sometimes she slept on the couch. When she made love, she was so soundless, so removed, he sometimes yearned to bite noise from her skin, to pull a sigh from her hair. Instead, he was gentle. He acted as though a false move would shatter her.

The move didn't make things much better for him, either. He escaped to the road. He kept telling himself that his life was new now, that he wasn't going to think about what had happened. He'd start to get pleasure from driving on the highway; he'd glance over at the other cars, and then, halfway to some new city, he'd have to pull the car over to the shoulder because he was so upset, because he had seen a baby in the car ahead of him, and his own car had suddenly filled with the scent of milk. He sat slumped over the wheel until the milky smell started to disappear, and then he bolted upright. "No," he pleaded. "Don't go. Don't."

When the car finally smelled like nothing more than a car, he drove to the nearest pay phone and called Dore. He couldn't make his mouth work very well. He made up some story about having forgotten some papers at home, just to keep her on the phone talking with him. He told her he missed her, he told her he loved her. Sometimes he asked her if she wanted to catch a plane and meet him at the hotel, but she always said no.

"You miss me?" he said. "You love me?"

"Don't I act like I do?" Dore said, and then she told him she had to go, there was someone at the door.

Nick was cheerful and friendly to his clients. He lied to his old contacts, telling them how well things were going, that he and Dore both loved Boston. To his new clients, he presented a picture of great activity. He detailed dinners that never happened because Dore didn't feel well, plays they didn't see because he couldn't focus his attention. He made it seem that he was happy, and sometimes, when he almost could believe what he was saying, he tried to stretch out the conversation just to make the feeling linger.

Away, without constant reminders, he could fool himself into thinking he had a very different life. He wasn't living with a woman who was more of a ghost than a partner; he hadn't lost a baby. He was just a salesman, a visitor in a city, with time to enjoy it. He tried to stretch the time out the way he stretched out conversations. He'd walk around trying to find the longest lines at restaurants, and once seated he'd read every item on the menu, then call the waitress over and make her explain even the simplest meals to him. Even then, he wouldn't order until she had come back three separate times, asking him with a steely gaze if he was ready yet. He never enjoyed the food. He took slow, careful bites, watching the other men in the place and wondering if they were happy, if they had wives who loved them, who let themselves be somehow indelibly marked by lovemaking, if they had daughters who were still alive, still safe.

He took over some new territory, wanting to stay as busy as possible. The only problem was that his boss wanted him to take over Pittsburgh, too, the one place he never wanted to return to. He wanted the new territory, he needed it, and in the end he told himself that he could go back and be just fine; It didn't have to matter that he had once been so unhappy there, because, after all, he was a new person now and none of that could touch him anymore. He wouldn't let it.

It felt so strange in Pittsburgh now. He walked past Marks, only it wasn't Marks anymore; it had been torn down and made into a porno theater. No one at the theater seemed to remember much about a student-run café. The girl at the ticket booth scoffed at Nick when he persisted; she told him to either buy a ticket or get the hell away, because his standing around was going to drive the customers away. "What customers?" Nick said, looking around the blank sidewalk. "See? You drove them off already," the girl said.

Nick couldn't bring himself to go past the home. He didn't want to see boys standing out in the yard, yearning toward him when he walked past, mistaking his interest for their salvation. He didn't want to walk into Mr. Rice's office and watch him fumble for Nick's name, trying to place the man he had once claimed was just like his own son.

He wouldn't go to his old house, and he wouldn't go anywhere near where his parents were buried. Being in the city where they were didn't make him feel any closer to them; if anything, it almost felt like a betrayal to come back to the place Tom had tried so hard to escape, the place he himself had managed to leave.

He walked to the stores where he used to buy his clothing, he passed the place where he used to get his haircuts, and then he went back to the hotel and called Dore. There was no answer. He didn't know where she went evenings. There was no Flora around Sommerville, no Ruby. Dore never even mentioned any neighbors she might know, any friends. He couldn't pinpoint his competition for her anymore, and he felt powerless. He called her three times, letting the phone ring and ring, and then he got his jacket and wandered over to town to get something to eat, to be among people.

He ended up in Shadyside. He remembered artists used to live here, students, but now he saw only a lone businessman, a few older women walking arm in arm. The Cluck-a-Buck, where he used to work, was now a psychedelic poster shop, but even this early in the evening it was closed. It was funny—even though the city had changed, he still didn't like it. He walked around. It was only eight o'clock, but the streets seemed so dead, the homes and apartments shut up tight, and he thought, Who could ever live in such a lonely city? Who could live here without going mad?

He searched for noise, finally finding a small Italian restaurant on a side street. The tables were cramped close; it was fairly crowded, fairly noisy, and it comforted Nick just to see it.

He was seated by the door at a small table for two, and he was studying the menu, line by line, when a woman tapped him on the shoulder. "Do you mind if we share a table?" she said. "It's just that

I'm in this terrible hurry." She stared down at him, anxious. "I eat really, really fast," she said.

Nick looked up at her for a moment. He had never seen anyone who had eyes like hers, so deep and black he couldn't make out the pupils, skin so pale it was practically white. An unruly mass of black hair tumbled down her back. She was dressed in black, too—one of those plain, sweatery dresses, hitched up and belted into a mini.

"Listen, you take the table," he said, wanting to prolong his release from the quiet, empty streets.

But she shook her head. "No, come on, I can't do that," she said, annoyed. "Please."

"Sit," Nick said, and she did, ignoring him, immediately picking up the menu, bending forward for some of the bread. She ordered quickly, and she didn't look up until the food came, and then only to clip back her hair. She smiled at him then. She said it made some people squeamish to eat with all that hair around; that even when she was growing up, her teachers used to call her up to their desks just to get her to pin her hair out of the way.

"Some of the kids thought I was a witch," she told Nick. She didn't know how it started. Maybe it was the hair, maybe the dark, ill-fitting clothing her mother bought her. She hadn't really minded people thinking she was the reason they found twenty dollars on the street. It was only when she was made the cause of someone's bad luck that she got angry.

"Kids thought I hexed them into failing a test, that I somehow made their dogs run away. What did I have to do with any of it? Some of the girls at school once offered me five dollars to make up love charms. I told them the truth, that I had no charm, but they didn't believe me. I needed the money. I wanted to buy a necklace. So I wrapped up some Queen Anne's lace in a red string, said some words over it, and then I took that money and tucked it into my waistband the way I thought a real businesswoman would." She took a sip of water. "My father was watching from the window, and when I came inside, he beat me with a tennis racket."

She grinned. "It didn't stop me." She told him her name was Leslie and that she was no more a witch than he was. She was a dressmaker—a designer—who worked out of her home. She had worked in New York City for a while and done fairly well, but she

hated the city, hadn't been able to cope with the pace or the pressure.

Nick wasn't interested in remembering his life, not during a light
and pleasant dinner, so he told her only outlines—that he sold children's books, that he lived near Boston. He was mute about Dore
and Susan.

"So listen," Leslie said. "Why don't you let me know the next
time you're in town and maybe I'll buy some books from you?" She
fished in her purse and pulled out a scrap of paper, a nibbled pencil,
and scrawled her number and address.

"You can buy any book I sell right in the stores," Nick said, but
Leslie shook her head; she said she liked things when they were most
direct.

"You like living here?" he said abruptly.

"I love it," she said. "I'd never leave here."

He was baffled. "But what do you do at night? The streets seem so
empty."

She laughed. "What does anyone do at night? I go to movies or
the theater, I visit friends, go out to eat—you know. Sometimes I
just get into an old robe at eight and watch TV." Nick shrugged and
she stiffened a little, defensive. "Listen, we have everything Boston
has and we're prettier."

His food arrived, and she didn't talk much after that, but Nick
still liked having her interesting face to look at while he ate, her
voice occasionally directed at him. She bolted her food, told him she
had to rush to get to a fitting, and when she finished her meal, she
abruptly unclipped her hair so it fell, casting shadows about her.
"Look," she said, standing. "Call me, why don't you. If you lose my
number, it's in the book. And I bet I can make you love this city the
way I do."

"Not a chance," Nick said, but he smiled at her, and she smiled
back before turning away. He watched her as she left; he saw how
she turned around once to meet his gaze, how in seeing him, her face
took on light.

He thought about her as he drove home. He remembered her hair,
the way she talked about spells, and it made him feel restless, as if
there were fireflies in his blood. But then, as things on the road

turned familiar, he began thinking about Dore, and he reached inside his pocket for the paper with Leslie's name and number and address. He rolled down his window and held the paper out, feeling the pull of the wind tugging it from his fingers, and then he let it go, let it carry back across the endless dark path of the highway. He tried to look back, to follow it, a simple strip of white along the highway, but then a car raced toward him, forcing his mind back on the road, back on Dore.

FIVE

• • •

Dore began thinking that maybe her redemption lay in getting pregnant. She'd do everything right this time. She'd quit her job and never go back; she'd stay at home reading beside the baby's crib, breathing when the baby breathed; and she'd strap her child against her own heartbeat so it would always be reminded of life, so it would never forget. When she climbed into bed, she curled about Nick. He moved, surprised. He was used to sleeping on the edge of the bed, used to being careful how he touched her for fear she'd get up and go sleep on the couch. She touched his face, she whispered against his skin, and she pulled him closer to her.

Nick wasn't sure how he felt about having a baby. The whole idea was disturbing and startling; he didn't want to think how he might react to another child, what memories it might force him to relive. But the thing of it was, he loved having Dore back again. He'd forget everything when he was holding her, stroking her buttery hair. He told himself over and over that she really did want him, that it wasn't just what she thought he could give her—and then sometimes, too, he thought that even if it was, a baby might bind them together again.

Sometimes, when they were making love, he'd sense Dore straining against him, and he thought suddenly of that woman in Pittsburgh, the one who kids used to think was a witch, and he imagined charms she might have for making babies bud and bloom, for rekindling love. And then Dore would be rolling away from him, panting, slick with sweat, and he'd slip out of her and feel so lost, so crazy with need, that he'd try to enter her again even though he was soft now. They didn't sleep entwined after lovemaking, they didn't whisper secrets anymore or trace the moonlight on the sheets. They were silent. Nick, one hand on Dore's thigh, swore he could hear her heart beating, but it was a kind of language he didn't understand anymore, and it made him grieve for her.

She wasn't conceiving. She bought books, she took her temperature ninety times a day and made charts, and finally, the two of them went to a doctor. Nick sat in the waiting room holding Dore's hand, telling her dirty jokes to get her to laugh, but in the end the doctor told them there was nothing wrong that a little relaxation wouldn't cure, that there was no reason they shouldn't be popping babies out. It made Dore tense up all the more. How could she possibly relax?

She waited until Nick was away on business and then she went to a psychologist who did hypnosis. But he made her talk about her childhood, he pulled stubborn answers from her about everything but Susan, and he finally suggested that hypnosis wasn't a good tool as far as she was concerned; the whole problem was that she was reacting to a mother she didn't much care for by refusing to be anything like her.

She visited a chiropractor, who assured her the problem was in her spine, who sat her on a green leather table and kneaded and worked her flesh, who manipulated her spine until she winced, sure it was cracking. Alarmed, she struggled upright, and when she stood, she could hardly walk; her whole back felt inflamed and dangerous. "You shouldn't have gotten up so quickly," the doctor accused. She wanted Dore to scoot right back up on the table so she could undo the damage she said Dore had brought on herself, but Dore wouldn't hear of it. She cabbed home, lying prone in the back seat, shaking her head at the driver, who kept shouting at her in broken English that he could take her to the hospital if she just said the word. When Nick walked in the door that evening, he found Dore on the couch with the heating pad. "I sprained my back," she told him.

And then, she missed one period, and then two, and her breasts began hurting. They enlarged so much that she had to go out and buy herself new bras, nearly two cup sizes larger. She couldn't zip her jeans, and her skirts bulged in front so she had to wear long, loose tops. Delirious, she blurted out to Nick that she was pregnant. "You saw a doctor?" he asked. She shook her head. She said she had just made the appointment—she had wanted to wait until she was sure. "I know I'm pregnant, I feel it," she said, pulling him down on the floor, rolling and bruising against the walls.

A baby, Nick thought. It might have made him more uneasy than he was, except for the way Dore had suddenly come back to life, to herself, and to him. She was ravenous in her lovemaking; she'd call him at work and tell him to come home and meet her in the bathtub. He couldn't get through the day without wanting her, needing her taste. He'd have to leave work because his whole body was pulsing. He'd drive home like a madman and then surprise her, kissing her belly, moving her against him. Now she wanted to talk afterward. She had all these wonderful, dreamy plans about taking the baby to France, about organizing a play group with some of the other women she had seen around the neighborhood. She went to work happy. She began discussing her students' papers with them, allowing them to cluster about her.

But when Dore went to the doctor, he told her that she wasn't pregnant—that the tests showed nothing. She was furious. She wanted to know what the swelling in her breasts was then, why she got so nauseated mornings that she had to keep saltines by her pillow. Why did her stomach swell out? Why was she dreaming about babies every time she shut her eyes? He shook his head, he told her he didn't know, and in the middle of his speech, Dore got up and strode out of his office. She told herself he was a quack, that he didn't know what he was talking about.

She made another appointment, with a woman doctor, who was more expensive, who had a plush, all-white office on Newberry Street. The doctor examined Dore and then had her come into the office for a talk. "You're not pregnant," she said. She told Dore it was what was called a "hysterical pregnancy," that it was a common phenomenon, mostly in African tribes, and that oddly enough it was the men who swelled up, carrying it to such extremes that they even seemed to go through labor and got as much attention as their wives.

"I'm not doing this for attention," Dore snapped.

The doctor shook her head. "Of course you're not," she said. "But you do want a baby, and your body did its best to oblige." She told Dore to go home and relax, to take hot baths and wait and the swelling and nausea would disappear. "Then we can start to work on really getting you pregnant," the doctor said, smiling. "Don't you worry."

Dore, silent, got up and left the doctor's office. All the way home, she kept her eyes unfocused. She didn't want to see any pregnant women in the streets, she didn't want to see any babies, and she didn't want anyone seeing her, knowing how shamed she felt, how betrayed.

Nick came home that night with roses for her, wrapped in green tissue, but she was in the kitchen, crying over onions. When he bent to kiss her, she shrugged him roughly from her. "I'm not pregnant," she said.

"You're not?" he said, and she told him it wasn't a real pregnancy, that her mind had done it to her body, and she didn't want to talk about any of it.

He was silent for a moment. "We could adopt," he said, but she shook her head; she said they'd have to get married for that.

"But I would marry you," he said. "I want to."

"I told you, I can't get married because of a baby."

"You don't make sense," he said, and she turned and looked at the floor.

"Sure, I do," she said.

Just like that, Dore gave up trying to become pregnant. She dieted like a crazy person, refusing to eat breakfast although her stomach twisted and growled, nibbling on toast for lunch, picking at her dinner until Nick told her she was being silly, that she looked wonderful, that a few extra pounds was probably healthy. "Why should I look pregnant when I'm not?" she said. She exercised every late afternoon, as soon as she got home from teaching, dancing around to old rock-and-roll albums in her living room until the people downstairs banged on their ceiling for her to stop. It made her feel lonely, hearing the banging; it somehow reminded her of the baby she wasn't to have, a baby made of air and imagination, who wasn't to be her healing after all.

She called Flora, but the number was out of service, and she took it as omen. She began walking about the neighborhood to keep herself from thinking. When Nick was out on the road, she missed him, but really what she missed was her past with him, those days in the trailer when just seeing him made her breath stitch up inside of her. When he came back from being on the road now, she always felt a faint flutter of pain. Although he said he loved her, although he said he didn't care that she wasn't pregnant, she didn't believe him. She didn't think he needed her anymore.

She wasn't sure why, but she began talking to her students. She sipped her morning coffee right at her desk and struck up a conversation with whatever kid was hanging around. She homed in on the details—the red-rimmed eyes of a girl, a brand-new inky tattoo on a shy boy's arm—and she asked question after question, surprising kids into answers, pulling out their confidences. She was good with them. She never gave advice, she never revealed her own opinion, but she listened so intently, the effect was mesmerizing. She couldn't help feeling nourished by all the need. It hooked her. She began getting to school a whole half-hour earlier just to expose herself to that much more student interest. Gradually, she began to reveal bits and pieces about herself. The kids were fascinated by her. They whispered among themselves. They tried to imagine their teacher living in a trailer, carrying some secret pain like a romantic Brontë heroine. They adored her; they began to spread the word that she was a good ear, that you could tell her anything and she wouldn't flinch or accuse you, or rush to call your parents or the principal. She treated you like a human being.

The kids began showing up in her neighborhood, walking back and forth in front of her apartment until she chanced to notice them, bumping right into her in the supermarket. It made her remember Ronnie Dazen again, how he tried to court her interest, only this time she didn't need to be courted, she almost always invited the students right into her apartment. She ended up disinfecting irritated tattoos, making strong tea for broken hearts and family miseries. She watched each kid gradually heal and then fade away, replaced by another wounded soul. She began giving out her phone number to a kid or two, telling them they could call her only if it was a dire emergency, and when her phone rang, she leaped to get it.

Nick would come home with his hands full of blooms for her.

Orange tiger lilies like small flames; white roses. He'd saunter into the living room and there would be four kids sprawled on the floor, leaning toward Dore. Dore would stop talking as soon as Nick came in, and the kids frankly stared. He felt like an intruder in his own home. He nodded curtly, and then he went into the kitchen, trying to jam the flowers into a jelly glass, all the time waiting for Dore to at least dip into the kitchen for a hurried kiss before she went back out to her students. But instead, the talk continued, low and secretive. "They need me," she told him when he asked about it. "They have parents," he said, but she gave him an odd, crimped smile; she turned from him.

There were phone calls. Late at night. Pleas that pulled her into her car, that had her driving to the bus station to pick up some kid who was too terrified to really run away, too scared or drunk to go home. Nick would sometimes wake up to find a stray ragamuffin sleeping on the sofa. He was polite at first, even concerned, but the kids were shy about him. When Dore ran out to get coffee, he'd sometimes approach one of them and try to be comforting, but they always gave him a blank, angry stare, and he sometimes felt they were angry with him for disturbing their privacy with Dore.

"Look, this has got to stop," he told Dore. Their apartment wasn't a halfway house; she wasn't a therapist. He told himself that the next time a kid came to their door, hungry for talk, for something cool and clean in a glass, he would tell the kid himself to go see Dore during school time, to make an appointment with a good psychologist. He told himself that—but then, of course, when the doorbell rang and he opened the door on some kid stammering out Dore's name, stumbling on some story, Nick always ushered them right in. Orphans of the storm, he kept thinking.

He saw Dore, talking, talking, talking. One night, passing by the living room, he heard Susan's name, and instantly he felt his heart freezing, his blood tamping its flow. He leaned along the wall where it was cool, and then he heard Dore say, "She died . . ." and then he strode forward, not seeing her, not bothering to get his jacket, and he got in the car and drove out to the Dairy Queen and just sat in the parking lot, a dime-size headache breeding behind his eyes.

He didn't know what to do. He wanted Dore back, he wanted her the way she used to be; but he didn't want the baby being part of it—he didn't want to have to remember, to have to see that face flickering across his mind, burning, a flame. This was Boston. Everything was supposed to be changed now, the pain was supposed to be past, as unvisited as the New Jersey trailer court.

When he came back home, his headache in full bloom, the kids had all gone. Dore was sleeping on the couch, a glass of tea beside her.

"Hey," he said, nuzzling her.

"Oh, don't wake me," she murmured, her face turning toward the pillow. "Just let me sleep." She started settling back into the couch, but he didn't want to go to bed alone, not tonight. He didn't want to have to bunch up her pillow beside him. He lifted her up and carried her into bed, and then he got in beside her and hooked her limp arm about him, as if she had done it herself.

The next time he was back in Pittsburgh, he found himself thinking about Leslie. What he wanted was a little laughter, someone to talk to while he ate dinner. He looked through the phone book at the hotel for her number, telling himself it was no big deal if he couldn't find her; he could go down to the hotel bar and float himself away on a few beers; he could swim upstairs to sleep. He found two numbers he thought might be hers, and he got Leslie on the very first try. She said of course she remembered him, and she didn't seem surprised that he had called. She didn't mention that it had been three months since they'd met. She said only that she had a fitting that night but could meet him later at the movies. *Children of Paradise* was playing and she had seen it only once.

Leslie, outside the theater, was in ripped jeans and a black sweater, her hair braided down her back like a spine. One of her sleeves had a safety pin in it, but her nails were buffed and clean, and when he got close to her, he caught some piny, mysterious scent.

She beamed when she saw him. "Well, hi!" she said. She chattered and bounded at him.

He was surprised that she really wanted to see the movie, that she didn't want to just go get coffee and talk. She said they could talk later, that the film would give them something to talk about. She made him sit in the first row—she said things looked more real that

way—and for one sharp moment he thought of Dore. Dore always
sat in the front row because of her poor sight. They never had to
rush to make a film, because the front rows were always the last to
fill.

But Leslie didn't watch films the way Dore did. She didn't touch
him or lean over to make comments; she didn't want him to put his
feet on top of hers because the circulation was jammed up and she
needed the weight to start things up. Instead, Leslie hunched toward
the screen, perfectly silent, ignoring him, and gradually Nick was
suckered into the story, too, and he forgot her there beside him, and
forgot Dore.

When the movie ended, he felt something tear in his heart. He
felt as if he were the one in the final reel, racing helplessly after the
departing carriage, crying the name of the one he loved, crying,
"Dore, Dore," and there was Dore riding in the carriage, her head
held up, an enigmatic smile on her face, oblivious to him. Abruptly,
he turned to Leslie, but she was already standing, looking past him
into the audience, and when he touched her, she turned to him,
smiling, embarrassed at the tears she was wiping away.

They walked outside. "Oh, my," she sighed, but she didn't want
to talk about the film. "It's all in here," she said, tapping her chest.
She walked with her hands in her pockets, her strides long. She
didn't ask him very much. She didn't even want to know how he
had liked the film. She seemed perfectly happy to see him, but he
had the feeling she would have been just as happy not to. She didn't
ask him how long he planned to stay, and when he told her anyway,
she simply nodded.

She was funny to walk with. She kept stalling in front of store
windows, mesmerized by a row of silky blouses, a fan of skirts. When
Nick faltered, when he tried to make some remark about the window, she glanced at him, amused, and continued walking. "I'm
sorry," she said, "but if I stare at anything long enough, I can copy
it. Unfortunately, not all of my clients want originals from me." She
said she had always had that talent. Her dolls had worn the same
spanking-white tennis outfits her parents wore.

Leslie saw Nick looking at her own outfit and she bristled. "It
doesn't matter for me," she said. "Clothing is for other people. I see
it on them. I can't tell the difference between silk or cotton on me,

but on someone else I feel it, I just know how it should be styled. I knew how to change all my friends' outfits so they'd look smashing, but I was always being sent home from school because my skirt was torn." She laughed, looking over at him.

He walked her to her house, a small brick home on Howe Street in Shadyside. It had a small porch, a small yard, and a white front gate that she told him she used to swing on when she was a little girl. "I grew up in this house," she said proudly.

"You did? And you still live here?" He couldn't imagine it, staying in one place that long, having a history that seamless.

"Well, I moved out when I was at design school. Parsons in New York. No one I knew wanted to leave the city, but every chance I got, I came home. I loved coming home. The house just felt good." She pushed back a stray hair.

"Then my parents moved to Arizona when my mother got arthritis, and they couldn't bear to sell the house. It was all paid for, and filled with their memories. My father thought selling it would be like having a piece of him die. I was through school by then, sharing an apartment with a girl I almost never saw, because she worked nights. I was working myself, for a small company designing women's golf clothing, trying to sketch my own designs at night. I was designing, but it wasn't enough. I just never felt very comfortable in New York, it never felt like home. When my father called and offered to give me the house, I got the next plane out. The house always felt like it was mine." She leaned on the gate.

"I have lots of clients here," she said. "It took a while. Word of mouth. Going to people's homes and showing them my book. I designed originals at reasonable prices—and sometimes, if I was short of cash, I did alterations.

"You know tennis?" she said abruptly. Nick shrugged. "Both my parents were champions." She said she had photos of the two of them holding up their loving cups, smiling into the crowds. They'd taken her to all the matches when she was little; she grew up teething on tennis balls and rackets, she grew up playing. "I wasn't very good, though," she said. "My skill was sewing."

She said her mother was the better player of the two, and when she was diagnosed as having crippling arthritis, she started smashing things. Her trophies, her dishes, her rackets. "She had to give up playing," Leslie said. "She'd take me to matches and we'd both sit in the bleachers and watch my father win, and sometimes she'd grab me and walk out because it was just too upsetting for her to watch.

"It affected his game, too, seeing her leave, seeing how her face changed there in the bleachers." Leslie sighed. "God, he loved her so much. He couldn't play as well as he used to. It was as if winning were suddenly a betrayal, so he started to lose. He wouldn't practice, because he saw how she'd tighten when he left her. In the end, they decided to go to Arizona because he thought the sun might heal her."

"Did it?" Nick said.

Leslie shook her head. "She bathed in sulfur springs, she saw faith healers and acupuncturists, she practiced positive thinking until she gave herself migraines, but she kept crippling up. She had to cut the front of her shoes out because her toes were so deformed. She couldn't move her hands because the fingers kept overlapping, locking on her.

"Finally, my father talked her into doing some coaching. She did it grudgingly at first, sure she'd have no students—because really, she couldn't demonstrate much, all she could do was speak and yell and prod. But she got students because of her name, and she built up a reputation, a kind of mystique. Everyone said that because she couldn't get up and play, it forced her students to stretch their minds, to imagine what the moves should look like, to dig the knowledge out of themselves. She raised holy hell when they did things wrong. But she praised, she gave good directions, and she started producing stars."

Leslie stretched in the moonlight. "They both coach now, they both love Arizona, and they both never get back here. I go to see them."

"Could I come in?" Nick said.

"No, I don't think so," Leslie said. She pulled keys from her pocket.

"We could sit on the porch," he said, thinking how cool and lovely it was tonight, how easy it would be to talk away the hours with her.

"No," she said again. She was silent for a few moments, fiddling with the keys in her palm. "Call me in a few days, why don't you," she said abruptly.

"What, from Boston?" he said. "I'll be gone by then."

She looked up, studying him, and then abruptly told him to come for breakfast tomorrow, that she liked to get up really early so she could have the whole day to work. "Come whatever time you want," she said. "I'm up and famished at six."

"I'm more nine o'clock," he said, and then she bent forward and touched his face, pulling away before he could see her expression.

He watched her go into the house, and then he went grudgingly back to the hotel, but he couldn't stop thinking about her. He lifted the phone to call Dore. It rang and rang. He hung up. The room was terrible—nothing-colored chenille bedspreads, green carpet. He knew exactly what would flicker on the TV right now, exactly how the water in the bathroom would taste in the glass after he had unpapered it. He didn't like it—the phone in his room not ringing, not going to ring; the night settling heavily about him.

He got his jacket and went outside and walked by the pool. It was still filled, even this late in the season, silent, coolly blue. He walked all around the complex, waiting for the night watchman or someone to come out and ask him who he was, just so he could tell him. They could swap stories, maybe even have a beer by the pool. It made him hopeful, and then he got irritated. Jesus.

He decided to go for a drive. He drove along the highway, blasting the radio, and he thought about Dore, about what she might be doing, where she might be. Maybe she had been right there when he called, listening to the ringing, knowing it was him and not picking up. And then, before he knew what he was doing, he found himself driving past Leslie's house.

It wasn't a bad place. Her lights, he noticed, were still blazing. Curious, he parked two houses away, rolling down his window a little. He liked being so close to her, and her not even knowing it. He could sleep right here and not feel so alone. He'd just have to wake himself up early enough to drive away and then come back, shaved and clean, to have breakfast with her. It was no problem. He could wake whenever he wanted. It was a talent he had cultivated back at the home, giving himself cues before he fell asleep, concentrating on a clock with the hands set at the hour he needed. It always worked. He'd wake at three in the morning just to sneak a cigarette, just to read undisturbed in the bathroom.

Lately he had been doing it with Dore, waking in the middle of the night, half hoping she might talk in her sleep, might say something, anything, that would convince him that she still loved him. And, oh, yes, he had done it with Susan, so he could bring her bottle before she even thought to cry for it. He remembered her soft, sleepy face when he woke her, the surprised pleasure when her mouth found the bottle, and his own delight in pleasing her.

He shut his eyes. Just for a moment, he thought.

Leslie, in the house she had inherited from her parents, the house she loved, had stopped playing the piano. It was just after three, but she wasn't sleepy at all. She was pulling down the blinds when she spotted the car, and, curious, she leaned against the window to study him.

She didn't have many men in her life. Her mother used to try to fix her up, getting strange men to call her on the phone with dinner invitations. Her clients sent their handsome sons to pick up dresses, to have suits designed when they didn't really need them. The mothers would later call on the pretense of asking about a hem, and then gradually they'd bring the conversation around to their sons. It always flustered Leslie. She never felt comfortable with any of them. She'd go to the films, to the restaurants, and once or twice she'd bring a man home with her, but in the morning she'd be restless. She'd sense too much male in the house, and she'd hurry the man up and out of her home before she got too used to him, before she expected anything.

She had been in love only once. She was eighteen. His name was Danny and he played football and was on the honor roll at school and her mother was teaching him tennis. Leslie played tennis a few times with Danny, but mostly the two of them went up to the grassy areas behind the courts and made love. He was terrified of getting her pregnant. He pulled condoms out of his pockets, and he had a brown paper bag with a can of foam in it. She laughed at him. She squirted the foam across the tops of the dandelions even though he told her to cut it out, that it wasn't funny. She didn't care. She wasn't going to have anything between herself and the feel of him, no layer of plastic, no chemicals. She insisted that she could will herself not to get pregnant, that he could help out by willing it, too.

They were both stubborn, but then she would be all over him, covering his face with kisses, opening his buttons, his pants, and then he didn't care either. Sometimes, afterward, she'd squirt some foam in because he was so solemn, and then they'd walk back down to her house, the foam leaking out of her, staining her pants so she'd have to ball them up and stuff them into the trash. They were exhausted, pleased with each other, and then her father would walk by and ask them if they had had a good game. Leslie always poked Danny in the arm. "It never hurts to practice," her father said, and they both had to look at the floor to keep from laughing.

She had designed her own prom gown. Black satin with ribbon at the hem. She was going to have her flowers dyed black, too. She didn't care that her mother said black was for funerals and not for proms, that everyone would look at her and whisper trashy things.

"They whisper now, I bet," Leslie said.

"You like that? Fine," Leslie's mother said.

The week before the prom, Danny went to visit his grandmother in Nebraska, and it was there that a tornado struck. The weathermen on the TV stations kept predicting how bad it would get, breaking into everyone's favorite programs, telling people what to do. Danny's grandmother, used to nature's turmoil, calmly packed bottles of water into the cellar, easy-open cans of tuna and juice.

Danny was riding around on a neighbor's motorbike, crossing a field in his hurry to get home. The sky was dirty-looking and the air felt clammy. He hadn't planned on getting back this late except he had wanted to talk to Leslie in private, away from his grandmother. He had gone all the way over to the drugstore in town. She didn't know about the tornado; she knew only that he whispered to her that he loved her, that he was going to swallow her whole when he saw her again. She had whispered what she was going to do to his body, how she was doing those things to him right now, in her mind, channeling them to him over the phone wires.

He hung up. He got on his bike and he was halfway across the field when the tornado struck. Terrified, he managed to bolt down into a ditch, peering up at the storm. He thought the world was ending, turned inside out. He saw trees cracking like matches, soaring up into the black swirl of air. He saw a dog, frantically barking, hurtling past him before his neck was snapped by the ferocity of the wind and he was still. Danny rolled into a ball of fear. He peed into his jeans, his heart slammed up against his chest, and his breath felt stitched up tight. He was in the ditch for over four hours, and then the black spiral moved away and the rains came. He couldn't move. He clung to the mud, he let the water fill in until he was soaking, until he was weeping and calling for Leslie, over and over.

He didn't make it home until the next day. He was muddy and chilled and he had to ring his grandmother's bell for ten minutes before she came to the door, and then her face went white when she saw him.

He was a celebrity in the town. His picture made the front page, and people said that TV should buy the rights to his story. It made Danny a little irritated when the talk turned, when people started saying it hadn't been such a terrible tornado anyway, and it wasn't such a miracle that he'd survived. The damage to the town was minimal—a few phone lines were down. Danny called Leslie, who had heard about the tornado on the news and had been white-knuckled by the phone. He told her he was taking the next flight out, home to her.

He went back to the field to get the motorbike. A neighbor told him to forget it, that a life was worth a lot more than a bike, but Danny went anyway. He found the bike in the field, a little battered, but he got it to run, and then he was racing it back, speeding and alive, until the bike struck one of the fallen power lines and he was instantly electrocuted.

Leslie refused to remember the details now. What she did recall was taking the black prom dress and burning it in her garage. When her father saw the smoke, he made her put out the fire, but he didn't yell at her. Instead, he took her and the rest of her ruined dress in the car to the incinerator by the plant in town and waited for her to drop it in, and then he drove her back home, the two of them silent.

It had done something to Leslie. She stopped expecting anything in relationships, stopped letting herself believe that a future could spin out of her like magical sugar. It was funny how it worked, but it made the boys around her, and later the men, fall hopessly, easily in love with her. In college, a man named Eddie fell in love with her, making a magnet of her disdain. He would stare dreamily at her in class, he would follow her to lunch and dinner. He kept asking her out, and when she refused, he made up excuses to come to see her: He had to get study notes; he had to get an assignment. She told him right from the start she wasn't interested in any man, but he told her he would kill himself if she didn't give him a chance.

She .thought he was crazy—and in truth, he was a little. He wound up in the infirmary with a pumped stomach from an overdose of antihistamine pills. When she came to see him, he was quiet, removed. The attempt had burned the fire out of him—and inexplicably, her own interest suddenly kindled.

She was like that a lot. She had liked Nick when she first met him because he seemed so transient in her life. The months she hadn't heard from him, she had thought about him, and when her mother had phoned with the name of some new young man that a friend of a friend knew, Leslie had said she was seeing someone.

She stared outside at Nick. She wasn't angry, the way she might have been. He would be gone again in a day, and then he'd either be back or he wouldn't. She stood up straight, she stretched, and then she went to get her jacket.

Nick was dreaming when he felt the knock at his window. He blinked. He jerked up. It was still dark outside. The music was sapped from the air, and when he turned, he saw Leslie studying him through the window. Her hair was impossibly long, impossibly black. "You're watching me," she said. He rolled down the window a little more, and then he pulled her to him and kissed her hard.

He didn't want to stop. He didn't care about the neighborhood. He pulled her into the car with him and slid his hand under her soft flannel shirt. Her body was damp; she smelled of powder. Who took a shower in the middle of the night? He was so used to Dore's silences, and here was Leslie, rough, moving, kicking out one leg so the horn honked, making low easy moans like she was dancing. He touched her, he tasted her, he kept his eyes forced open, afraid if he shut them he would see Dore's face shimmering back to him. When he entered her, she gave a small cry. She threw her head back and pushed herself against him, and then he stroked her eyelids until she opened them, until she saw him.

Afterward, stunned, he sat up. "Oh, God, I'm sorry," he said. "I never meant—"

She put her hand over his mouth. She said that she was sleepy. She wanted to go inside. Her bed was freshly made; she had changed the sheets just that morning. It was a bed big enough for two. He shook his head no, and she didn't ask him why. She burrowed up against him, and in minutes she was sleeping. He watched her, absolutely amazed, and then he tentatively touched her shoulder. She didn't move. He settled back against the door, looking out at the vague light of the stars, and after a long while he slept, too, as best he could.

When he woke—his back stiff, his left leg cramping so he had to stamp the pins and needles from it—she was gone. His mouth tasted funny. When he peered at himself in the rearview mirror, his eyes looked old, his skin sallow. He didn't know what to do—whether to ring her bell and take her to breakfast, or leave her a note, or just drive and drive and drive back to Dore.

He got out of the car. Across the street, a little boy was pushing dirt with a stick. He made a face at Nick and then sat down on the curb, rat-a-tatting his stick like a drumbeat. Nick started up Leslie's walk, wondering what she'd do when she saw him, how he'd feel when he saw her face. And then the door suddenly opened and there she was, in blue jeans and a rose-colored sweater, her hair wound up on top of her head.

"I've got to get to a fitting," she said, rushing, stooping to buckle a shoe. She looked at him. "No breakfast," she said cheerfully.

"I'm going to call you," he said, and she smiled, she dipped one shoulder.

"No, really, I am," he said, and then she leaned toward him and gently kissed him before she brushed past him to get to her car.

"I'll be here," she called out, and then she raced the motor and pulled out of the driveway, leaving him standing there, watching her, unsure.

SIX

• • •

Nick hadn't counted on missing Leslie the way he did. He couldn't stop thinking about her. She was an undertow sucking at his heels, pulling him inexorably toward her. She jammed up his thoughts, appearing when he least expected it. He'd be trying to tally his sales for the month, making rows of figures, and he'd think *Leslie*. He'd be driving, looking for an exit sign, two hours late, totally lost, and he'd see a green road sign, and when he looked closer, Leslie's face would suddenly bloom into his mind. She made him see her in every woman with unruly black hair, in every pair of bottomless black eyes.

He told himself it was all craziness, and when he went to Pittsburgh—three times, then half a dozen—he told himself he was simply looking her up because of the warmth she always offered, because with her he seemed to shed his past as easily as a winter coat. When he was with her, he forgot how Susan had once risen from the bathroom steam, he forgot how Dore was transforming into a stranger he couldn't reach.

He told Leslie as much as he could. He talked about Tom and Helen, he told her about the home, and he sketched his first New York City apartment for her. She, in turn, opened up her house to him, showing him where she had written her name in indelible ink when she was six, where she had buried a doll in the backyard, a body that was still there as far as she knew. She towed him about the city, making him ride up and down the incline on Mount Washington, squiring him to the zoo, to the park, to the river, where she rented a boat. Every five minutes, she demanded, "Isn't this wonderful?" "Yes," he said, meaning her, meaning how light he felt, meaning the only reason to tolerate the city was because she was in it. "Pittsburgh *is* a great place," she said.

At home, he was confused, on edge. He kept trying with Dore, trying to get back to her. He even gave up one or two trips to Pittsburgh, although Leslie's face yearned across his mind. He took Dore to dinner, spent long evenings at home with her, but she was so silent, so reserved, it made him miss Leslie even more. "Talk to me," he said, sitting with her on the couch, stroking her pale hair.

"Talk to you about what?" she responded flatly.

"Anything," he said.

She looked at him. "You don't mean that," she said.

"Yes, I do."

She asked, abruptly, "You think this is a new life?"

"Sure it is," he said.

She shook her head, sinking down into the couch. "Susan was gone in the trailer and she's gone here. What's so different about that?" Dore wiped one hand across her face, and Nick started plundering his pockets, looking for a cigarette.

"You can't talk about it anymore, can you?" Dore said. "Or you won't."

He was silent for a moment. "I don't want to remember anymore," he said quietly. "I don't want to be reminded all the time."

"But I do," said Dore quickly. "I want to be reminded now. I want to remember everything about her, every detail—the Pampers, the powder, the toys she liked in her bath. I'm afraid if I don't, she'll just get fainter and fainter in my mind, she'll disappear for good and I'll never find her, never."

"Stop looking," Nick said, and then Dore's face abruptly closed and he couldn't reach across the space to pull her back. She got up, she left the room, and then he heard the TV going and she was as distant from him as another country.

Sometimes he worried that she might leave him. Every time he came into the house, he tensed, half expecting to find her things gone, a note crumpled and bleeding ink into a damp water glass in the kitchen. He'd start speeding when he was driving home from business trips. He'd sometimes show up when her school was letting out. He sat in the car in front of the school, and when she came out, she was surrounded by students and her face was illuminated, laughing, and he saw how her smile faltered when she saw him, how she took a step back.

Sometimes when he was most lonely, when she was in the other room grading papers or reading, when they had spent another silent evening, he'd find himself looking through his travel logs, running his fingers across the pages until he came to a Pittsburgh entry. It always triggered something. It always made him feel a little better.

Leslie was having her own problems. She didn't trust the way she felt about Nick. He began calling her now, odd hours, from places she had never heard of, and he'd want to talk and talk. It'd be four in the morning, and she'd make him wait while she fixed herself coffee, while she got a sticky bun from the bread box and a clean fork to eat it with. He said he just wanted to hear her voice, but when she talked, he was so silent that sometimes she thought he had drifted off to sleep, and she'd go silent, too, waiting for him to speak, to make himself real to her again.

He was always the one doing the calling. At first, she wouldn't even let herself ask him where he could be reached, and he never offered her the information. Oh, she didn't really care—she thought the relationship was simply what it was, and it would be stupid to try to make any more out of it. When she saw him, it was wonderful; and when she didn't . . . well, she had her own life—she had, as her mother would say, her own sweet self. She wandered aimlessly about the house, fiddling with sewing projects, with jacket facings that wouldn't lie flat, with zippers that snagged. She miscut things. She had to toss pieces out, because suddenly, for the first time, fixing them seemed like too much effort.

She didn't want to be in love. At least not with someone in and out of her life like this. Have you heard the one about the traveling salesman? she told herself, trying to lighten her own gloom. She told clients she would finally go out with whatever sons they had in mind to fix her up with, and although the men came, showing up in jackets and ties, with roses and candy, nothing took, and every time Nick came back to town, she was glad to see him.

One night she had a dream about Danny. He was crouched under a crackling tornado, burrowing into the ground, and there she was, too, about ten feet away, in her black prom dress, pinned in place by the maddened wind. She shouted his name, and suddenly the wind stilled and he heard her, and he started to stand, half-smiling, his whole body relaxing. As soon as he was straight, the vortex began screaming toward him, swallowing him up, and she was crying, crying, and her own sound woke her, and then it was suddenly Nick's name she was crying, Nick's name making her throat raw.

She thought love was making her ill. The work she adored suddenly irritated her. She didn't like the feel of certain kinds of cloth anymore, the way silk swished, the nub of corduroy. She talked a sixteen-year-old bride into a linen dress just so she wouldn't have to handle all that lace. She assured the girl that linen was really so much more adult, so much more soigné. The girl didn't have the foggiest idea what *soigné* meant, but she was easily swayed by it. Leslie talked the girl's mother into cotton because, she said, it could be worn as a day dress, too, and was more practical than silk. But then the cotton, too, began to annoy her, and the linen made her hands swell and burn, so that it took her twice as long as usual to finish the dresses.

When her clients left her house, Leslie collapsed. She had deadlines to meet, but she couldn't work at all. She burrowed into the couch and slept dreamlessly. She filled the tub with bubbles and slept there, too, her magazine drowning down toward the bottom. When clients called, complaining, frantic about dinner suits and party frocks, Leslie would stay up all night and work, her head pounding. She chewed on aspirin and fingernails while she sewed. She felt her fingers betraying her into ruining necklines and hems, and she ripped out almost half the work she finished.

Leslie didn't feel like eating much anymore. She forced down salads, made herself eat an apple every morning, choking it down. At night she felt feverish; she kicked off sheets and blankets and then shivered without them. When Nick was with her, he worried. He kept asking her if she wanted to go to a doctor, but she told him of course not, she was fine. She didn't want to talk about illness when she was with him; she didn't want concern eating away their time together. And, too, she wasn't sure how he'd react to adversity, what pain of hers he might be willing to share. She didn't know, either, how he'd react to her being in love, what he might want to do or not do about it, and that scared her even more.

It wasn't until another few weeks, another visit from Nick, that she finally recognized what was wrong, realized it wasn't just love doing this to her. It was love growing, sustained within her. She was pregnant.

She had no idea what to do. On some days she took it all as a kind of sign, a sign of permanence to her relationship with Nick, and then, a minute or so later, she was sure Nick would see it as an unwelcome claim and never come back to her. It all made her half-crazy. She was super-aware of the life inside her, but she couldn't manage to spit the news out to Nick. Sometimes she'd try to will him to know; she'd sit on her porch and think the baby out across the night to him.

She rode her bike to the library and read book after book on motherhood. She read articles about what you should name the baby, about the power certain names held, the way the wrong name could damage a child for life. Allison, she thought, Rob, Betty, Beth. She read about parenting, and once, she shyly dipped into a book about weddings. She gorged on such books, and then, uneasy, she'd wander over to the other shelves and get out books about money management, about investing, about the single parent in the Sixties. She went to her bank one day and spent an hour and a half talking to a woman in a blue plaid suit about trust funds and college funds.

At night, she lay with her hands on her belly and missed Nick. She willed him to call her, to visit her on the spur of the moment, telling her he knew. She curled up small in the big bed, she tossed her way into sleep, and when she woke in the morning, she kept her eyes closed and reached an arm across a length of bed, begging her fingers to touch Nick, there, beside her.

She got up alone. She stumbled into the kitchen and called Information for Nick's work number. Maybe she could talk the operator into giving her the home number he always said was unlisted, he always said he never answered. He'd answer her call this time, she thought; he'd answer it if she had to let it ring and ring and ring eight million times over.

Dore no longer let her students camp at the house. Her time was more her own now. She treated Nick like a sad memory, like someone who had died right along with Susan. She sat out evenings on the porch and missed him, and then sometimes Nick would come out and sit beside her, and it would just make her miss him all the more. It wasn't the same. She didn't want to spill out her thoughts to him. She couldn't bear his baffled, yearning face; his stiff, retreating silences whenever she tried to talk about Susan. She thought he didn't know one thing about her misery, he didn't know one thing about his own pain.

She'd stand up and leave him sitting there. She'd walk to the end of the block and then back again, and she always felt a little relieved to find the porch empty when she came back. She'd sit down again and dream up into the sky.

At night, she liked to read on the couch. She fell asleep there with just a light blanket over her. She began waking up even earlier, getting to school nearly an hour before she had to. She didn't mind being alone, she didn't mind Nick's business trips anymore. By herself, everything was less tense. She knew what to expect.

She knew she was drifting from him, but she knew he was drifting, too. She began thinking about escape, about going away somewhere, taking a leave from school. She thought about going to Mexico. It was hot and pretty there; the sun could burn away memory, peel it away like skin, leaving you a whole new layer of life. The more she thought about it, the more she wanted to go.

She told the school first, and then she blurted out to Nick that she was taking a leave. He nodded. "Just let me see how much time I can take off," he said to her. But Dore shook her head; she said she wanted to be away by herself, that she wanted to think. "Think about what?" said Nick, frozen, but she walked past him, touching his shoulder in the way you might touch anyone, a friend, a casual stranger.

"So when do you think you'll be coming back?" he said, his voice trailing, waiting for her to fill in the date, the time, the hope.

She shrugged, she said she didn't know, and when she packed, he saw how calmly she folded. "We both need the time," she said, wearily, as if she didn't believe it.

"Don't go," he said, but she kept moving about the apartment, taking things from hangers. She left behind photos, wool sweaters, her favorite pair of red earrings, and he told himself it would be all right then, she'd be back.

When she left, a week later, he was at work, half furious, half missing her. When he came home that evening, the house felt empty. He missed her; he missed the times when he hadn't been able to pass a school kid without feeling her so clear and sharp inside of him that it hurt. When the phone rang, he picked it up, expecting a client, and there was Leslie's voice on the wire. "I have something important to tell you," she said.

Nick walked outside, head down, seeing nothing, his heart wild. It was crazy, crazy, Dore leaving his life like this, Leslie entering it in a way that was too permanent to ignore. He remembered once in the home, a baby dying, and then another appearing, just one hour after the funeral, brought into Mr. Rice's office by the social worker who had found her, abandoned in an alley. "Happiness out of grief," Mr. Rice had said, dandling the baby, showing her off. "It turns on and off like a light switch." Nick pulled in a breath of night air. A baby, a baby. It made him feel this incredible sense of possibility. A real child instead of a ghost, a woman who loved you instead of one who kept walking away.

He had taken control, talking to Leslie. He had told her not to worry, that he'd be right there, and then he could feel something changing in her, something alive and moving over the wires, and she had stammered out that she loved him. Oh, God. She had never said that to him before, and as soon as she said it, it was like that light switch, clicking something on in him. He loved her, he had for a while now, but he loved Dore, too, and he didn't know what to do about any of it.

He worried the situation, weighed it. It was a second chance. Dore might not return; a large part of her had left him a long time back. He could have a whole other family, a woman who clearly loved him, a child, a life. He could marry her, too; he could give it all a permanence it wouldn't be so easy to drift away from. And the baby—his baby—well, he'd never leave it with a sitter, he'd never let it out of his sight. He'd be such a spectacular father, nothing would dare to hurt it. He thought suddenly of Dore, struggling to get pregnant, crying in bed after lovemaking, or sometimes before, making him so guilty, he couldn't get hard.

He felt almost feverish. He'd make good as a father, good as a husband. He felt for a moment as though he were promising something to Susan, and to Dore, too, off in Mexico.

He had no idea what to tell Dore, how to leave her. She hadn't left him any number, any city, only the whole vast country of Mexico in which to find her. He called Leslie every evening, soothing her, making up emergencies that kept him from being there at that very moment, and then as soon as he hung up, he'd start composing his goodbye letters.

It gave him an odd strength, leaving Dore before she left him. He wouldn't take a single thing from the apartment, he'd let her have it all. Oh, maybe he'd take books. Photographs. He thought about the picture of Dore he had on his desk. He had taken it the week he met her, when he was already dizzy in love. She was smiling fearlessly into the camera. What could he possibly tell Leslie about that face? Could he say it was the face of an old friend, a neighbor? Could he say it was the face of his first love? Leslie was private enough herself not to ask more than he was willing to tell, but just that small bit of information, that naming, might be dangerous. He might as well tell her all of it, and in the telling, he'd give his past sudden new power over him, give all that pain entry into a new present, and he didn't want to feel it anymore, not Susan dying all over again, not the love dying. None of it.

In the end, it was Dore who found *him*. She called one night when he was asleep. "Remember me?" she said.

He sat up, clicking on the light, pulled by her voice.

"I was going to write you," she said. "Then sometimes I thought I'd just stay and stay and not tell you, but I was afraid you'd come and find me, and I didn't always want to be looking over my shoulder thinking I saw a detective in every friendly face." She started crying. "I don't want to be found," she said. "I'm tired of everything. I don't want boys pulling up their T-shirts pretending to scratch, all the time watching me to see if I'm getting turned on. I don't want love-sick compositions from girls." She sighed.

"Dore—" Nick said, but she interrupted him.

"God help me," she said, "but I can't do it alone; you have to help me out a little here." She was silent for a moment. "I just want to be by myself for a while. We don't have to say it's forever. We could call it a separation. I mean, we could get back together, couldn't we? We could work things out. Maybe you could see a therapist or something, talk it out in Boston, and then come here and talk it out with me."

"Dore," Nick said. "It's all right."

"Right," she said, bitterly. "And cows can fly."

"Don't say that," he said. "Do you want to give me an address or a phone?"

"No," she said. "I don't."

"I won't stay in the apartment," he said. "I'm going to get some new kind of job, move away."

"Oh," she said. "Look, don't tell me your address, all right? If I have it, I might write."

He didn't want her to hang up. He suddenly wished she would come back and stay in the apartment, just so he would know where she was. He wished he could take her along with him to Leslie's. "I still love you," he said abruptly. "Isn't that horrible?"

"Yes," she said. "Yes, it is." And then she hung up, leaving him only the empty hum of the wires.

He didn't get any new kind of job. All he did was switch from one publisher to another, only now he would be handling more than just kids' books, he'd be selling an adult list as well. The home office was in Philadelphia, and it was enough of a change to make him feel he was completing his new life, and it was enough of a stasis to make him feel safe.

He packed Dore's things and put them in storage, sending the information along to Dore's parents. Then he rented the place to three college girls, leaving them his share of the furniture and the dishes.

He left the day after he rented the place, and when he got into his car, he couldn't help it, he kept seeing Dore in Mexico. She'd be eating at a café, her skin brown as it had never been. He tried to picture her with some man, but every man became himself. He couldn't imagine her without him, he couldn't.

He had taken no pictures of her with him, not one photo of Susan. And here he was, driving, moving toward a city he had always hated, moving toward a woman he now loved, and a child.

On a damp Saturday afternoon, Nick and Leslie married. The ceremony was performed in a judge's chambers, and the two of them stood very close together, fingers linked. The only other people there were Leslie's parents. Leslie's mother had a Brownie camera strapped loosely about her neck. She sat because the arthritis in her legs bothered her. She leaned forward to snap a few pictures, then handed the camera over to her husband and wept quietly into her hands.

Nick was astonishingly aware of Leslie beside him. He had thought the ceremony was going to be very casual; he had told Leslie he was going to wear his favorite black jacket and his black sneakers. When she was secretive about her own dress, he had simply assumed that she wanted to surprise him. And here she was, in glimmering blue satin, a formal wedding dress, beaded in a paler blue, covered in lace. He had never seen anything like that dress; he had never imagined Leslie so beautiful.

She beamed and beamed when she saw the expression on his face. She told him the dress wasn't just for him, but for herself, too. Some nights, while Nick slept, she had carefully gotten out of bed and padded to her sewing room. She had painstakingly beaded the satin, squinting as she grew more and more sleepy, half-certain she was ruining her sight and spoiling the dress. After a few more hours, she'd collapse back into bed, her head knotted. She woke with headaches so terrible she would have to bind ice chips into a scarf about her head, freezing the pain just enough so she could get back to work again.

He couldn't believe it when they were finally married. Leslie hadn't wanted rings at first, insisting that they distracted from the natural beauty of the hand, but Nick had said that rings were important, a piece of jewelry like that carried magic.

He insisted on a honeymoon, too, although Leslie said it wasn't necessary, taking her up to a cabin someone at work loaned him. There wasn't much to do—the air was too cold to swim in the lake, but they could walk, they could sit inside, and every time Nick felt her watching him, every time she told him she loved him, he felt as if he had somehow gained a reprieve.

They moved back into Leslie's home. Nick had wanted to find a new place, so they both could start out fresh, but although Leslie agreed, he had seen her face whenever he scanned the real-estate section, whenever he pointed out the places he circled in red. Every house they looked at had made her cramp up and get wary. She'd pace out the rooms, narrowing her eyes, squinting against the light she said was much too poor to sew in, running her fingers over the walls she claimed were already chinking off powdery plaster. She found flaw after flaw that no one but she seemed to notice. She said the places were too expensive, too charmless, too small, and in the end they just stopped looking.

She told Nick it didn't matter—they could redo the house, paint every room a new color for all she cared, get all new things. They went to a few stores, they sat in leather chairs and Haitian-cotton couches, and they even bought four gallons of blue paint. In the end, though, the paint was stacked in the basement, not one stick of furniture was ever bought, and the house was left the way it had always been, exactly the way Leslie loved it.

It took some getting used to, living in Pittsburgh, actually having to be there day to day. It wasn't where he wanted to be, but it was part of the territory his job gave him, and with a baby coming on, he couldn't afford to quit. He kept sending feelers out about other jobs; he'd read the papers with the same restlessness he had once watched in his father. But nothing seemed to happen. He reminded himself the city was different, that he was different, too, and that his wife, his child, could make any city livable. Still, he couldn't help feeling angry when the Sunday *New York Times* came out and he saw all the shows and films sprawled across the pages; he couldn't help his claustrophobia when night came on and the streets emptied to a chilling quiet. He'd try to fill the space with the raw blast of the stereo, he'd go for walks with Leslie, talking loudly, stamping his feet, filling the city's vacuum.

The city seemed to suffer from an inferiority complex, too. Every once in a while, Nick would see glossy articles about transplanted New Yorkers or San Franciscans who thought there was just no place prettier than Pittsburgh. "They dragged me here kicking and screaming," said one man—a plastic surgeon from Los Angeles. "Now they'd have to forklift me out of here." Women from Boston claimed Pittsburgh had every bit as much fashion as their old city had. You could buy T-shirts or posters emblazoned with the city's newest slo-gan, "New York might be the Big Apple, but Pittsburgh—what a plum!" Leslie thought he was being silly. "Come on, it's not so bad," she said. "Aren't you happy?" And seeing her, he was.

He liked living with her, waking up to find her beside him, com-ing home to her at night. But sharing the house still took some getting used to. He was always stepping on pins, pricking them into his feet. Needles caught in the nap of the rug, found their way into the cracks of the bathroom tiles. He checked his shoes before he put them on; he shook out all the sheets before he would sleep in them; and still he dreamed about rolling over onto a pin and blinding him-self, about wolfing down morning eggs and puncturing his gut with a stray needle.

Only sometimes did he feel himself unraveling. He'd be out on the street and a woman with short, pale hair would pass by and he'd root to the sidewalk, paralyzed, watching how easily she moved from him. He was even half-sure he saw Dore once or twice. He knew she wasn't in Boston, at least not yet; but even so, when he had business there, he crammed his time with activity so he wouldn't even think to find her. He took detours around their old routes.

Whenever he came home from one of his business trips, he was newly determined to tell Leslie about Dore. There was nothing so terrible about his past, nothing to keep from anyone. But as soon as he opened his mouth, he felt a sudden new clip of pain, stopping his heart, his breath, his speech. Leslie remained clear, cool, un-disturbed.

Dore's grip kept loosening, though, replaced by Leslie, her gold wedding band, the soft swell of her belly, and he felt as if this in-credible miracle had happened to him without his even being aware of it happening. Leslie was so different from Dore. He could walk into the house and no matter what client was there, revolving slowly in a half-finished skirt, peering at some sketches, Leslie never shut him out. She winked at him, she removed pins from her mouth so she could introduce him to her client. She never waited for Nick to leave; instead, she pulled him into the gossip, made him laugh so hard he couldn't ever imagine leaving her.

Leslie had a special sewing room, but there were always design projects scattered about the house. She had a portable machine that she moved all over the house, sometimes sewing in the kitchen when it was sunny, sometimes in the living room when she felt like seeing who might walk by. Her own clothing was always indifferent, but his began changing. He'd pull out an old denim shirt and find it had a shimmery new row of mother-of-pearl buttons. Before the weather turned frosty, there was a new heavy wool coat hanging in the closet for him, a cashmere shirt.

Leslie would watch him put her creations on. She couldn't relax until she had seen him walk around; she said she could tell if he liked the clothes by the way he moved in them. Nick was astounded. He asked her how and when she had done such wizardry, but she just laughed, pleased.

He hated traveling, hated leaving her. Sometimes it felt even worse than it had with Dore. He wanted Leslie to come with him, but she wouldn't. She said she didn't really like hotels; she liked staying home and sewing, dreaming about her husband. When he was at a hotel, he would miss her so much, his whole body would tighten up into his heart, moving in one single beat of desire. When he called her on the phone, she was delighted to hear his voice, yet pulled back to one of her designs, and it fueled his adoration, his need for her.

She loved being pregnant. She wanted to make love. She wanted to admire her own Buddha belly as she stood naked in front of the mirror, and as she grew, he sometimes thought that she wasn't just carrying a baby, she was carrying their whole life together, nurturing it, giving it life.

Nick's daughter was born during one of the worst rainstorms Pittsburgh had ever seen. Some of the streets were badly flooded, and Nick, not trusting himself to drive, hailed a cab to take Leslie and him to the hospital. He sat in back with Leslie, who had her eyes squinched shut, her hands gripped about her belly.

On the radio, the news talked disasters. The Vietnam war was escalating. Students were rioting at Columbia and Berkeley. A couple wading in a lake in the rain had been struck by lightning. One was instantly killed, the other hovered on the critical list. The station wouldn't divulge any names until the parents had been notified. "Dumb shit kids," the cabbie muttered. A cat had been found an-

grily swimming in the river. The announcer described the cat's pecu-
liar dime-size black markings, and gave a number you could call if
you wanted to claim it. He said that everyone at the Animal Rescue
League had just fallen head over heels with the cat, that they had
named him "Rainy Day."

Nick, staring out the window, saw yellow slickers, umbrellas abandoned like bones along the roadway. Gliding sheets of water hit the
windows and the cabdriver sped and cursed and slammed on the
breaks.

The baby was born in the hospital ten hours later. Leslie's mother,
when Nick called her, cried and told Nick that it was an excellent
omen, being born in a storm, that it meant their daughter was a
child of danger, that nothing could ever hurt her, because she was
now protected. Nick felt a silly flush of relief. He went to tell Leslie,
who laughed and said her mother was unduly superstitious. "When I
was little, she wouldn't let me stitch up a tear in her blouse if she was
wearing it. She said the needle wouldn't just be mending a blouse
but stitching right through her brain." Leslie smiled at him. She was
pale and lovely in her bed, dressed in a favorite faded nightgown she
had insisted on wearing. She had her hair loose and tangled about
her. "Go and see your girl," she told him, "and then get back here
and be with your other one."

He saw the baby, one small red face among the others. He pressed
his nose against the glass. The nurse held her up, and then abruptly
he felt something snaking up along his spine, he saw the baby's features shimmy, and for a second she looked like Susan. He bolted
back from the glass, bumping into a nervous father, who apologized,
as if it had been his fault and not Nick's. Terrified, Nick moved back
toward the glass, and when he dared to look at the baby again, she
looked only like herself, only like his and Leslie's baby. He motioned
to the nurse that it was all right, that she could put the baby down,
and then, without daring a second look, he started walking, up and
down the floor. When he finally returned to Leslie, he sat on the
edge of her bed, taking her hand.

"Isn't she perfect?" Leslie demanded.

He lifted up her hand and kissed it. "She's like no other," he said.

SEVEN

• • •

They named the baby Robin, a name Leslie liked. Leslie slept a lot at first, so Nick hired a professional nurse to live in and help out. The nurse was a dour, middle-aged prune of a woman named Aggie Mason, and the very first thing she did was try to coax Leslie into a haircut. She said that now that Leslie was a mother, she'd be too busy to fuss with her hair.

"But it's no fuss," Leslie said. "It's wash and drip dry."

The nurse frowned. She said a mother should look mature and responsible, and not have hair long enough to strangle a baby. "I know a child who was rushed to surgery with stomach cramps and they had to cut her open," Aggie said. "Know what they found?" She paused, dramatically. "A hair ball. As big as my fist."

Leslie stifled a laugh. "My husband loves my hair," she said.

"Oh, husbands," Aggie said, and this time Leslie laughed.

Nick was grateful for the nurse. He liked it that she was older, that she had looked after countless babies in her time, and that she was overcautious. She liked things running smoothly, efficiently, safely. She stayed in the spare room and kept it meticulously clean. She vacuumed the whole house twice just to get rid of all the pins. She warned Leslie about making the house babyproof, about getting a lock for the sewing room so she could seal it up when she wasn't using it. "One room for sewing is smarter than using the whole house," Aggie said. "Especially with a little one." Leslie told her she was much too weary right now to even think about doing a hem, much less any project.

Nick liked the nurse more and more. He was sure nothing could ever happen to Robin while she was there. And it was funny, but with Aggie there, he felt safe to go in and look at his girl. Aggie distrusted him, though. Every time he went near the baby, she followed him. She barely let him hold Robin before she took the baby from him, reminding him that it was nap time or feeding time or some other kind of time that he wasn't supposed to be a part of.

Aggie was with them for two months. Nick begged her to stay on an extra month or so, but Leslie insisted that she was strong enough to handle things.

Nick was surprised at how easy it was for Aggie to leave. He had thought baby nurses got attached to their charges. He had read about nurses writing to the kids they had looked after for years after they left, visiting and calling, and even ending up taking care of the kids of their kids. All Aggie did was present Leslie with a list of stores that sold sterilized bottles and carried the right brand of diaper at the right price. She pecked Robin on one downy cheek and then got her suitcase and carried it herself to a waiting cab. Nick wanted to drive her to the train himself, but she shook her head, said she liked to end things at the place where they were ending. Nick opened the door of the cab, and as she scooted in, he said, "You'll miss her, won't you?"

Aggie smiled. "Only until the second I take the new one into my arms," she said. Then she settled herself in and turned to wave to Leslie, who was standing in the doorway, Robin in her arms. Leslie lifted Robin's baby hand and waved it. "Say goodbye," she said.

Robin didn't look like either one of them. She had red curls, gray eyes, and skin so fair that Leslie had to put a sun block on her just to carry her out to the car. Robin burned anyway. It made Leslie wince to see a baby all red like that, but Robin was strangely oblivious. She never seemed to mind. She was that way about other things, too. She'd sleep in diapers so soggy that she'd wake chafed and raw. She'd bruise her mouth against the rails of her crib and never cry.

"Do you think there's something wrong with her?" Leslie worried to her mother.

"Oh, for heaven's sake, count your blessings," Leslie's mother said. "So she doesn't cry. Big deal." Then she regaled Leslie with a long and irritating story about what a crier Leslie had been, how she had once stuffed her own ears with cotton just to get a moment or two of peace.

Robin was, as Leslie's mother kept saying, a child of danger, a child protected. And she seemed to grow more and more nervy. Before Leslie could stop her, Robin tried to crawl onto the neighbor's foul-tempered cat, Ralph, who scratched everything he came in contact with. Oddly, Ralph merely yawned and twitched free, leaving the baby surprised and blinking. Robin was curious about all the things she should leave alone—wall sockets, the knife Nick used to carve the meat, Leslie's endless supply of pins. She reached, she grabbed, she sometimes got, but she was never harmed.

Like the water baby she was, Robin couldn't get enough of water. She relaxed in her bath, becoming stiff and cranky only when Leslie tried to pluck her out. When it rained, Leslie swore Robin perked up. Leslie would sometimes carry her over to the big picture window in the living room and the baby would stare, mesmerized by the raindrops smearing paths down the blurry glass.

Leslie adored her daughter, but sometimes she had an uneasy feeling that the adoration wasn't quite mutual, that Robin could do fine on her own, thank you. It bothered Leslie that the baby never cried out its need for her; Leslie always had to go and check to see if Robin was wet or hungry. It seemed a slight to her.

Robin wasn't an affectionate baby, either. All through her pregnancy, Leslie had daydreamed about what a comfort a baby would be when Nick was on the road. But now the house seemed lonelier than ever. Robin didn't like Leslie's constant touch; she pulled away from hugs and kisses. Leslie tried to bring Robin into the bed with her, but Robin struggled and screamed; she wouldn't quiet down until she was back in her own room, alone and content.

Leslie couldn't help it—she began to think she had the wrong baby, that the hospital had made some mistake. She had read about such things. Once, in the dentist's office she had read a whole article in *Woman's Day* about such a mistake: two boy babies given to the wrong parents. One of the mothers kept thinking something wasn't quite right—just a mother's instinct—and did a little investigating.

She found that her baby's footprint didn't match the one made shortly after her baby's birth. There was a big scandal. The hospital was sued, and both babies were returned to their rightful parents, but who knew what damage had been done?

Of course, that had happened at a tiny hospital in some little headache of a town she'd never heard of. Robin had been born at Magee, the best hospital in Pittsburgh. Still, Leslie kept thinking about it. A loving little girl in someone else's home, a baby who dreamed of her rightful mother's kisses, of a lap to cradle in.

Leslie got up her courage and called Magee. At first she pretended she was doing research. She spoke to someone in PR about the likelihood of such an event, but the woman was annoyed. Things like that happened once in a blue moon, she said, and certainly never at Magee.

Leslie wouldn't give up. She took new prints of Robin's feet, and then requested a set from the hospital. When they came, she saw they were identical. She sat on the couch, missing Nick, lonely for her daughter, and then she bunched up a pillow along her chest, like a baby, and she wept.

It was different for Nick. He had loved the baby when she was just an idea, just a swelling in his wife's body. He had fallen more in love with Leslie and his life with her as the pregnancy went along, and if he had been a little unnerved by Robin's birth, well, Aggie's rigid control had calmed a lot of his fears.

Now, though, with Aggie gone, Robin seemed completely left open to life, and he had this vague new fear. He couldn't admit it to Leslie. He kept trying to remind himself that Leslie's mother had said Robin was a child protected, but sometimes he'd catch a glimpse of Robin's fiery hair and could almost swear he saw flame, a whole crazy corona of it about her head. He'd hear her burble, and layered within her small voice he heard Susan. It made him crazy. Late at night, he'd jerk awake, riding on all these mad thoughts about Robin being Susan reincarnated, about it being a new kind of test. He was going to have to make sure nothing bad ever happened to this second chance of a girl. He was going to have to be doubly careful.

He tried. He double- and triple-checked the locks on the doors and the windows. When he rode with Robin in the car, he made sure she was strapped into her car seat in back. When he was away, he'd call Leslie in the middle of the night because he missed her, and because he wanted her to go and check on Robin. "Hey, I do my job here," Leslie said, and he laughed and made some lame joke; he didn't tell her that he needed to know that Robin was still alive. When he came home, he was always a little startled to see the baby creeping toward him, unharmed.

At night he slipped into her room to make sure she was still breathing. He'd crouch over her crib, watching her small chest rise and fall. He'd place one finger near her damp mouth to feel her breath. He wanted to sleep beside her so he could match his breaths to hers, so the strength of his heartbeat might feed hers.

She let him pick her up. She yawned like a cat. In the middle of the night, he sat in the rocker and whispered to her and sang. She curled around him. He was half-asleep one evening when he saw Leslie. At first he thought it was just a dream. She was naked, shadowed in the doorway, her hair a wash of ink over her pale skin. "Leslie," he said, and then Robin stirred and he set her gently back in her crib.

"I bet she didn't want to be put back there, did she?" Leslie said. "Not by you."

Nick stroked Leslie's hair from one shoulder and bent to kiss her bare skin.

"I love you more than she does," Leslie said.

Robin grew. She was astonishingly healthy. She turned three, then four, escaping mumps and measles, chicken pox and the flu; even the few colds she did contract seemed to evaporate within days. But the funny thing was, the healthier she became and the firmer her hold to life, the more uneasy Nick was. He couldn't help thinking of it as borrowed time; he couldn't quite believe that she was really his for any sort of duration. The more birthdays she celebrated, the surer he was of their impending end. He told himself she had passed the danger point. She was older now than Susan had ever had a chance to be. He should relax now, loosen up, but he found himself still apprehensive.

He didn't want to be a bad father. He didn't want his wife wondering about him, his daughter scarred. He took her to the playground and tried not to see the rusty nails studded into the swings, the germs on the slides. At the zoo, he worried about the bears escaping; on trains, he saw gunmen. He couldn't enjoy himself; he kept hurrying Robin, until she got cranky.

He punished her only once. She was playing with matches, oblivious to his approach, and he yanked them from her fingers and smacked her so hard that she tumbled against the wall, hitting her head. She didn't cry—she seldom did—but she wouldn't approach him for days afterward. He couldn't bring himself to apologize, and he scoured the house for matches, tossing them all out, pack by pack. Later he heard Leslie speaking quietly to Robin, calming her with some story about Mr. Fire and Silly Milly, and he loved her for doing what he himself could not.

He did tell Robin stories, though—his father's tales about strange lands. He'd feel himself reeling right back through time. He'd remember the raw, scratchy feeling of Tom's shirt, the way his father's aftershave smelled. He made up his own stories for Robin, too—tales involving the two of them. They went on wonderful adventures to strange planets; they could change themselves into animals just by twitching their noses.

It was so easy being father and daughter in those stories. It was simple to face dangers, because he could control them all, he knew just how everything would come out: He and Robin were always rescued "just in the Nick of time." Oh, how he loved that phrase! It made him feel like he had some secret rule over the whole universe. He created dangers and then bottomed them out into amusements. He had villains, but they all secretly yearned to be heroes, and indeed turned into heroes at the slightest provocation. He loved making up stories for Robin, and she was enchanted. She would sit still and silent for hours, letting him transport her into his secret worlds.

Robin loved having her father home. If there was any problem at all for her, it had to do with her mother and not with him. With Nick around, Leslie suddenly seemed to stop seeing Robin. The kisses that were sometimes so rough that they made Robin feel wounded, the love nips and tickles and songs, all suddenly seemed to stop.

At first, Robin didn't mind much. She was glad enough to spend all day in her room looking at the colored paper maps Nick brought her, tracing the blue lines he had drawn of his routes so she'd know where he went. But then, when she was tired and wanted her mother, when she felt like a hug, Leslie was preoccupied, cooking something strange for dinner, dressed in something she didn't want Robin to wrinkle. Robin stood in the hall watching her, confused. Usually, all she had to do was just be in the house and Leslie would seek her out, pinpointing her location, finding her in seconds even when Robin was hiding. But now Robin had to stamp her feet or clap her hands just to get her mother to turn around and see her.

It was as if she had become invisible. She'd line up all her plastic animals across her mother's side of the bed, but when Leslie came into the room, it was to spritz more perfume across the back of her neck, or run a comb through her hair. She stared dreamily past her. When she left the room, she casually ruffled Robin's hair. "Look at my zoo," Robin said, but Leslie was gone, and suddenly Robin didn't feel like playing with her animals anymore. She cried, a little hurt, but Leslie had gone outside to get something from the car and didn't hear her.

At dinner, Robin tried to talk, and then deliberately spilled her milk into a drippy white puddle on the cloth, but Leslie didn't scold her the way she usually would. "Oh, Robin" was all she said, and then she mopped it up, telling Nick a story about one of her clients, her eyes dancing.

Leslie's affection didn't disappear—she never less than adored her daughter. But Robin was with her all the time. Nick's presence was rarer, and she channeled all of her energy into charming him so that he might stay a day or two longer, so that when he was on the road, he might remember just how lovely it had been with her at home, and come back to her that much sooner.

Sometimes they took family vacations, usually at the shore. Robin would play outside the cottage, and when she came back in, Leslie and Nick would be sipping iced coffee at the table, bent toward each other, talking so quietly that Robin would suddenly shout. They both looked over at her then. "Well, what's this?" Nick said, beckoning her to him, but Leslie told her to scoot and wash up for dinner. Leslie danced with Nick in the kitchen. She tucked Robin into bed and kissed her tenderly goodnight, but then she locked the bed-

room door behind her and Nick so Robin couldn't come in mornings.

Things changed almost as soon as Nick left for business again.
Leslie got very quiet. She spent a day or so by herself in her sewing
room, she fed Robin dinner and put her to bed, but it wasn't until
another day had passed that she suddenly seemed to see Robin again.
And then she wouldn't let her alone. She wanted to be with Robin
all the time. She wanted to take Robin to the park, she wanted the
two of them to bake cookies. She hugged and kissed Robin, she sang
songs, but Robin, remembering how cool Leslie had been to her,
how hurt and shut out she had felt, was wary. She expected every
hug that Leslie gave her to suddenly stop; she couldn't trust the stories or the kisses.

It always took Robin a while to warm to Leslie when Nick was
gone, and Leslie told herself that was natural, that she just missed
her father and it had nothing to do with her. Leslie worked to reclaim her daughter, praising her drawings, buying her blocks and
paper dolls.

Robin, despite herself, would gradually creep into her mother's lap
when she felt blue. She crawled into bed with her when she heard
strange noises, and sometimes she would throw her arms about Leslie
for a hug. But even so, it somehow wasn't enough for Leslie. There
was always something in Robin that pulled away from Leslie before
Leslie was ready to let her go. She'd be holding Robin and then she'd
feel Robin start to pull away, and she would automatically tighten
her grip, but Robin would always struggle free, always leave her.
When Robin closed the door to her room, she didn't like it when
Leslie opened it again, and she was upset when Leslie followed her
into the backyard, behind the shrubs.

"It was my secret place!" Robin complained.

"Well, now it's ours," Leslie said, but she noticed that Robin
never went back there again.

Leslie told herself that it wasn't just her. She had seen Robin with
her friends, telling them in a serious adult voice that they had to go
home because she wanted to play alone now. Leslie, watching the
baffled faces of the other children, felt like inviting them in and
making them brownies, felt like telling them, "I know how you
feel."

It made her angry sometimes. She was lonely. She missed Nick so much. She should have had at least the comfort of a loving daughter. When she saw Robin pulling away, she snapped at her, finding the soft spots that were easy to wound. Tugging a brush through Robin's hair, she groaned, "Where did you get such a mop?" She said it couldn't come from her or from Nick, that it was orphan hair, belonging to no one, and Robin, stung, snapped away from the brush.

It bothered Leslie, too, the way Robin pushed past her to rush to Nick when he came home. But then Nick would come up the walk, smiling at her, and sweep her so close to him that she could hear his heart, and then she'd see nothing, no one, but him, and it would be all right.

The first thing Robin wanted from Nick was the tapes he made for her. When he was on the road, he wrote scraps of stories on the back of his appointment book; pieces of plot found their way onto napkins in the places where he took his clients to dine. The writing relaxed him, made him feel bound to his daughter, and he felt this odd kind of happiness. He bought a portable tape recorder and began concocting stories in his hotel rooms, in the car as he drove the endless miles homeward. He thought she could listen to his voice now even when he was away. He'd never really leave her that way. Other men might bring their kids teddy bears or rubber balls, but Nick brought tapes, celluloid pieces of his heart.

Robin grew attached to the recorder, sitting in front of it, amazed and delighted and adoring. But sometimes she seemed to prefer the tape to Nick himself. He wasn't so sure how he felt about that. He felt stupid going into her room and sitting with her, listening to his own voice, small and tinny in the recorder. He stood outside the door for a bit, feeling like a voyeur, thinking that when the tape was over he would stride in and tell her a fresh story himself. But then he heard the sudden whir and click of the rewind, and there was his voice again, telling the same story. Leslie, gliding past, pins in her mouth, frowned.

Robin grew up on ghosts. Every year Nick tracked her height, making a small pencil dot over her head on the kitchen wall, but there was no way of keeping track of his presence, no way of being sure where he was. She was in second grade and it still confused her, having her father's voice there on the machine, or booming over the telephone wires at her, while all the time his body was somewhere else. Leslie inadvertently made it worse. She was trying to reassure Robin, who was crying, missing Nick. Leslie told her it wasn't as if Nick were gone, because, really, he left parts of himself behind. No, not just in the machine. Why, if you shut your eyes, Leslie said, you could feel him right there in the room with you.

She meant it as a comfort, but Robin lay awake in her bed that night, tensed for her father, wondering what he would do when he came upon her, whether this presence would have a body like his or be like the monsters she sometimes saw lurking on TV. She got up and put on her best nightgown, the one with the pink and blue ducks. She tried to brush her hair, and she doused herself with the sweet-scented toilet water Leslie had given her. It was purple tinted, housed in a glass poodle she tilted along her neck.

She got back into bed and forced herself to stay awake, suddenly afraid, suddenly remembering spirits like Santa Claus, who knew if you were nice or naughty and who withheld gifts; or like God, who wrote down what you did for punishments to come. You couldn't defend yourself against someone you couldn't see. Robin bunched the covers about her head so that only her nose poked out. She shivered in her fear.

In the morning, she was sure she saw proof that Nick's presence had been at work. A book was in the wrong place, and one of his flannel shirts had fallen into a pile from the hanger. She was afraid of his ghost, afraid she'd do something wrong and the ghost would leave and the real Nick would never come home. When Nick did arrive back, she was suspicious. She waited for him to tell her something bad she had done, and when he didn't, she tried to relax.

She began thinking her father wasn't the only ghost in the house. She was suddenly convinced that a wild and dangerous pack of wolves lived in the basement. She knew they were invisible; she knew they wore blue jeans and checked red shirts and walked upright on two legs and spat tobacco. And worse, she knew they had guns. When Leslie bounded downstairs to collect the wash, Robin lurked in the hallways, her heart racing. The few times she had to go down to the basement by herself, for her bike, or a doll, she made sure to carry handfuls of the hamburger meat Leslie had planned for her dinner, strips of bologna she was supposed to take to school for lunch. She scattered the meat in the corners, her peace offering. When the food drew mice, Robin said nothing. Traps were set, the mice were gone, but Robin knew that things had presence. She could go downstairs and still feel those mice, just as she still felt the wolves, just as she felt her father—there and always, just out of her grasp.

Nick's schedule kept changing. A buyer would reschedule an appointment and he'd be home two days later than he had planned. A meeting would spill into the night, and rather than drive home when he was so exhausted, he would just stay over in a hotel. Robin didn't really understand it. She only knew that he wasn't home when he was supposed to be—that one moment there would be an extra place set for him at the dining-room table, there would be candles, and the next moment Leslie would be taking the plate away, removing the candles, and her face would be sad. Robin wasn't sure what Nick did when he was away, although he had explained it to her. She only knew that he had said it was fun, and he always had stories about the wonderful places he visited. It suddenly began to worry her. If the places were so wonderful, what would keep him from staying there? What would make him come home at all?

Robin began getting depressed every time she saw Nick's suitcase on the bed. "Oh, now, I'll be back before you even know it," he told her, but he whistled as he packed. He seemed to have more energy when he was leaving. It was those times he'd want to swoop her into the air, want to kiss and tickle her and sing her wild snatches of song. She'd walk by the living room and see him waltzing with Leslie, dipping her down so low, her hair brushed the rug.

Robin waited until Nick was in the bathroom, fiddling in the medicine cabinet for his aspirin and after-shave, and then she'd sneak something of hers into his suitcase. A sock, a blue hair ribbon, anything with her imprint on it so he'd remember her. Homing devices. And when he did come home, she felt grimly satisfied. He never said anything to her about her sock or her ribbon or her whatever that had traveled with him. He simply put them back in her room, and if she was there, he dotted her face with a kiss.

She didn't trust the sound of his car in the morning anymore. She couldn't be certain that this wasn't one of his going-away days. She would dash to follow, the stones in the sidewalk ribbing her bare soles, her robe flapping open, her hair tumbling about her. When he spotted her, he slowed down, unlatching the front door for her to get in. She panted, unable to speak. He didn't have to ask her what she thought she was doing. He simply waited for her to clutch back her breath and then he took out his appointment book and showed her all his Pittsburgh appointments for the whole week, that he wasn't going to be out of town once. He watched her, and then he took the pen and wrote, with a flourish, "Tuesday, dinner with Robin." He looped the car back toward the house where Leslie was wearily standing in the front yard. "Come on, Robin," she said. She walked around to Nick's side of the door and kissed him. "Can't say I blame her," Leslie said, smiling. Robin scowled and kicked at the bushes.

It made Nick a little crazy. He couldn't get in the car without getting right out again to check behind the wheels, to look underneath and make sure Robin wasn't crouched there. Once, he found her sleeping in the back seat. He kept hiding the car keys, but she always seemed to know where to find them.

He didn't know what to do about her. She came home from school with drawings of her family, but sometimes his own face was missing. He remembered the trailer-court drawings with a pang; he remembered Dore's laughter when she told him how Ruby's kids had drawn their father in a skirt. He asked Robin why he wasn't on the page, but she just shrugged. "You're wherever it is you go," she said.

Robin calmed down a little as she grew. Nick watched her, and by the time she was in fifth grade, she had stopped trailing the car, she didn't put her ribbons into his suitcase as much, and for a while he thought the problem was over. But then, he and Leslie were called to Robin's school for a conference. Robin was a smart little girl who brought home gold stars on almost all her papers, but Robin's teacher, a thin young man with blond hair, told Nick that Robin had a problem with telling the truth. He said he had warned her and warned her about lying, but she persisted.

"What are you talking about?" said Nick. "Robin doesn't lie."

The teacher told him that Robin persisted in telling everyone that she was really an orphan and lived in a cardboard box under a bridge. Nick started. "Are things all right at home?" the teacher asked.

"Everything is fine," Leslie said sharply. She wouldn't discuss it. She told the teacher Robin had been blessed with a wild imagination, and as a teacher, why wasn't he trying to cultivate such a gift instead of trying to break it down?

"I'll talk to her," Nick said, his voice low. When he stood up, the room seemed to move. Leslie was silent all the way to the car. She slid inside and leaned against her window.

He took up her hand and laid it against his cheek, and then she turned to look at him, her eyes narrowed. "I'm with her all the time," she said. "You're the one who's always gone. You don't see how she gets when you're gone, how she pines." She took her hand from him. "You don't see how I get, either." She sighed. "Can't you work here in Pittsburgh? Do you dislike the city that much? Can't you be plain old nine-to-five?"

Nick rested his head on the steering wheel. "I don't know," he said. He was silent for a moment, remembering what it was like to be in a hotel room, lying across a crumple of sheets, shaping his pillow as though it were Leslie against him, missing her so much it was sometimes like a disease eating away at him. He couldn't tell her how things had changed; how when he was away, he convinced himself nothing could happen to them. When the phone rang in his hotel room, he never once thought it was the police wanting him to come identify some bodies. It was as if being away from his family was a weird kind of protection for them and for him. Home, he'd watch Leslie, worrying that she was ruining her eyes squinting over a sewing machine, uneasy when she didn't come straight to bed but puttered around downstairs. It was at home that he thought to lean over and place a hand on her chest to make sure it still beat; at home that he felt the dangers lurking, waiting for opportunity.

Leslie moved closer to him, scooting across the seat. Her hair smelled piny. Last week it had smelled of vanilla. She was a fanatic about shampoos. She had fifteen or sixteen different plastic bottles lined up along the slippery edge of the tub. He never knew what her hair would smell like, and it was a surprise about her that he loved.

He bent and kissed her hair, her neck, her face. "I love you," he said, as if that were an answer.

He didn't talk to Robin—he wasn't sure what to say to her. For a while he simply watched her. She read a lot, so quickly she went through a book a day. He'd come home and find her in the backyard poring over a book. She read at dinner if he and Leslie let her; she was reading in her bed when he came to tuck her in. It never bothered him, but Leslie claimed it was too much escape. She yelled at Robin to get outside and play in the sun, and not to do it with a book, either. She told Nick that Robin's teachers didn't believe the level of books she read. They were too old for her, too demanding.

Nick didn't mind. He had always brought her books from his job. Now he brought home selections from the adult lists, which she grabbed up and polished off in hours.

Once, he took a day off from work and showed up at her school. He told the principal there was a dire family emergency and he had to get Robin out of class. It wasn't such a lie when he thought about it. The principal was about to wave a monitor over to fetch Robin when Nick interrupted. He wanted to know if it was possible for him to go to the class and get Robin himself. He said she was a nervous girl, that it would reassure her to see him right off. The principal said the best he could do was to allow Nick to go with the monitor, but Nick would still have to wait outside. "It's just less disruptive," the principal said. "You understand."

Nick walked down the hall with a ten-year-old boy covered in freckles. The kid didn't say one word to Nick, and refused to even look at him as he strode purposefully down the hall, swinging his arms as if he would strike anyone in his way. When they got to the class, he pivoted to Nick. "Wait here," he said, in a voice so military that Nick felt like saluting. But he waited, and he peered through the glass ribbon along the door, and there was Robin, in the second row, her hair coming out of its braids, the ribbons undone, her dress rumpled. When she spotted him, he made a big production of waving so the other kids would see. Robin blinked. She got up and slowly came out with the monitor, and when the door opened, Nick waved at her teacher.

They didn't say a word until after they had left the monitor, and then Robin squinted up at Nick, uncertain. "So how does lunch sound?" he said. "I thought you and I should have a whole day to ourselves."

She seemed to switch on. She kept asking him was he really serious, were they really going someplace or was it just to the dentist? She didn't calm down. Not when he took her for hot dogs, not during some silly kid movie about a talking typewriter that solved mysteries. He drove back toward the house. "Mind if I pick up your mother and we all have dinner?" he asked. She gave him a doubtful smile, but she said nothing.

He got Leslie. They went to a family-style place, with lots of red plastic baby chairs, a big messy salad bar with kids milling around, throwing lettuce at each other while waitresses gave them beleaguered smiles. He held Leslie's hand, he winked at Robin. He kept looking at all the other families, grinning, letting them grin back, telling himself that he fit into a place like this just as well as anybody else; that anyone here could take one look at the three of them and not think anything was a bit out of place.

He told himself that from now on he was going to take Robin with him someplace one day each month. He had plans. He got tickets for the aquarium; he brought home tennis rackets and reserved court space, telling Robin to think how surprised her granny would be to hear she was playing.

But then, suddenly, the earth seemed to spit up its dangers. Nothing was as easy as that first day alone with her when he took her out of school. He'd be on the court and he'd lob a ball and it would strike her, just in the soft of her belly, but it would unnerve him so much, he'd tell her that daddy didn't feel well, and he'd take her home to Leslie; then he'd get in the car and drive down to Point State Park and sit by the fountain. He'd try again, taking her to a movie, but the kids in front would act up, shooting rubber bands, and he couldn't help it, he'd think, There goes her eye, and he'd make Robin get up and leave with him.

He knew he was probably making her crazy, stopping and starting like that, but he never stopped asking her to go places, and although he usually didn't carry through his plans, she always agreed to go with him; she seemed to look forward to it.

He ran, his old trailer-court habit, to calm himself down. He bought himself new black sweats, expensive running shoes, and a stopwatch so he could time himself. It did calm him. He looked forward to the running, until one night he heard one of the neighborhood dogs barking, and he turned, and there, behind him, struggling to keep up was Robin. He was startled and angry, and then he saw the panic in her face, the sweat beaded on her brow as she panted to reach him, and he stopped. He waited for her to catch up.

"Where are you going?" she gasped. She had a stitch in one side, she said she felt like throwing up, and he walked the rest of the way home with her, his legs achy, yearning to break free and run.

EIGHT

• • •

Leslie always felt discouraged when Nick left on business. She knew how Robin tried to keep him at home, and she knew that she herself was just too stubborn to attempt the same. She had never wanted to travel with him before, but now, sometimes, she thought how easy it would be to hire a sitter, pack a bag, and take off with him. She didn't care if they went to some hick town; she didn't care if it rained the whole time. She could take her sketch pad and do some designs in the hotel room; she could visit the local shops and see if they'd take some of her designs on commission. Nick, though, never asked her to go until he was already there, and then it was because of the loneliness in the night. He'd call her, the pull in his voice reminding her how she missed him, but she was never quite willing to join him then; she never quite felt that his asking her when he was already there was very fair.

She took care of things, she managed. She always told herself that this time things were going to be different between Robin and her; this time they would really use the time to get close.

She started out all right. She missed Nick. She wanted Robin's company, so she was tolerant when Robin played her new James Taylor album over and over. After all, she was playing it in the living room, where Leslie was; she was sitting in a chair right next to her. Leslie took Robin shopping, and tried not to feel wounded when Robin chose cheaply made denim shirts and bell-bottom jeans, when she said she didn't need to see the designs Leslie had sketched for her, because all she wanted to wear were the things Leslie had just bought for her.

They cooked dinner together sometimes. They stayed up on week-ends watching the late-night horror movie, sharing popcorn, hugging when the film got scary. But Leslie couldn't seem to keep things working for very long. Whatever was good between them started souring with the first of Nick's calls. As soon as Leslie heard his voice, her yearning for him flowered, her loneliness intensified. But he was so casual on the phone, and then he kept asking for Robin, and it did something to her. She wanted him to whisper something private to her, tell her how much he missed her, how he remem-bered their nights. Instead, he asked if Robin's cold was any better, if she had stayed home from school, if she dressed warmly.

"If you're so worried, stay home," Leslie said, her voice flat, and then his tone changed, too, he seemed less glad to talk to her, and the call seemed spoiled. She was restless with anger, blaming him a little, blaming herself, and then Robin took the phone, turning her back to Leslie, whispering so Leslie couldn't hear, and Leslie's anger found another target.

She told herself it was crazy, that she couldn't really be jealous of her own daughter; she wouldn't let such a thing happen. But when Nick came home, she saw how he always had something for Robin— a tape, a book, a poster. He whispered to Leslie that he was the gift for her, but they never got to bed until after Robin was asleep, and by then Nick was too tired to do more than stroke her, whispering that he would make it up to her in the morning. He left her to lie awake and remember one clear, cool night when he had slept two houses away from her in his car because he hadn't been able to tear himself away.

She hated herself for it, but sometimes when Nick called from a nearby gas station saying he'd be home in two seconds from his busi-ness trip, she wouldn't tell Robin. She'd send her out for milk just so she could be alone with him for a while. Sometimes, too, when she was on the phone with Nick, she lied and told him Robin was out, when really she was just upstairs in the shower. Once, she was caught in her lie. She turned to see Robin in the hall. "I'm here," Robin said angrily, taking the phone from Leslie. "I was outside."

Leslie made some excuse, and later that evening she took Robin to a movie, whatever one Robin wanted to see, but she couldn't meet her daughter's eyes, and she was grateful for the dark theater.

Leslie sometimes felt as if she were on a roller coaster. The anger would suddenly drop from her and she'd feel how much she loved her girl, how much she wanted to be close. But Robin was used to her mother turning on and off to her—used to her being preoccupied with Nick when he was home, and seeming to need Robin only when Nick was away. Robin had learned to fend for herself from years of practice, and although she did love Leslie, she still couldn't quite trust her.

Leslie's attempts to get close always turned clumsy. She watched Robin peering anxiously at herself in the mirror when she thought no one was watching. She saw how her daughter sometimes seemed too eager to please when they had company. And sometimes, too, it made her ache to see how silent Robin became after a phone call from her father; she'd feel twinges of guilt that she had ever thought to keep Robin away from Nick. She's just a lonely little girl, she thought. But when Leslie went to put her arms about her, Robin, suspicious, stiffened, and then before she knew it, Leslie started to criticize her for wearing a stained blouse, for not combing her hair, until Robin jerked away.

Even when Robin did let her get close, something went wrong. Robin would come home crying about something, wanting comfort, and Leslie would sit with her, talking in a low voice, feeling so suddenly close to her daughter that she took on her sorrow and ended up being the one who needed comforting. It made Robin furious. "It's *my* problem!" she cried.

"Can't I even feel for you?" Leslie asked, stung.

"You're not doing that, you're taking over," Robin said.

But Leslie didn't see it as taking over. Not then, and not when she rearranged things in Robin's room to make the space seem larger, not when she kept pulling up the blinds Robin pulled down. Robin, who was used to coming and going as she pleased when Nick was home, who was even encouraged to stay over at friends' homes, was now expected to stay put in the house. Every time she found reasons to go out, Leslie found reasons for her to stay. Robin couldn't go to the library, because Leslie had to dash out and someone had to stay to let a client in. Robin couldn't visit a friend until she had helped Leslie with the dishes. And then it would be too late for Robin to go anywhere, they'd both be tense from trying to have their own way, and in the end, both of them would be as alone in the house that evening as if they had no family at all.

When Robin was twelve, she decided to adopt another family altogether. She was in seventh grade, and her best friend was a girl named Mandy Hartford. Mandy was an only child, too, and she had absolutely everything she wanted. She told Robin it was because no one had ever really expected her to exist at all; her parents said she was a miracle baby. Her mother, Evie, had suffered three miscarriages before Mandy was finally born, and when she got pregnant with Mandy, she had taken to her bed as if she were Sophia Loren. The doctor said that was hardly necessary, but Evie was taking no chances. She wouldn't move, not even to go to the bathroom. She made her husband carry her; she hired a girl from the neighborhood. She was in bed for eight months, but she remained cheerful because she believed emotions could affect the unborn. She ate meals from a hot plate by her bed. She closed her eyes for fifteen minutes a day and willed herself a healthy baby.

Mandy confided to Robin that her mother wouldn't sleep with Mandy's father, Jake, during her entire pregnancy; she made him camp out in the spare room on a lumpy couch that kept throwing his back out. Robin, shocked that Mandy knew such a thing, stared. Sometimes, Mandy whispered, her father even cried. But when Mandy was born, they threw a big party and Evie pranced around on what she called her sea legs and there wasn't ever enough anyone could do for Mandy.

Robin began spending more and more time at Mandy's, calling Leslie when Mandy's mother had already cooked extra dinner especially for her, when it was too late for Leslie to object. Robin adored Mandy. They made prank calls on Mandy's white Princess phone. They had secret pacts where they swore eternal friendship. Robin saw how it was at Mandy's home, and she began to think that Mandy had the kind of life she should have had herself, the kind of parents.

Evie treated Robin as if she were another daughter. She gave her the run of the house, let her do whatever she pleased, and when she saw Robin was upset about something, she didn't push. She sat beside Robin and quietly took her hand, saying nothing, but just being there, and it always made Robin feel a lot better. She didn't turn on and off the way Leslie did; if she was in a bad mood, she still smiled at Robin, still gave her impulsive hugs the same way she did with Mandy.

Jake made her doubt Nick in new and disturbing ways. He was always home nights. Once she had even heard him canceling a business trip for no other reason than he wanted to be home with his family. Robin went home that evening brooding about it. She approached Nick and asked him if he would stay home from his next trip, just one time, just for her. He ruffled her hair. "Why, I can't do that, baby," he said.

"Well, could you take me with you, then?" she said. She thought that would be more fun anyway, because the stories of the places he visited always mesmerized her.

"Come on, you have school," he said, and she turned from him.

Jake took Mandy and Robin everywhere. He spoiled Robin the same way he did Mandy, bringing them both chocolates and comics. When Robin talked, he didn't move; he concentrated on her as if there were nothing else worth his attention. And he took them both shopping. He picked up bright silk shirts and held them up against Mandy, and when Mandy found the one she wanted, he told her to buy it in two colors. When he saw Robin wistfully fingering the shirts, he sent her and Mandy downstairs, telling them he had some personal business to take care of, and when he came down, he handed Robin a brown bag.

"What's this?" she asked.

"Beats me," Jake said. "Why don't you just open it?"

She did, and a red silk shirt spilled out into her hands.

She took it home, delighted, but Leslie was not pleased. "That's some expensive present," she said, looking at the tag. "I could make you this for half what it cost." She folded the blouse up. "I just don't feel comfortable about this. You take it back, say thank you, and that's that."

Robin hated her. "Look, I'll make you one just like it," Leslie said.

"I don't want one you made," Robin said.

Leslie sighed. "Fine, have nothing then."

Robin took the blouse back and Jake was very solemn, but he told her that he had no intention of taking the shirt back; instead, he'd keep it in the spare room for her, so that anytime she felt like wearing it, she could.

Robin began collecting more and more things that she kept at Mandy's. Sweaters, skirts, even a hamster that was named and kept in a cage. When she wore the clothing home, she felt daring and special, and she lied to Leslie, telling her it was something Mandy had loaned her. Her mother knew how spoiled Mandy was—something they were beginning to argue about. Mandy would beg for this and that, and then wear it once before she decided it was no good. Evie couldn't bear to throw anything away. She was sure Mandy would change her mind, so she kept all the clothing in mothproof plastic bags in the basement.

The first time Robin had been at the house, Evie had taken her on a clothing tour, showing her the furs Mandy had discarded, a tweed jacket from just a week ago. "Throw that junk out, would you?" Mandy said, but Evie said she would like hell, and she kept trying to get Mandy to try the things on again.

Robin began to think of Mandy's home as her real life, and her life with Leslie as some movie bound to end. She kept her world at Mandy's like a secret. Sometimes she told herself that Evie and Jake were her real parents—she had been born when they had thought Evie had miscarried; an evil nurse had sold her. Or maybe Jake had had an affair and she was the product, given away at birth. She studied Jake; she watched Evie; she stood in front of a mirror trying to squint her features into theirs.

She felt more a part of Mandy's family than her own. As soon as she stepped into the house, she felt herself change. She'd go into the closet and pull out one of the shirts Jake had bought her; she'd go and see to her hamster; and she'd dip her fingers into the cookie jar as if they belonged there. She could take a shower without asking anyone. She could flop onto any bed in the house and read. She could use Mandy's phone and shut the door for privacy. When Jake came home, she ran to the front along with Mandy, and fished in his pockets the same way Mandy did.

Every Friday, Robin went over for dinner. Evie really couldn't cook. Robin was used to Leslie's garden snap beans and fresh fish, to lightly braised meats and salads, and here was Evie making a big presentation out of corned-beef hash and canned peas. Robin would always grab a peanut butter sandwich before she came over, wolfing it down as she sped to her friend's, so that by the time dinner rolled around, she wasn't all that hungry anyway. Both she and Mandy picked at the food. Mandy was always on some new crazy diet, though she was thin enough, and Robin followed her lead.

Still, Robin loved the dinners. Jake told jokes and teased. He kept asking when Robin would be old enough to run off and marry him. "I'm old enough right now," Robin said. Everyone laughed, everyone interrupted everyone else. She and Mandy did the dishes, but it was kind of fun. They blasted rock on the radio; they made up lists about what ten boys they would like to go out with, what five boys they would like to kiss. Robin thought, Jake, Jake, but she didn't dare say it.

"You're gone an awful lot," Leslie said. She didn't like Mandy much. She had overheard her call Evie an old goat because Evie had brought home a sweater that Mandy claimed was burgundy and not magenta as she had wanted. Leslie insisted that Mandy come over sometimes, but when she did, the two girls stayed in Robin's room, and when Nick was home, Robin seemed angry.

Missing Nick made Leslie want to flood her time with work. She told her clients she was available to their friends. She took out small ads in the local papers, and gradually business increased.

Sometimes, when Nick was away and Robin was at Mandy's, Leslie was sure she was starting to go mad. She tried to talk clients into coming over in the evenings. "I just got a cancellation," she said breathlessly over the phone. "There won't be another opening like this for a month." She tried to sound like she was giving out favors, but she felt the silence on the phone. Clients rarely came. They had husbands who were taking them out someplace nice for dinner. They had kids who had to be squired to the school play or to Brownies. They had their own night classes over at Pitt.

Leslie couldn't stay alone in the house on nights like that. So she walked. She put her hair in one long, sloppy braid; she put on Nick's black leather jacket that always smelled of him when she lifted the collar up against her nose. She slowly made her way up and down the streets of Shadyside. She sometimes walked up the series of steep hills that led to Squirrel Hill itself. She walked slowly to make the time last, to stretch it out like gum.

She liked Wednesday nights the best. The shops were always open along Walnut Street until ten, and she liked to wander in and out of them, gliding like a ghost, touching skirts and sweaters, the very feel of the cloth a comfort to her. It made her feel good to see expensive clothing so cheaply made, to know a seam wouldn't hold for more than a month, to see how faddy a design really was. It gave her own work extra value to her, made her feel special. She walked past the coffee shops and looked in at the couples. She felt the easy lure of company. She imagined people happy.

Sometimes, too, she imagined she was close to Robin. She imagined Robin coming to talk to her about her problems, to tell her that she didn't really hate her at all, it was just adolescence. She thought about Nick telling her he was going to settle down to a desk job in Pittsburgh because nothing was more important to him than she was. Nothing, nothing.

By the time she had circled back to the house, she was restless and angry. She started packing a small overnight bag, jamming in a clean sweater, a fresh pair of socks. Then she called Mandy's mother and said she had to go out of town and would it be all right for Robin to spend the night there? "No prob," said Evie, and when Leslie hung up the phone, she felt light, dazzled with sudden new hope.

It didn't take long to get to Harrisburg, where Nick was. When she got to his hotel, though, the man at the desk wouldn't let her up to Nick's room. He said Mr. Austen was out, and he didn't care that she had a driver's license with the same last name. He said Mr. Austen was out. "I can't let you up unless he's up there himself. If you want to wait in the bar, you're welcome to."

So she waited in the bar, sitting in a booth, snacking on stale goldfish crackers tumbled into a plastic bowl, sipping a weak bloody mary. Every once in a while, a man would approach her and offer to buy her a drink. She wouldn't look up—she pretended she didn't hear the soft invitations. Someone dipped toward her, and she sprang up, scattering the goldfish across the table, and there was Nick, uncertainly smiling.

"Surprise," she said weakly. If he asked what she was doing here, she would kill him. If he didn't seem glad, she would go home and pack her bags and take Robin and go and live in the mountains someplace. They could live on Milky Ways.

Instead, he gave her a real kiss and led her to the elevator, carrying her bag, and as they passed the desk clerk, Leslie turned and gave him a hard, deliberate stare.

The room was small and done in faded blues. Nick made a big deal of showing her the small white refrigerator filled with soft drinks and beer, the soap and shampoo in the shower, the complimentary toothbrush wrapped in cellophane. And then he grabbed her and rolled her with him onto the clean bathroom floor, so if she looked up she could see the papered glass by the sink, the folded white towels he hadn't used yet. He burrowed into her hair, started undoing her braid, and Leslie sighed, letting out all her fears in a rush of air.

Nick woke in the middle of the night. For a moment he didn't know where he was. The room seemed strange, dangerously unfamiliar. Leslie was curled on the far side of the bed. When he touched her, she moaned and curled up tighter. She made him think about Robin, made his mind drift into disasters. He felt like getting up and calling her, waking her at whatever friend's she was camping out with, letting her voice soothe him.

He got up and sat in the chair by the window. There were heavy blinds, but it didn't matter. There was no view. He was glad to see Leslie. He loved her. But it was funny, too, how much simpler it was to love her at a distance, how much safer when he could imagine her invincible in his mind, when he didn't have to see her shaken or stumbling. He got back into bed and wrapped his body about her as protectively as he could.

It wasn't much of a morning. Nick had too much to do, and it discomfited him having Leslie sitting there on the edge of the bed, watching him rush about, her serious black eyes unblinking. She had wanted to laze in bed with him that morning. When he bolted at the alarm, his appointments worrying in his mind, she had stiffened. Now she was silent—judgmental, he felt.

He tried. He squired her to a soggy breakfast, but he had to stop her from ordering a second cup of coffee or he would be late. He dropped her off at a movie theater and then dashed for his first meeting. But he couldn't concentrate. He kept seeing Leslie sitting in an empty theater, watching a bad movie. At every store he walked out of, he knew he had lost sales. By the time he was through for the day, he was irritated. She shouldn't have come.

They were both stony during the ride home. Leslie was annoyed that Nick wouldn't stop for dinner, he was in such a hurry to pick up Robin. "She's a big, capable girl," Leslie said, but Nick was silent. They were halfway home when Leslie fell asleep, her eyes rolling into dream. It was tornado weather all over again, only this time she was the one down in the ditch, alone, calling for Nick, calling for Robin, and all around her there was only the sound of the wind, screaming its way toward her.

Nick felt Leslie changing. When he looked at her, he remembered everything about her—the way she combed her hair with her fingers because it snagged on plastic combs; the way she would pull on one of his sweaters even if it didn't match her skirt; the smell of her hair, her touch. When she moved, when she spoke to him now, she seemed somehow different. She didn't ask to visit anymore. She didn't call him several times a night at his hotel. Sometimes when he came home, he was surprised to find the house empty and a note tacked up for him—the phone number of a client she was visiting. His dinner would be a dish in the oven, a boiler bag in a pot on the stove.

He missed her. He didn't want her to get up mornings, but kept her in bed with him. He made love to her, lapping at her until she cried out, and then he kept her taste in his mouth as long as he could. But it was suddenly metallic and unfamiliar. It worried him so he would have to keep her in bed even longer; he wouldn't let her get up to shower until she just kicked the covers back and pushed herself free.

He wanted Leslie to last. She still hypnotized him. He remembered how her face used to fill his mind those last months with Dore, how he couldn't bear to drive away from her. She was drifting and he didn't know where she was headed, didn't know how to bring her back to him.

Sometimes he worried she'd leave the way Dore had. He could sit right beside her and suddenly he'd be missing her, as if she had left him already. He felt as if he were being slowly erased.

And then, of course, there was Robin. She had turned thirteen when he was on the road; she was a teenager now, already whispering about boys. Kids that age ran off to New York City and lived on the streets until they were turned into hookers or found strangled in the seamy pit of the subway. Kids that age got themselves pregnant and had babies of their own to edge them into adulthood.

He slunk about the house watching her. He went into her room when she wasn't there, ignoring the KEEP OUT sign that drove Leslie mad. It was tattery on the edges from all the times Leslie had yanked it off. He found *The Facts of Love and Life for Teens* on her bureau, and leafed through it, trying to gauge which pages looked the most wilted, the most read. Married people had intercourse twice a week, it said. He snorted. That wasn't very much, that was impoverished. There were all these line drawings in the book. Girls shaking their heads no so adamantly that there were wiggly lines emanating from their heads like halos. Flat-chested girls woefully staring at big bras in store windows. He put the book down and lay on Robin's bed. He leaned against her headboard. If she had a diary, would he read it? He felt this sudden rapid clip of tension about what might be scrawled there. His fingers burrowed under the mattress, but he found nothing.

She wasn't a little girl anymore. She was more than half a dozen times older than Susan had ever gotten to be, and still he felt that she might leave any minute, he was aware of the danger of getting too close. He watched her at dinner that night and suddenly saw how lovely she was becoming, with her flash of red hair, her serious deep eyes, and he thought how soon there would be boys coming around. He felt as though a milestone he hadn't ever been looking for was somehow passing. She was at that age now where parents didn't fit. He reached across the table to touch her, and ended up startling her so much that she toppled her glass of grape juice, pooling it across the table. She jerked up. "God, will you *watch*," Leslie sniped, but it was at Robin and not at him.

He began to look forward to the little things he could do that didn't act as disturbances, that Robin sometimes didn't even notice. If he was careful, he could kiss her hair as she brushed past him to get to school; he could stand at the window and watch her striding past the house, her long legs as coltish as Leslie's, her hair nearly as wild. He looked in at her when she was sleeping, before she got up mornings, and he prowled through the photo albums until it began to chill him a little, seeing how she had managed to grow; how, so far, she had been safe.

She was angry a lot now. When they all went to dinner and he took Leslie's hand, she scowled and grumped, but when he tried to take hers, she pulled away. She told him she was no baby.

"You'll always be my baby," Leslie said, and Robin frowned and walked ahead.

"I can't help it," Leslie said to Nick. "She will." But Nick, who considered babyhood the most dangerous of all possible states, felt soothed by Robin's denial.

NINE

• • •

As they got older, things began changing between Mandy and Robin. In ninth grade, when they were both fourteen, Mandy suddenly began wearing makeup, layering on frosted blusher and green eyeshadow. She clipped her hair into elaborate styles and fooled with long, sparkling earrings that her mother was always telling her were going to ruin her earlobes. She had a boyfriend who drove a yellow Camaro, who wanted everyone to call him Head. After the skis, Mandy claimed, and also because he had such a big head, made even larger by a bushy corona of hair. Sometimes, though, Mandy confided that the name was because of the things he did to her, the things he liked done to him.

"I'm not calling him Head," Robin said. But it didn't really matter what she called him, because he ignored her. When she spoke to him, he looked at Mandy. When she touched his wrist to get his attention, he put his own hand on Mandy's thigh. Robin went over to Mandy's less and less. Jake was as friendly to Head as he was to her; Evie as mothering. Mandy wouldn't make any plans with Robin until she had checked to see what Head wanted to do, and what Head wanted usually involved a dark place and something for two.

Robin didn't have any other close friends, and she didn't like coming right home from school. Leslie trailed her, wanting her to go shopping, to come take a walk with her. She was always asking questions, always prying, and sometimes she would go into sudden heated rages, yelling at Robin about the dust under her bed, about the den-

131

tal bill caused by all the candy wrappers she found in Robin's pockets. When the phone rang and it was Nick, Leslie would grab the phone from her, curling her back, suddenly acting as if there were no one else around.

There's no place on earth for me, Robin thought. She was always trying to escape from Leslie's smothering attention, always trying to make her father like her. She didn't know what it was she had done, but she knew she must have done something to make him so distant. He had stopped telling her stories, making her tapes, a long time ago, and when she tried to play the tapes now, it just ended up making her feel blue. Sometimes at night, when he was sitting outside, looking at the sky, she'd feel a little lonely and go out and sit beside him. His whole body seemed to tense up. He made small talk with her for a while, and then kissed her cheek and went back inside, and it all made her feel more alone than she had felt before she came out to be with him.

Whom could she live with? She had no relatives except an arthritic grandmother and a grandfather, who lived out in the desert, called twice a year, and never could manage to visit. They were very old now. Robin knew Leslie worried about her parents because when they died, she'd be as orphaned as Nick was. Robin didn't know them that well, although she did remember a few visits when she was younger. She remembered her grandmother carefully telling her the whole story of her birth, reminding her that she was protected, a child of danger.

Robin had once asked Leslie about it, and Leslie had told her she was much too smart a girl to believe in any superstition like that. But Robin did anyway—it comforted her. She tried to strengthen what power she was supposed to have. She made herself a beaded leather bracelet and blessed it herself so it might act as an amulet, a reminder that she was special. She told herself that if her life was different from anyone else's, if it was more lonely, then maybe it was supposed to be; maybe it was just part of the price you had to pay for being really unique.

She didn't make any new girlfriends, but suddenly, there were boys. She was attracted to the ones who didn't fit in, the wilder boys who wore black leather jackets even when it was ninety degrees outside, the boys who didn't even go to the regular high school but attended the vocational school just in back. Everyone said it was because they were too stupid to make it in regular school, that they were all outcasts who couldn't even cut it in the remedial program.

Robin didn't think that. She was curious about them. They learned trades: They could take apart a car and put it back together so it ran as good as new; they could wire a whole house if they liked. She felt drawn to these outcasts; she liked the way they carried their label defiantly, proud. There were only a few girls in the program, but there were stories about them, too. They carried nail files to fight with, or orange sticks that they rubbed against the sidewalk into points. The boys didn't have to carry anything at all.

Robin, protected, walked past the vocational school every day on her way to class. The weather was warm now, and the mechanic students were working on a car outside. Her coltish legs shone under her short skirt, her red hair caught and tumbled the light. Some mornings she felt bold. She'd go right up to a boy she thought looked interesting and start talking to him. She'd ask him about the car, about what he was doing. She even leaned under the hood to look. The boy was always so startled that a girl from the regular school would talk to him with something other than disdain that he almost always fell in love.

She saw the vocational boys after school—for walks, for a Coke and a piece of pie at Jerry's Sweet Shop. At first there was no one special. She saw two different boys in one week, or sometimes one particular boy for a week straight until someone else caught her eye. She wrote name after name in her books, and some in the palm of her hand so she could close her fingers around them and keep them hidden. She never slept with any of the boys, although she was certainly pressured, and although almost all the kids assumed that she did. Mandy, passing her in the hall one day, stopped her and told her that she was getting herself good and talked about, and that Head had even stood up for her.

"You can't just hang all over guys," Mandy said. "You got to be a little cool about it."

"What do *you* know?" Robin said. She didn't tell Mandy that the reason she hung on to the boys so much was because she was sure if she didn't, they would float away from her; that having boy after boy lessened the chance that she'd be alone.

The boys left her, of course. They were always leaving her, just when she'd convinced herself she loved them. When they started getting twitchy, turning back to the girls they knew would part their legs for them, Robin concentrated her energies. She wrote desperate prayers into a journal to her grandmother, to the guardian angel she was sure she had. Please, please, let Ron come see me at lunch and apologize. Please, please, let Timmy smile. And when a boy did what she had prayed, she felt protected again, she felt strong.

Robin never told Leslie about her boys. She was the one to call them, keeping her conversations clean of names or details. She was the one to go to *their* houses, *their* meeting spots. And then, there was one boy who stuck around longer than the rest, one boy Robin really, really liked, and for him, she opened her life up a little—she took him to her home.

His name was Rick. He was sixteen, with dirty-blond hair, one side shaved close against his skull. He wore battered brown work shoes with steel toes he claimed were for fighting and not for protection like the auto-body manual said. He had a reputation. The other kids stayed clear of him. He was said to have put his own father in the hospital because he had caught him beating up his mother one day. He was said to have been suspended from the regular high school for slicing up a student who had pulled a gun on him. But he didn't seem dangerous to Robin. If he fought, he fought for principles, it seemed to her. Every time she saw him, he was quietly tinkering with a car in the parking lot. He would look up and see her, give her a dazed, sleepy smile. He talked to her more and more. He began walking her to class, walking her home, talking to her about small engines, about spark plugs and motorbikes.

He was protective about her. He didn't seem to mind that she wouldn't sleep with him, and he never pretended that she did, not even to the other vokies who had gone out with her, the ones who had never managed to even unbutton her blouse. He told Robin she was a refreshing change from the girls he was used to, that it underlined how different she was from everyone. "Yeah, different," Robin said. He held her hands; he told her he'd wait for her to make whatever moves she wanted. "You're a loner, just like me. You make your own rules," he said.

He talked to her about cars. He told her he could match up any person in the world with a car.

"What matches me?" Robin asked.

He squinted over at her. "Oh, a nice little VW, something compact that whips around, that lets you know you're never in control."

Robin smiled; she pulled on his hand.

He was sensitive about not being smart enough for her. He saw all the books she stashed in her purse, saw that she was always reading when he came to pick her up at the drugstore after school. She read in the coffee shop when he went to the can. She read walking down the street, for Christ's sake, dodging people, so skilled she didn't even have to lift her nose up. He brought her paperback editions of Kafka stories he had underlined and made comments in. Most of the comments he lifted from the *Cliffs Notes* he bought for himself. He memorized bits so he could say something intelligent to her, and when he couldn't remember, he lied. He told her that Faulkner had loved cars and was almost a mechanic. He told her that Fitzgerald rode a Harley. He was very polite with her, very solicitous.

Robin adored him. She never told him, but she really couldn't have cared less whether he read anything at all. She didn't care if he knew the difference between Kafka and comics. When he talked that way, she just let her attention glaze over; she concentrated on the shape of his hand, the bark of his neck. She liked it best when he talked about the two of them together—about the body shop they could run, the house they could live in, filled with dogs and cats and music. And she loved it best when he was just staring at her as if he couldn't believe his good fortune, as if he would never leave her, no matter what she did, no matter how she was. "Say it," she commanded. "Tell me again." She swooned on his words. He loves me, she thought.

The first time Leslie saw Rick, he was coming up the walk holding her baby's hand and blowing smoke rings. She stopped sewing and strode out onto the front walk, her hair unraveling from its topknot, her blue dress streaky with tailor's chalk. He dropped Robin's hand, but he didn't put out the cigarette; he kept insolently drawing on it, and he let his eyes slide over Leslie. Leslie noticed the tight fit of his jeans, the shirt he had half unbuttoned, the threatening stance of his boots. Rick kept one hand in his pocket, but he answered Leslie's questions so politely, he almost made her like him a little. But then, he started talking about the vocational school, and when it was time to go, he just jerked Robin to him, tumbling her off-balance, kissing her as if he didn't even see Leslie standing in the sun. When he strode off, he was humming something low and dangerous in his throat.

In the house, Leslie told Robin she didn't like him. "A girl as smart as you can find someone better."

"I have Rick, I don't need anyone."

"You're not seeing him," said Leslie.

"I am," said Robin, her mouth tight.

When Nick came home, the house was quiet. He found Robin in the backyard, in a green dress he hadn't seen before. "You look pretty," he said, and then he saw how red her eyes were. "What is it?" he asked, alarmed.

"Nothing," she said helplessly, and then burst into tears.

"Ah," he said, "that explains everything."

He sat down beside her. The only time he could remember really talking to her was when she was just a baby, when he'd liked to whisper his secrets into her crib and just imagine her response; or when he talked to her through his stories, the way he still did—only now she didn't listen, she didn't hear him.

"I hate this," Robin said abruptly, plucking at tufts of grass.

"Hate what?"

She looked at him for a moment. "I don't know. . . . Love," she said.

Nick leaned his back against the stiff, gnarly bark of the willow. Love. She was in love. He wanted to take her inside, and as soon as they stepped through the door, he wanted her to be five years old again, with a flurry of uncombable curls; he wanted her to be a baby he could rock in his arms and breathe over as she slept so her breathing would match his. He washed one hand over his face.

"What's the matter," she asked. "Are you mad at me?"

"I was just remembering," he said.

"Was Mom your first love?" Robin asked and suddenly Nick felt himself spiraling back, to a long white corridor, a long, pale blonde, blind-man's-bluffing her way along the wall, catching him so he couldn't move, so he couldn't do a single thing but pin himself in place and wait for her to release him.

"It was a long time ago," he said.

"Really? You loved someone else?" She was charmed, she wanted him to tell her about it; but he just shook his head—he said they were talking about Robin right now, and not him.

She seemed loosened up. She started hesitantly telling him about this boy she was seeing, about how he made her feel, how confusing it all was.

The more details she unfolded, the more uneasy Nick became, until he suddenly stopped her speech. "Listen," he said, "you're only fourteen."

"How old were you?" she asked.

"I don't think I want you seeing this boy," he said. She snapped up, like a door slamming. She strode across the grass, around to the side of the house, leaving him alone in the back. Where she had been sitting, the grass was pressed down, still warm, and he placed his hand on it for a minute before he, too, got up.

When Leslie came home, exhausted, he wanted to talk to her about the boy. He told her he had asked Robin not to see him, and when Leslie heard that, she flung her arms about him. "You did?" she said, smiling. He held her, he kissed her neck, and upstairs he heard Robin's angry silence, and it made him hug Leslie tighter.

Rick was used to parents not liking him, used to sneaking around. He knew how to orchestrate meetings with Robin—after school at the coffee shop, early morning before school started, weekends when she was supposed to baby-sit. It could all be worked out, but what he couldn't get used to was the way Robin was reacting. She cried without reason. They'd be having a perfectly good time just swinging on the ropes by the old school, and then she'd dip her head, and the next thing he knew, her eyes were a blur of tears.

She was difficult to comfort. He bought her ice cream and windup toys; he skipped classes just so he could eat lunch with her. "What do you care what your parents say?" He smoothed her hair. "What do they matter?"

He made himself angrier and angrier by scratching away at the situation like it was a rash he couldn't cure. He told Robin that his father used to be that way, trying to run everyone's life, and then there had been this thing that happened to him, and after that, things had changed—his father acted like a decent human being now.

"What thing?" Robin asked. She had heard the story whispered in school, but she wanted Rick to tell it to her, wanted to hear his version.

He shrugged. He told her that what had happened didn't matter; what counted was how his father had changed. "We all get along now," he told her. He kicked at a stone, making furrows in the dirt. He held her hand. "I don't like anyone making you sad," he said. "This has got to stop."

Robin, looking up, thought he meant her crying, and it made her tense.

At home, Robin moped. Nick tried to talk with her before he went on the road, but she was curt with him; she nodded and kept her eyes glassy and unreadable. The whole drive out, he kept her photo up against the dash. He tried to imagine her rushing off to a movie with a girlfriend, trying on a skirt in some brightly lit department store—anything, everything, but Robin sleepily wrapped up in the arms of that boy, making her body a secret for him to discover.

Leslie couldn't escape as easily. Her daughter was home with her, an open wound she couldn't get near enough to heal. Robin pushed out of the house. She said she was going to the library, but when she came back home, her hands were empty of books and she was flushed. She said she was going to study at a friend's. She took her math book, she even left the phone number where she was going to be, and sometimes, hating herself, Leslie would call on the pretense of offering to come pick Robin up. No matter when she called, Robin was always in the bathroom or had just left—there was always some reason why she couldn't come to the phone. And when Robin got home, she'd walk by Leslie without explanation. "Do you think I'm a fool?" Leslie cried. "Don't you think I know where you've been?"

"I've been at Debra's," Robin said.

Leslie didn't know what to do. Robin looked terrible. She wasn't sleeping nights. Leslie heard her walking around, making tea, eating cookies. In the morning the kitchen would be seeded with crumbs, and Robin had circles under her eyes.

One afternoon she simply forbade Robin to go to the library, but Robin stormed past her, breaking the glass in the front door, stepping over the pieces in her defiant hurry to get out. Leslie jumped into the car and tried to follow her. She didn't care if someone broke into the house and took everything. She drove up and down all the streets she thought Robin might travel, but her daughter seemed to have disappeared. She drove for over an hour. She tried and tried to dredge up that boy's last name so she could at least call Information from a pay phone and try to get his address. She could drive out to his house and confront him. She could confront his mother; the two of them could stand out on the front porch and wait for him to swagger home. He'd have Robin's scent on his clothes, in his pores; Leslie would have to place her two hands about his neck and squeeze just to free her.

Leslie kept traveling the same routes, over and over, until on one street a woman in blue curlers and red stretch pants stepped right in front of Leslie's car and flagged it down. Leslie stopped, bewildered, and rolled down her window.

"Are you lost?" the woman asked. "You sure do look it."

"No, I . . . I'm just looking for my daughter," Leslie said. Her voice foundered; she felt the woman's palpable interest.

"Not many kids come by this block," the woman finally said. "You'd better try Moran Road, just that way." She pointed. "That's where they cause their trouble."

Leslie continued to drive until the streetlights set a dreamy film of light dappling against the sky. She glanced at her watch and saw that it was 9:30, and that for the first time in her entire life she had missed a fitting. Grace Thomas. She had a temper, too.

The lights were all off when she got home. She parked the car in the front instead of putting it in the garage, in case she had to go out searching for Robin again. She stayed in the car for a moment, her head resting against the steering wheel, and then, wearily, she went into the house. When she clicked on the light, she saw Robin, sleeping on the couch. Leslie was so grateful to see her that she turned off the light and simply sat there in the darkness, watching her. She kept wondering what she could do to make Robin happy, to make Robin at least like her a little. After a bit, she slept herself, but she kept waking—she heard things rustling outside, noises. She blinked in the dark until she could make Robin out again, Robin, who was sleeping as if there were nothing simpler in the world. Gradually the noises faded, and Leslie slowed down into sleep, deep and dreamless.

The next day was Saturday. Neither of them mentioned the night, not even when Nick called, insisting on speaking to Robin. Leslie couldn't tell what he was saying, only that Robin kept saying yes.

All morning they were careful about each other. Leslie waited around for the glass man, and Robin made no attempt to go anywhere, not even outside, but took a paperback novel and sat in the kitchen reading. She hadn't even tried to call up that boy on the phone, hadn't once glanced out the window the way she usually did, with eyes focused so far beyond what Leslie could see that Leslie would never be able to follow.

Leslie decided to do something. When the glass was in, she got the car keys and came into the kitchen and abruptly asked Robin if she'd like to learn to drive. "Just in the schoolyard," Leslie said. She thought driving was an adult thing, a symbol of her trust.

Robin looked at Leslie in amazement. "I can't even take driver's ed yet," Robin said.

"It's fine," Leslie said. "I'll be right beside you. It'll be my worry, not yours." She jangled the keys. "It'll be our secret."

Robin hesitated for a moment and then got up. "Deal," she said.

Leslie drove them to the old schoolyard. No one would be there. Robin could drive around and around, practice parking and turns. The car pulled a little, and Leslie swore, pumping the gas, turning to smile at Robin to show her the curse had nothing to do with her. She remembered her own driving lessons. Lord. Her father shouting and cursing as she backed into a bus. He had humiliated her by making her get out of the car, right in the middle of the road, while he did the maneuver himself, all the time still yelling at her from his window, drawing everyone's eyes right to her. She had never wanted to drive after that, and she had refused to get into a car with him. She had taken driver's ed at school only because she could get a credit for it, and because the instructor was also her math teacher, who always liked her because she got straight A's.

"Okay, you take the wheel," Leslie said. She stopped the car in the middle of the schoolyard. It pulled again, but she figured it was probably due for a tune-up. She scooted across and let Robin take the wheel. "Easy now," she said.

Robin was a slow and deliberate driver. Leslie kept telling her how great she was doing, partly because every time she said so, Robin turned and smiled. Teaching Robin also gave Leslie excuses to touch her. She put one hand on Robin's to help her turn; she sometimes had to touch Robin's leg to remind her to brake; and never once— oh, the miracle of it—did Robin move from her. She just glanced at Leslie and laughed.

They must have been out there only about a half-hour when the accident happened. Robin was driving down a long slope when suddenly the brakes failed. She couldn't move, she panicked, and Leslie crunched her own foot down on Robin's to pump the brakes. When that didn't work, she tried to reach the emergency brake, but it was all the way over on the left. The car wasn't going that fast, and the road was lined with grass, so Leslie opened Robin's door and roughly shoved her out. Then she jerked the wheel all the way to the right and tumbled herself out of the car.

The car dented against a tree. Nobody was hurt. Leslie's jeans were ripped at the knees; Robin had one long scratch running across her cheek. Leslie, startled by Robin's crumpled shoulders, put her arm about her and rocked her a little. "It's not your fault," she said. She pulled her up and led her back to the road, brushing off the back of her sweater, which was seeded with dry, dying leaves. They disintegrated the moment she touched them. "Come on," Leslie said. "We'll go call a tow truck."

It didn't take the mechanic very long to figure out that the car had been tampered with. When he came out to talk to Leslie, wiping his greasy hands along a spanking-white jumpsuit, Leslie was sure he was about to scold her for not taking regular care of her car. Instead, he kept watching her, studying her curiously as if he couldn't quite believe a young suburban wife would have this much menace in her life. He told her how lucky she was that she hadn't been on the highway and hadn't been driving fast. And then he told her what an expert job had been done on her brakes. He said he couldn't remember seeing anything like this, and if he were her, he wouldn't do any driving for a while; he would watch himself.

"Tampered? What are you talking about?" Leslie said. She wouldn't believe him; she thought he was just some stupid kid— what did he know? She left the car there and took a cab home, but during the whole ride back, she felt vaguely uneasy. She kept thinking about that one night when she had left the car out in front of the house; she kept remembering the noises. And then a sudden queasy intuition made her straighten up, so violently that the cabbie twisted around to ask if she was all right, if she wanted him to pull over so she could catch her breath.

Robin, lying on her back in the grass beside Rick, holding his hand, was telling him the accident story, embellishing it so it seemed she had practically died. She made him trace the scratch on her face; she added bruises and cuts she now claimed had miraculously faded; she made up a visit to the emergency room, a ride in an ambulance. She thought he'd pamper her silly. Instead, he unlaced his fingers from hers and sat up, stitching his brow. When he stood up, she pulled him down, but he wouldn't look at her. "You sorry I'm alive?" she asked. She was only kidding, but he jerked toward her, his eyes aflame.

He didn't make sense. He started talking about how he wanted to live in the country, how even Pittsburgh, dinky as it was, was too much of a town for him. He wanted to be somewhere surrounded by silence, where all you saw in the distance was one red light blinking out civilization, and even then it would be too far away to touch you. He'd have cars to work on, maybe a small shop with a few customers he knew.

"Are you listening to anything I'm saying?" Robin asked. "I nearly *died.*"

She told him how great her mother had been about it, how they had both agreed not to tell her father, because anything like that would set him off for weeks. "You wait," she said to Rick. "I bet she has you over for dinner soon." She nestled up against him. "God, I love you," she said.

He twisted her to face him. "Listen," he said, "when people love each other, they can tell each other anything, right? They can forgive."

She blinked at him. "You want to tell me what's going on with you?" she said.

"You're like a volcano in my blood," he said, and she giggled until she saw his face; then she felt the breath rush out of her. "You don't understand," he said. "You haven't been with anyone else, you don't know what it's like for someone like me to love someone like you, what it's like not sleeping with you because I don't want you thinking that's the only reason I'm with you. I'm the one that's doing the waiting, that's making the sacrifices—I'm the one who knows just what it is I'm missing out on."

He got up; he stormed in place. "Sometimes, in the night, you know, all that wanting just wakes me up. I feel like I'm burning alive. I have to go to the kitchen and chip ice out of the freezer and swallow it just to cool down. It never helps."

He said sometimes he tried to call her, even though it was late, and then her mother's voice, so hard, so cold, made him so angry, he'd just hang up on her. He said he knew her father didn't have any use for him either. He had never even met him, but fathers were always funny about their daughters.

"I didn't know what to do," he said. "But it seemed so crazy. I mean, here we were, loving each other and not being able to be together when all the time we've been—I don't know—*innocent.*" He licked at his lips.

"At first, I was just going to go over to the house, trickle stones at your window, and get you to come out with me for an hour. I didn't though," he said. "I didn't even tell you how I was suffering, because I didn't want you thinking I was weak, a pussy."

"You should have told me," Robin whispered to him, but he didn't hear her, he was riding on his story.

"And then, that day you came to see me, crying about the broken door, about your mother—you remember that?"

Robin nodded. He had bought her a Coke and told her everything was going to be fine. He had kissed both her eyes. One, then the other, so gently, she could feel his lashes dust her skin. He had made her go home, had told her they would have to be sly and bide their time.

"I came to talk to your mother, to have it out," he said. "The car was in front."

Robin sat up.

"I was going to go to the door, I was going to, but then I kept hearing in my mind just how it would go, I kept thinking what a waste it would be—she'd be more angry at me than before. It made me so mad I couldn't see straight. I decided to go home, cool off, and then think what to do, but by the time I got home, I was even madder. I kept thinking about your mother, keeping you from me, making you break the goddamned front door just because you were trying to get to me—to *me*—and the next thing I was doing was getting some tools, going back to the car—"

"*Stop!*" said Robin. "Don't tell me another word!"

She stood up, backing away from him a little, but he snatched up her left hand and pulled her toward him. "Listen, I had to do it," he told her. "What other way did I have? I didn't do it to hurt anyone. I just thought—well, a little scare. That's what I thought. Like leaving my calling card."

Robin pulled away from him. She didn't think she could think straight anymore; she didn't think she could breathe or eat or do anything ever again. "I was in that car," she said. "I was driving."

"Don't tell me that!" he cried. "I can't hear that!"

"I was driving!"

"Do you want to make me crazy? I'd die before I'd hurt you. Do you want me to slit my throat with my knife?" He dug in his pocket and pulled out his knife. Robin knocked it from his hand. "Did I make you hang out with my friends? Did I make you sleep with me? Did I ever hit you?"

"That was my *mother*," Robin said. "Who told you that wouldn't hurt me? Who told you I wanted her hurt or scared or anything?" She couldn't look at Rick anymore. He hurt her eyes. "Get away from me," she said, her voice snagging in her throat. "Just get away. Don't you look at me or talk to me or even think about me anymore. You hear me? I don't even want you having me in your daydreams."

She started walking away, and he followed, desperate, not speaking, trying to get her to just look at him. He touched her arm, her leg, but with each touch, she flinched as if burned.

"You *told* me" he said, "what a suffocating bitch she was, that you hated her. You said she never left you alone."

"You don't know anything," Robin said.

"Yes I do. I know you."

"Get *away* from me." She flailed one arm wildly at him, the way she might shoo an animal. "We're separate. I don't want to see you."

She had never seen him cry before. She had never seen any boy cry, really, and when she saw his tears, something caught inside of her. She thought how easy it would be to touch him, but she forced herself to keep walking, even after she sensed he had stopped following.

"You'll call me!" he shouted. "You're the one who'll come begging and then we'll see whose turn it is to shut off, we'll see who sends who away!" When Robin didn't speak, he shouted again. "Who likes you? Who ever liked a stupid twat like you?"

She shut her eyes and kept walking, blinded. It wasn't fair, having to choose her mother against him. It wasn't fair that he would do something she could never explain to herself. For a moment she wished herself back in the belly of the car, back to the moment when the brakes failed. She willed it to speed, to hurtle recklessly down a twisting, turning highway, gaining on the raw, broken side of a mountain. The crash, when it came, would be nothing more than a blinking away of her life, a clean erasure of all the memory she was now going to have to bear.

For a while, it brought her closer to Leslie. She thought it was her own guilty efforts—her staying at home, her hesitant help at dinner. Instead of reading in her room, she'd venture out into the living room where Leslie was stitching facings. She'd plop herself down on a nearby chair and crack open her book. She felt protective of her mother. She didn't sleep nights for a while, just waiting for something to happen. She wasn't afraid for herself. She saw Rick lingering around the high school, but now when he saw her, he scowled and made a big production out of turning his back to her. Sometimes she'd come out of school and see him with his arm about another girl, but she still felt his eyes trailing her and she knew that the other girl might just as well have been a newspaper for all the attention and desire he was showing her.

She never discussed the accident with Leslie, and she certainly never told Nick. Leslie had filed a report with the police, but later she insisted that the mechanic had been wrong, that there had simply been a problem with the car, and anyway, it was fine now, so what was the problem? She never told Robin how easily she had managed to put the pieces together.

She went into Robin's room one day while Robin was at school and prowled guiltily through her papers until she scavenged his last name. There it was. Pruitt. Like spit, she thought. She went to the phone book and carefully traced down his address with her finger. She knew from Robin that he liked to hang out in his driveway, tinkering with an old car.

She waited until one afternoon when Robin was at the dentist. She wasn't going to do much. She was going to threaten him, tell him she'd see him in juvenile court if he so much as called Robin again. And if he wasn't there, she'd ring the bell and talk to his parents, or she'd sit out on the porch and wait for him.

When she turned into his street, she saw him, there in the driveway, swabbing down an old green car with a red rag. He stiffened when he saw her, but Leslie parked, got out, and strode toward him.

He denied everything, of course. He even had the balls to threaten her right back, to accuse her of defamation of character and tell her she'd be good and sorry if she didn't shut up. When she remained unfazed, he threatened to beat her up.

"Ha!" said Leslie. "You beat me up. Ha!" She was secretly terrified. She could feel the quick thrill of fear; the air seemed charged. "You stay the hell away from my daughter. You come near her and I swear I'll kill you myself."

"Your daughter," he snorted. "Who wants your daughter!" His eyes turned hard and glassy, and then, to Leslie's shock, he started crying. He was furious with himself. He kept trying to twist away from her so she wouldn't see his face. She was half expecting him to tell her some story about allergies, but he just kept repeating that no one in his right mind would want anything to do with Robin. "Like mother, like daughter," he spat out, and Leslie felt another quick snap of surprise, realizing that Robin must have gotten to Rick first.

She was so touched, so amazed, it made her suddenly gentle. "It's all right," she said out loud, half to Rick, half to herself. "It's going to be all right."

"Get out," he said.

She turned and walked back to the car. She drove home half in a dream, and when she came into the living room, Robin was there, reading one of Leslie's novels. Leslie didn't say anything, just walked over and rested one hand against her daughter's hair for a moment, until Robin touched her hand, and then she went upstairs to sew.

TEN

• • •

Nick couldn't help it, but he always thought of the bookshops he visited as his own. He knew all the layouts; he knew the windows and how light struck the displays; he knew where the dust was most likely to settle. Every visit, he gave himself lots of time so he could prowl about the shop and see how things were doing. He made minihomes of each shop, relatives out of every buyer, and he felt this tremendous flush of pleasure every time he walked through a door, every time a buyer walked toward him with a hand out to grasp his.

Really, he considered the book buyers caretakers of his shops, and he enjoyed giving them advice. He didn't like the way a new line of books was just junked onto the shelves. He hated a window cluttered with tiny Styrofoam men holding up the books. Some of the buyers listened. One girl was just as happy to have Nick climb into the greasy front window to set up a display the way he said would do the most good. She was just as content to have him be the one to pick out all the dead flies that had kamakazeed into the fluorescent lights. The truth was, she didn't give a hoot what he put into the window as long as he was the one doing it.

Nick talked to the customers. He'd try to figure out what kind of book they needed to read and then go and find it, popping it into a pair of surprised hands. He found comic novels for depressed-looking women; he pulled out murder mysteries for bored-looking men; he suggested kids' books to grandmothers. Once, he started telling a little girl one of the stories he had told Robin a long time ago, but halfway through it he began to feel guilty, as if he had somehow betrayed something, and he had to excuse himself, making up something about needing to see someone in the back.

But lately there were complaints. At one shop, he had seen a thin, anemic-looking blonde in a white coat hunching surreptitiously over books. Curious, he trailed her a little, until he got close enough to see her unfurling a long loop of pink stickers with JESUS SAVES printed on them. She was furtively pasting them into the pages.

It enraged Nick. He knew you couldn't pull off a sticker without lifting up print, too. He saw the books she went after—books on abortion, books by Sartre, for Christ's sake—and he grabbed the girl's arm. "Hey, who you touching?" she said, jerking around, socking him squarely in the eye before she sprinted out of the shop.

The buyer, a new man, gave Nick a paper towel soaked in cold water for his eye, already blooming into blues. He was cross, though. He told Nick it was none of his business, that what he should have done was just call the manager. "It's not your responsibility," he said, miffed. "And we never touch customers. That's how you get sued." After that, he was never as friendly to Nick, never as glad to see him in the store.

There were other complaints. Nick's boss told him buyers didn't appreciate Nick homing in on their clients, fiddling around with their shops. They didn't like the way he kept rescuing what he called the "orphan books," the novels no one but him had ever heard of, the poetry volumes that were lucky to sell one or two copies, and then displaying them beside the best-sellers. People wanted to be left alone to browse; they wanted to pick out their own books. If they wanted to read nothing but trash, that was their business, wasn't it? "The buyers say you bother people so much they don't come into the store as often. Can't you just do your job? You're a wonderful sales rep. Isn't that enough?"

It made Nick feel a little lost. He began bringing home pieces of his bookshops—fiction, mysteries, first novels, and travel books—packing the whole back seat of the car. He liked looking in the rearview mirror and seeing all those books as he drove home. He stacked them in the bathroom, tucked them into the kitchen cabinets, on top of the refrigerator, and by the napkin holder on the table. He never remembered where each book was, but it didn't matter. He just liked being able to walk into any room in the house and be surrounded by books. He liked being able to pluck up any book and know it was worth reading.

Everyone in the house read. He never forbade Robin to read at the dinner table, and he set up a special stand so Leslie could read at her design table. The silence in the house didn't matter so much if everyone was reading his books.

But even that began to change. If the bookshops were getting away from him, he felt as if his family was, too. Oh, they still read, but more and more when he called home there was no answer. Sometimes Robin picked up the phone, but she often told him that Leslie was out walking. "Walking?" Nick had said the last time he'd called. "But it's eleven at night." Pittsburgh streets emptied at eight. People were in robes watching TV, and Shadyside was wooded, it bred shadows.

"It's okay," Robin said. "She always does. The neighbors watch for her."

Nick didn't like it—Leslie loping fearlessly through Shadyside's deserted streets, Robin thinking her mother was under the protection of neighbors they didn't even know. He pressed her for details. What did Leslie wear on these walks? Who did Robin actually think watched her, and how did she know? He imagined people watching Leslie, but instead of comfort, he felt a sudden new chill.

"Do you miss me?" Robin suddenly blurted.

Nick felt something cramp inside of him. "What kind of a question is that?" he said. There was another moment of silence, a noise, and then Leslie's voice, out of breath, came on the line.

"Please don't go walking," he said.

"Please don't go away," she said.

"That's no kind of deal."

"We'll talk when you get home," she said.

They never did talk, not really. Leslie, in her habit of walking, couldn't seem to stop, not even when Nick was home. He offered to go with her, but she let him come along only once, and then he felt as if he were trailing after her, rather than walking with her. She walked too fast for conversation, staring dreamy-eyed in front of her, and he had this feeling that because of his presence, neighbors who might have been looking after her, watching her through the film of their curtains, had just turned away.

He began to tell her when he might call, so she could get her walks out of the way, or save them until afterward. Still, she was difficult to reach.

He was in Boston one night, dialing her. He wished she would answer. He wished he had someone else to call. When he was a kid at the home, he'd had a little red notebook into which he had copied the numbers of half the pay phones in Pittsburgh. People who were lonely always answered ringing pay phones and almost always would talk to you. He had never admitted he was an orphan, had never admitted he was lonely, and he'd had some good conversations until he'd run out of dimes. Things had changed, though. He didn't feel comfortable anymore calling pay phone numbers, and the one time he himself had answered a ringing pay phone, a raspy male voice had asked him if he wanted a blowjob.

Idly, he dialed his boss's number, then dialed a book buyer he liked, but no one answered. He didn't know why, but he suddenly began dialing his old number, the one he had shared with Dore. He knew she wasn't there, but it made him think about her again, it made him remember, and he called information to see if she was still in Boston. To his surprise, she was listed in Chelsea.

He dialed the number, and when he heard her voice, he hung up. He felt dizzy, felt the present crazily starting to recede. Leslie, he thought, but Leslie wasn't there beside him, Leslie wasn't on the other end of a phone whispering all the things she wanted to do to him. Leslie was out walking in the night, striding alone under the eyes of his neighbors. He called Dore again, nerved up, and this time her sturdy voice belled out that one more crank call and she was going to get her gun and shoot the phone out. She hung up.

He found himself dialing her number all the next day, never with any luck. He tried as soon as he woke up, right before an appointment; he even excused himself during a business lunch, leaving his catalog with the buyer while he dashed outside to make a quick call. He couldn't help himself. He just felt the need to know if a man would answer, calling out, "Honey, I've got it," if a child would pick up and plaintively call for mommy. No one picked up, though, until the evening, and then it was a young voice. He froze until he heard the voice call politely, "Miss . . ." and then he relaxed. Dore must still be teaching.

He wrote her address on a piece of paper, his hand trembling. He wondered what she looked like, if she had let her hair grow, if she still wore those glass earrings that trapped the light in small halos. He didn't go visit her, not then. He didn't even call her again until another month had passed and he was back in Boston. He drove by her apartment. He told himself he just wanted to see how she was living, what kind of a neighborhood it was. It was perfectly all right to still be concerned about someone you had once loved, wasn't it? He strained to see the numbers on the buildings.

Her place was brick, small, well kept, and he drove right past it. He didn't want her to see him. He remembered when he had first fallen in love with her, how the impossible fact of someone loving him that way had transformed everything. The air had smelled different—he used to swear he could feel it around him. Colors had shimmered. He had walked around the city wanting to stop people and tell them about her. He had felt that he was two people—himself and her—and that no matter what he did, no matter what happened in his whole life, he could never lose her.

He drove to Cambridge, parking, walking over to a burger joint. He'd eat some lunch; he'd think about what it was he really wanted to do. And then, no matter what it turned out to be, he would leave. He would go home to his wife and his daughter.

Dore was teaching English as a second language the day Nick came back into her life. It was a fairly new job for her, and she was still dumbfounded that they had hired her. She knew no Spanish, no Japanese, but the administrator had told her it didn't matter, that ignorance was a plus because it would force her to be a better teacher, and force the class to be better students. She nodded, then went out and bought herself some elementary language texts and began teaching herself.

She had two classes—a beginning class that stared at her, and an advanced class that didn't. Her students ranged from a sixty-year-old doorman at the Ritz to the sixteen-year-old daughter of a South American dictator. She liked the doorman, but the girl gave her haughty looks and finally left the school abruptly because of a military coup at home.

Dore took her classes on field trips. She made them go into McDonald's and order; she made them stop people on the street and ask for the time. Her students never called her anything but "Teacher," and although some told her their problems, none came to her house or even phoned her. She told herself it was progress.

The day before she saw Nick again, one of her students gave her a present. She was a sad, soft-eyed girl named Ria, just sixteen, but married. She and her husband had been living in her mother's house in Puerto Rico. She had once told Dore that she married him because her mother said he was a good choice, and they had moved into the house because her mother said Ria couldn't do laundry or cook well enough to please a man, so she would do it for her. Ria also told Dore that when she was little, she had had epileptic fits, but her mother, shamed, had never told the school. Ria had nearly died because no one knew what to do with her. She had come to the United States for just six months, on her mother's savings, staying long enough to learn English because companies in Puerto Rico paid more money for that kind of skill. "Go," her mother had told her. "I can take care of your husband."

Ria had told Dore this her first day, waiting until the other students had left. She whispered her life to Dore, dredging in her dictionary to find the words, but she never spoke in class, and when Dore called on her, Ria looked at her in reproach.

Now Ria handed Dore a brown bag and dipped her head. She said she had to go back to Puerto Rico; her mother was ill and could no longer tend Ria's husband. Her eyes were terrified, dazed. "Open the bag, Teacher," she said.

Dore did, pulling out a flimsy pale green blouse with short, puffy sleeves, a riot of green and orange embroidery on the bodice. Dore thought she had never in her life seen anything so hideous, but she held it up against her and exclaimed how lovely it was, until she was almost crying. Ria, pleased, blushed.

Dore spent half the night trying to figure out something to wear with the blouse the next day. She looked terrible in it. The sleeves were ridiculously girlish, and the material pulled across her breasts no matter how she plucked at it.

She ended up wearing a black jacket over the blouse, keeping it close around her until Ria came into the class; then Dore took it off. She taught in the horrible blouse, sweating half-moons under the arms, smiling over at Ria, who looked around, pleased. As soon as class was over, she struggled into her jacket again.

She dashed out to her car, sped home so she could change. She parked, and then she saw Nick, standing there, shimmering in her poor vision like a mirage.

They went to a coffee shop, Dore wrapping her jacket over the blouse, trying to hide the dizzy colors of the embroidery. She didn't feel comfortable being with Nick, and she didn't want him coming to her place. She knew how it would be. His scent would get into the folds of her drapes so it could never come out. His sound would move in and out of the creaks the apartment sometimes made at night. She'd see him in the corners; she wouldn't be able to turn on the lights without feeling him there, just out of reach.

Nick told her he was in Boston on business. "Business right in front of my apartment?" Dore said. She watched him skim off the milky layer of his cappuccino. "You haven't by any chance been calling me, have you? Calling and hanging up?"

"Someone's been doing that?" Nick said.

They didn't really talk about themselves at first. Nick felt the same way he had when he was at the home and prowling the teashops for company, making up a history for himself, a past that might unlock the kind of present he wanted. He told Dore he lived in Philadelphia now, that he still sold books, and then he noticed Dore's face changing, and he stopped. "Hey," he said, and abruptly she started to cry.

She wouldn't let him touch her. She lowered her head and covered her face with her two hands. The waitress waltzed by, raising one eyebrow at Nick, lifting the coffeepot toward him, but he shook his head at her. He wanted to touch Dore, but he was afraid. He kept edging his hand across the table toward her. He was halfway there when she opened her eyes. She smiled weakly at him. "Hard day at work," she said.

"Sure, I know," he said.

She fiddled with the saltshaker, and then she started telling him how it was for her after he had left. After Mexico, she had gone to live in France for a year, because in France it hadn't bothered her so much seeing all those mothers and babies—after all, they were French babies, French mothers. Besides, everything was in a language she didn't understand, so she couldn't possibly imagine they were blaming her. Nick grabbed one of her fingers. "Let's just drive," he said.

He had no idea where he was going to take her; he just liked having her in the car with him. For a moment he could think he was driving her back home to the trailer, back across a bridge of memory into the past.

"What is it?" she asked. "You look so funny."

"You look the same," he said, "like time just stopped."

"No," she said. "I don't." She put her hands in her lap and then looked over at him. "I had a banker for a while," she said. "He was perfectly nice—he brought me flowers and took me out to dinner. I thought he liked me. But then he said something about my being the best friend he could ever have, and then he never called me again. The last I heard, he had gotten married." She looked over at Nick. "Did you find anyone as good as me?" she blurted.

"No one like you," Nick said. He didn't know what to say to her. If he could just shut his eyes, if he could just think, maybe all the answers he needed would come to him. He couldn't stop looking over at her. He didn't want to make her uneasy, so he kept pretending to glance over at the traffic, when actually he was looking at her eyes, her face, her hands balled into her lap.

He felt that without even trying, he was in love with her all over again, or maybe it was just that he had never quite stopped.

He knew he didn't want Dore to have anybody, that he was glad the banker had disappeared. And being with her, he didn't feel like he had anybody but her either.

"You're so lovely," he said.

"Don't, please," said Dore. "Talk to who I am now. Not to who I was."

"I am," said Nick. "I am talking to who you are now."

"Whom you remember," she said.

"Whom I never forgot," he said, and as soon as he said it, he felt it was true. "You told me to leave you," he said. "Remember? You said you couldn't do it yourself, that I had to do it for you."

"Oh, I don't want to remember this," Dore said. "I don't want to think about it." She sat up straighter. "Nick, this is too confusing for me. Please, I can't be with you anymore tonight. Would you drive me home?"

Home, he thought. The trailer and Flora and a baby burbling in a crib. A woman with eyes so black you couldn't see the pupils, you could never be sure what she was thinking; a daughter who grew and survived only as long as she was a mystery to you, a girl almost old enough to leave. He shut his eyes.

"All right?" Dore said.

"Why wouldn't I be?" he said, and turned down toward her street.

He stood outside her apartment after she went in, trying to imagine just what sorts of things she'd do inside. He hadn't kissed her. He'd told her he'd be back in town, implying that he'd call her, but clamping his voice down so it sounded casual, as if they were nothing more than old friends, as if their lives hadn't once unraveled together.

It was easy enough to persuade his boss to send him to Boston more often. There were new bookshops sprouting up all along Commonwealth Avenue, all along Harvard Square. There were new "alternative schools." He had a whole list of them he had culled from Dore, who knew about such things. His boss thought Nick was finally becoming a go-getter, and he was delighted. He gave Nick bonuses, which Nick promptly spent on dinners for Dore, on white tulips.

He didn't know what he was doing, except he couldn't stop. As soon as he drove into Boston, his mood buoyed. Anything was possible. He could stride into strange shops and sell them half his stock before they realized they didn't need it. He felt that Boston had a frantic new pace, and it was only later that he realized it wasn't Boston doing the speeding, it was he. Dore made everything seem dizzy, like some obstacle course he had to get through as fast as possible to make his way to her. Everything began reminding him of her. He'd eat a muffin at the Pewter Pot and he'd remember the cookies Ruby had brought over on a blue plate; he'd see women with short, athletic haircuts and he'd see the nape of Dore's neck. He couldn't walk past an optician's office without thinking of her.

He fetched her at school, selling the headmaster a few basic grammars, leaving his catalogs and his card, and although he talked about books, he talked mostly about Dore. The headmaster told Nick how pleased everyone was with her, that he practically had to threaten students into the next level because they hated to leave her. "I know how they feel," Nick said.

He watched Dore coming out. He couldn't explain it, but he felt as if he had been waiting and waiting for her, that every breath of air he had ever taken had been thick with all those nights with her, and he hadn't even realized it until he had seen her again. Loving her again made him feel safe, buttressed against loss. It made things possible.

While Leslie never asked much, Dore wanted to know about everything, and sometimes, rather than lie, he told her he couldn't seem to think about anything but her. "Oh, phooey on that," she said, but he could tell she was pleased. She pressed him, though. She wanted to know why it was so difficult to get him at home (he had given her the phone number of a friend who was in Europe for the year), why she always had to call the main office. And she wanted to know, over and over, just what they thought they were doing, just how he expected things to end.

"Who said anything about ending?" Nick said. "We're just going slow, getting surprised."

She gave him a long, even look. "Surprised?" she said.

"I love you," he said, but she wouldn't say it back; she kept telling him that when she knew how things were going, then she would tell him how she felt, and not before. He tried to trick her into it. He asked her when they were tumbling entwined across her floor; he whispered to her just as she was drowsing off to sleep and defenseless; but then the look of terror that flickered into her face made him feel suddenly scared.

He told himself anything was possible, that the best thing was not to focus on any outcome at all, just let things happen. He thought of Flora in the trailer park, with her threads and her cards; he remembered her telling him he'd have a whole family of girls.

He never really thought of himself as having an affair. It was an ugly, unromantic word; and besides, how did you have an affair with someone you had once lived for and had a child with and shared a

whole life with? An affair was cheating, leaving less for one person
so you might have more for another, and he didn't think he was
doing that. If anything, being so happy made him generous, made
him feel closer in a way to Leslie. He brought her baby roses and
tulips; he walked with her at night, and found her silences didn't eat
away at him the way they used to. He waited them out now, or
teased her from them until she smiled and draped her hands about
his face.

He felt so protected that he began taking new note of Robin. He
kept remembering her as a little girl, how she used to feel inside his
coat pockets looking for toys, always taking instead the things he
carried for himself—his pen, a small notebook, an inky itinerary
sheet. He never knew what she did with those things, why she even
wanted them. He only remembered her screaming in fury when
Leslie tried to take them away. He remembered how she used to
watch him, how he'd sometimes feel her eyes on him when he was in
another room, another city.

Robin didn't ask him for anything anymore. She didn't meet him
at the door. When he came home, she was in her room, the stereo
on, but her headphones keeping her room so quiet that you wouldn't
even know she existed. Sometimes she was out at the "Y" swimming;
she'd come home sulky, her hair smelling of chlorine.

Little girls you could cart to the zoo or the museum; you could
prop them up beside you in the bleachers while a baseball game
droned on in front of you. He had no idea what you did with teenagers, how you spoke with them. He ended up asking her to meet
him for dinner one night when Leslie had a wedding-gown fitting to
attend to and was going to be gone a long while. He told Robin he'd
take her to the Pasta Palace, a new Italian place in Shadyside.

She showed up for dinner in a black dress and metallic blue shoes,
a silver clip in the wilds of her hair. The dinner was supposed to be
special, but it really didn't go very well. He was nervous with his
own daughter, and she kept looking at him as if she expected something to happen.

They were leaving the restaurant when he ran into a client. Bill
Glassman, who owned the Squirrel Hill Bookmart. He took one look
at Robin and started making a fuss. He knew her name, which startled Robin because she had no idea who he was at all. He started out

with the usual pleasantries—how pretty she was, how he had always assumed Nick was doing the usual fatherly bragging, but really, she was a breathtaker. And then, while Robin stood rooted there, amazed, he began to tell her about her life. He knew what grade she was in, he knew she swam, and he knew that she loved Jane Austen. He knew things she never thought to tell anyone about, like how she drew pictures on the backs of envelopes and liked to make shadow drawings on the misty windows. He knew almost all the outside details of her life because Nick had never stopped collecting them, because he had memorized the facts of her existence and then happily spilled them out in conversation, almost as if he were convincing himself that he played a part in all of it.

Robin swayed on the heels of her shoes, shocked, glancing from Bill to Nick and back again, all the while listening to her past being played back to her by a total stranger. Before he left, Bill shook her hand and then Nick's. "You come by the store," he told Robin. "I'll fix you up with all the Jane Austen you want." A little dazed, Robin moved closer to Nick.

While they walked, she kept glancing over at him, waiting for him to say something, but all he said was, wasn't Bill a damned nice guy, and that Robin ought to stop by the shop, he had a good selection. He looked at her, beaming, but she stayed silent. At one point she stumbled, and he wrapped his arm about her for a moment. "I've got you," he said.

ELEVEN

• • •

Robin began buying her books at the Squirrel Hill Bookmart. Every time she wandered in, she looked around for Bill, and every time he saw her, he always had some new story about her life to relate back to her. He showed her off to the clerks, asked her opinions about displays, and sometimes, too, he talked about Nick. He told her stories he thought she already knew—about Nick having to share a room with a drunkard at the "Y" in Philadelphia because of a hotel strike; about Nick riding and riding the swan boats in Boston, a grown man charming a gaggle of little kids. He told her how much Nick loved Boston, and asked her if she felt the same way. Robin was ashamed to admit she had never been there. "Sure," she said. "It's a great city." He sent her home with an armful of new books and regards to "that father of yours."

At home, she was restless. When Nick came home that evening, she asked him abruptly if he would take her to Boston sometimes.

"Boston? Why Boston?"

"I'd like to see it," she said. "Maybe I'll want to go to college there."

"It's just a city," Nick said, but Dore flickered along his mind.

"It is not," she said. "You're smiling."

He sighed. "Why all this sudden interest?"

"I don't know," she said. "Maybe I want to go someplace new. Maybe I want to be with you. Just me and you."

He looked at her. "Listen, you wouldn't have a good time there.

160

It's dull and it's dirty." He scratched at his face. "It's about time for *all* of us to take a vacation. Maybe we could all go to Philadelphia for a long weekend soon. What about that?"

"Sure," she said, turning.

It really bothered her that Nick wouldn't take her. She didn't ask him about it again, but she trailed him aimlessly about the house, a shadow, until finally he turned around and gave her another reason why he couldn't take her to Boston, why she wouldn't like it. "I didn't even ask you," she said. He looked discomfited. "Well, you didn't have to," he said.

Less than a month later, he left for Boston. She knew what time he was leaving in the morning, and she set her alarm to rouse her, but when it shocked her awake and she woozily peered out her window into the dim morning light, she saw that he was already settled in his car, the motor already running. And then, before she could rush into her robe and slippers, before she could shout out the window for him to wait, he was gone.

All that week, things angered her. When she tried to comb her hair, the teeth caught in the tangles and broke off in her hand. When she put on mascara, the brush poked her in the eye. She wouldn't get on the phone when Nick called, and then later, when she changed her mind and called him herself, he was always out.

Leslie always took on more work when Nick was gone, coming home later with her hands full of rustling silks and textured cottons. At night, though, she liked having Robin in the house with her. She bought ice cream, she made popcorn—she'd do anything to have Robin keep her company. She kept the good TV in her bedroom, so when they both sat up watching old movies, there was always the possibility that Robin would fall asleep in bed with her, that she could quietly shut the set off and cover Robin, that she could wake in the night and have a body next to her.

On Saturday morning, the day before Nick was due back, Leslie told Robin that he had called to say he was going to be another few days. Leslie was at the kitchen table, nursing a cup of coffee, a bottle of aspirin spilled out in front of her. When she looked at Robin, she frowned.

"Did he say how come?" Robin asked.

Leslie shrugged. "And where are you going?"

"To the library," Robin said. "Swimming maybe."

"Dinner's at six," Leslie said.

"I'll probably just get a hamburger in town."

Leslie put her cup down, stroking her brow. "You just be here at six, please."

Something prickled along Robin's spine. She heard Leslie telling her again about dinner, about getting home early and helping around the house, and then she turned and went out the door, into the blissful cool of the morning.

She didn't realize she was going to Boston until five that evening. She couldn't stop thinking about her father, about Leslie waiting at home for her. It was a weekend. If she left now, she could be there a whole day before she had to come back. She could call him to say she was coming; she could get him to call Leslie for her. She fiddled in her jeans for some change, and then, thinking better of it, stood up and began collecting her things. She'd take care of it when she got there. Leslie wasn't expecting her for another hour, and Nick . . . well, Nick wasn't expecting her at all.

It would take Robin fifteen hours to get to Boston. She was wary hitching out of Pittsburgh. She kept trying to squint into oncoming cars before she jammed her thumb out, making sure she didn't recognize a client of Leslie's, a friend of her father's, or anyone who might know her. Whenever she saw a car that looked vaguely familiar, she tucked her head down and hunched around from the road, as if the wind were too fierce for her.

She had never hitched before and she had a feeling that maybe she wasn't doing it right. She tried to keep her stance loose and confident and tough, and she tried to look so pretty, a driver couldn't help but slow down. Once, when she was still going with Rick, when they were eating lunch behind the vocational school, she had overheard some of the vocational girls talking about hitching, idly discussing what they would and wouldn't do. You wouldn't get into a car with more than one guy; you had to check for door handles on the insides before you got in; and it was a good idea to lean in just enough to sniff out any alcohol scenting the air. No old cars; no real new cars, either, because that could mean someone so rich they might feel they could do whatever they wanted. Matronly women were good; girls your own age; truck drivers, who could be counted on not only to be polite but to buy you dinner at a truck stop. The girls had told a few horror stories, but Robin discarded those now; she still thought nothing bad could ever happen to her.

A car whizzed by her, slowed for a moment, and she saw a red glove suddenly poke out the window and beckon to her. She raced toward it, but just as she got to the door, just as she was about to peer in, the car suddenly jolted ahead, speeding, leaving her standing in the road, her hand outstretched.

Her first ride was from a middle-aged man in a green suit. There were handles on all the doors, he smelled only of lime aftershave, and for the whole two hours he drove without once touching her. He sneaked anxious peaks at her, though, and when he spoke, he called her "princess." Then, abruptly, he asked if she knew what *fellatio* meant, and Robin sat up straight in her seat. She started gauging the hurt she'd endure if she leaped from the car, but then he said kindly that it was understandable that a young girl like her might not know, and he said it meant when a woman goes down on a man. "You know what that means, going down?" he asked, and then he said that he meant sucking cock. "The woman takes the penis right into her mouth. No teeth, though," he said. "She has to kind of tuck them away." Robin put her hand on the door, but he just switched on the radio and started to hum. He never asked her another question, he never did anything more than hum, and when he left her off, he told her she was a very nice girl. He smiled. And he waved at her when he drove off.

By the time the next ride came, she was so cold she just got in without checking faces or door handles. She got ride after ride, from women who lectured her about Richard Speck and the nine nurses, and once from a girl only a little older than she herself was, who told Robin about a maniac loose who liked to cut off the nipples of young girls and keep them preserved in solution in his trunk.

Some of the rides were pleasant. A woman bought her soup and a sandwich at a diner, insisting that she was hungry herself and that it was up to Robin whether she ate or waited inside a frosty car. A trucker brought her to his home, a split-level with red-white-and-blue shag carpeting. His wife gave Robin hot cocoa with marshmallows dotting into foam, and a grilled cheese sandwich, while he made a few phone calls. "It isn't safe, what you're doing," the trucker's wife told Robin. She wanted her to call home and get the first bus back. "Oh, it's all right, I'm invincible," Robin said.

"Nobody's that," said the wife.

Robin climbed back into the truck and slept while he drove her the rest of the way to Boston. By the time they arrived, the air was dusky, and she felt a little disoriented, homesick for something familiar.

She knew the name of Nick's hotel, and she asked a few people for directions. It startled her, how many people were on the streets this early, how much noise. She walked past the gardens, and when she saw the swan boats, she got a small, sharp thrill. But when she got to them, the man told her they weren't open yet; he said to come back in a few hours. Everything felt so different here. The people seemed to be harboring some secret knowledge she didn't know how to access, and she felt unsure and out of place.

She took her time walking to her father's hotel. She practiced in her mind how he might take her visit. He'd finally share the wonders of one of his cities with her. He'd be delighted. He'd swoop her off to dinner, take her to a mall or whatever they had here and buy her a dress to wear. Or maybe, maybe he'd be furious. Maybe he'd make her call Leslie and apologize. She'd get yelled at in stereo, but then the squall would flutter away and she'd still be here in this wondrous city with her father, on her way out to eat. Maybe, too, she would end up here when she went to college, and then he'd be the one to visit *her*, he'd be the one missing *her* because she just wasn't at home anymore.

"Hey, bright eyes," someone said, and, startled, she dipped her head. "Hey, pretty bitty," the voice said, and she strode past, not looking at the face that went with the voice. She remembered Rick's stories about big cities. Women walking past men who would spit beer into their hair. Things falling from windows—shopping carts weighted with bricks. A woman in the subway screaming because someone had thrown a bag of manure on her, no one even able to get close enough to help because of the stench. Robin shook the images away; she reminded herself just who she was, just what could and could not hurt her.

She was on Tremont Street, waiting for the light to change, pressed into a crowd so she could barely move, when there, across the street, she spotted her father. She elbowed forward a little. Someone cursed and pushed her back. "Jesus, are you out of your mind?" a woman said to her. "You can get killed on these streets crossing at the lights, let alone against them."

Robin, pinned into place, tried to lift one hand into a wave, tried to call out, but all the noise smothered her sound. She strained up on tiptoe, and then there was her father again, in a clearing by the park, only he wasn't alone. He was holding someone, a woman, bending her toward him as if there were no one else on the street but the two of them, moving her into a kiss.

Robin froze. The light clicked, the crowd moved like a tide, straining against her, but she couldn't get her legs to work, suddenly couldn't remember how to breathe, how to speak, how to do anything. "Move it," someone said, jostling her, but she couldn't. She couldn't do anything but watch the woman peeling away from her father, lifting up to kiss him again, on his forehead, on his nose, on his mouth, long and deep. The two of them separated, as smoothly as a seam, gliding in opposite directions, and then, without thinking, Robin began to follow the woman.

Dore was running herself a bath, sifting in rose bath salts, bubbling the water pink, when the doorbell rang. "Shit," she said. It was only nine. She had warned Nick not to even think of calling her until ten. She needed the time to calm herself down from seeing him, to think about what it was she wanted to do about it. Every time he came back into her life, it was like an assault. She'd work herself up in knots, and then somehow he'd manage to loosen them up just by being with her. She'd get used to him again, feel the same old comfort starting to surround her like a blanket, and then he'd be gone and she'd have to pretend it wasn't killing her, wasn't ruining her life. The bath helped. The heat of it soaked out the lust and the need and the dreamy yearning; it let her rise up from the water like some Aphrodite reborn. She could feel alone with herself again. Alone and strong. She swished her hand in the water, lifting up bubbles, and the bell rang again.

Let the damned thing ring. Whoever it was would get tired and go away. Or they'd phone her. Her friends knew how she was about her privacy—they could be banging at her door and she wouldn't answer if she was reading or watching an old movie on TV. You couldn't get her to do anything she didn't want to. Maybe the bell wasn't even for her. There were kids who came into the foyer to smoke dope and sometimes bumped up against a bell. Dore ruffed her hair, snapped her jeans, and then heard the buzzer downstairs, steps in the hallway, along the stairs, and finally a loud, insistent knocking at her door. Who the hell let someone in on her bell? She wiped her hands against her jeans and went to the door, wrenching it open, glaring.

There, standing in front of her, was a young girl, her hair wild, her face a little dirty, her hands balled into fists. Dore let out a breath. Ah, she was used to this—this was familiar. She knew the look on that face all too well, the way the body was held, the pain contorted there. She could probably repeat this girl's story back to her, word for word. She didn't recognize the girl, but it didn't matter. She must be a friend of a friend of a friend of one of her old students. They all knew she wouldn't turn them away.

"Come on in," she said, and the girl did.

Dore led her into the living room and sat her down. She knew what to do. "Wait just one sec," she said, and went into the kitchen, quickly popping tea bags into blue china cups, hurrying the water to a boil. When she came out again with two cups on a tray, balancing a plate of chocolate snaps, she smiled. She fitted one of the cups into the girl's hand. "Are you all right?" Dore asked. The girl stayed silent, but Dore was used to that, too.

The girl kept looking around, her face pinched and tight. Dore's place was small, cluttered with books and photographs, snapshots taken in Woolworth's four-for-a-dollar booth because she was too impatient to pose for a real picture. The girl got up and went to the shelf, her back to Dore. She was still for so long that finally Dore got up and lightly touched her. The girl seemed to contract. In her hand was a recent photograph of Nick, laughing into the camera. It had been taken just about a month ago, on a sunny day when they had driven out to the Cape. They were on a deserted beach, and Dore had been happy.

"Who's this?" the girl asked, her voice low.

Dore started to take the photo, but the girl's grip was strong.

"Oh," said Dore, "that's my favorite runaway." She smiled at the girl, who promptly burst into tears, letting the picture flutter down from her hands.

Dore wrapped her arms about the girl and let her cry against her. It always amazed her, how easy it was to comfort a stranger, how when you had nothing to lose, you could give everything. All these young bodies somehow just fit against her. Their heads rested against her neck, their chests were so close she could feel their hearts beating right through her. God help her, but it was heady.

Girls were the hardest for her. Sometimes, after they left, after she had helped them call their parents in another state, paying for the calls herself, after she had given advice until they smiled, after they had names and numbers of doctors tucked into their jeans, the apartment seemed so empty, it was an affront. She sometimes calculated ages. She'd think, This blonde must be twelve, the brunette, fourteen, and when they got close to the age Susan would have been, it started to hurt. She couldn't stop herself, she felt the comparisons rising to the surface like cream. This one had hair like Susan would have had, thick and dark, pulled into a braid. This one loved to paint, the way she always imagined Susan would have. She made herself crazy with it.

"I wish you were my mother," girls told her. They made her a model, they loved her for the few hours they were at the house, and then they disappeared. Sometimes she got stray postcards, scribbles proclaiming that someone would never forget her, but of course the someone always, inevitably, did. The visits were always one-time, and she always felt as if she had somehow come up short, as if she had failed yet again.

She took sleeping pills sometimes, the mild kind they sold over the counter, and as she rolled toward her dreams, she began thinking about Susan. What if she hadn't died at all? What if she had been revived in some stark white room, kidnapped by a childless woman wandering the floors, pulled by her yearning to any small heartbeat? What if one of these girls forever showing up at her house was Susan, fully grown now, sent by fate, somehow meant to test her? Christians swore they could see Jesus in everyone. They were supposed to be kind to beggars and drunkards because anyone could be Jesus. What you do to him, you do to me. Her girls, Dore called them, her girls.

Every one of them a potential Susan, a chance to make up for not having loved her enough, for not having been there to avert disaster.

The girl moved against Dore. Dore led her to the couch and sat her down. "You cry all you need," she said.

The girl needed a lot. Dore sat there, her arm falling pins-and-needles asleep under the girl. This one would take some time in her telling, Dore thought.

When the girl finally lifted her head, she looked shamed and wouldn't meet Dore's eyes. Dore reached out and tilted the girl's chin up. "What could be that bad?" Dore asked.

The girl looked angry, confused. She stood up and then sat right down again. "The man in the picture," she said. "Who is he?"

Boy pain, Dore thought, another open wound of the heart. "He's an old friend," Dore said.

"A friend?"

"The best kind," Dore said. "I love him."

"But like a friend," the girl said, sitting up. "You love him like a friend."

"Well, more than that," Dore began, but the girl was suddenly staring at her, making her uncomfortable.

"You know his family?" the girl said.

"His family? No, he's an orphan."

The girl started crying again, and Dore hunched toward her. "Listen, is this about a boy? Is that what's wrong?" The girl seemed to sink down into herself. "Look, you can't let men run you," Dore said, then stopped, Nick's face moving into her mind. "Right, Dore," she said, and the girl looked up.

"Do you want to tell me?" Dore asked.

The girl rocked a little. "How did you meet him?"

She's hedging, Dore thought. "You really want to hear this? You're sure you really wouldn't rather be doing the telling?"

"No," the girl said, "I wouldn't. I wouldn't at all."

So Dore started telling stories about Nick. How they had met, how happy they had been, their life in the trailer. She didn't talk about Susan. The girl kept looking down into her lap, threading her fingers, and then abruptly she bolted for the door.

"Hey!" Dore cried, getting up, and the girl stopped, freeze-framed like a deer in a blinding light. Dore fished around in the end-table drawer and pulled out a pencil and some crimped paper. Smoothing it, she hastily scribbled her name and her phone. "You have a place you can stay?" she asked. The girl nodded. "Well, I'll just write out the address of the "Y" anyhow," Dore said. "You never know, and it's so cheap." She handed the paper to the girl, who slowly took it. "You call if you need to talk. Anytime. And you can come back if you want to." Dore sighed. "You want to tell me your name? Just the first one so if you call, I'll know it?"

"No, no, I can't," the girl said.

"Wait again," Dore said, and went to the bedroom to get some money. She came out and pressed ten dollars into the girl's hand. "In case you get hungry."

"I can't take this," the girl said.

"You just did," Dore said, and the girl hesitated for a moment and then tucked it into her shirt. She put her hand on the door, and then Dore impulsively hugged her. She felt the girl stiffen. "How old are you?" Dore asked, but the girl pulled on the door and was gone.

Dore leaned along the wall, listening to the clatter of steps down the stairs. She went to the window and looked out, watching the girl stride down the street, seeing her pull out the paper Dore had given her and study it for a moment. Dore wondered what the matter was with this one, what could hurt so much she couldn't find a voice to it. Anyway, Dore thought, it would be a story, wouldn't it, to tell Nick when he got there.

For a while Robin just walked. She kept feeling Dore's arms about her, seeing Dore's face. That woman didn't know Nick had a family, didn't know where he lived or who Robin was, and yet she had a sure, simple claim to him anyway. Robin was a complete stranger to her, and yet she had let her into the apartment without even asking how she'd found her way to this door. She had given her money and an address and endless comforts without insisting on an explanation. Robin took out the piece of paper again and looked at the phone number, at Dore's name scribbled across the top. She still wasn't sure what was going on now between this woman and her father, only that something somehow was, and if there was anyone to hate about it, it was her father.

She walked, concocting accidents for him. She'd push him into

the path of a subway. She'd wait for him in front of Dore's so he'd
know as soon as he saw her eyes blazing flame why she was so angry;
and then, just as some lying explanation spilled from his lips, she'd
stab him with a fork she had stolen from a restaurant. She thought
about Leslie, and suddenly she was furious with her, too, for not
knowing, for letting all this happen.

She didn't want to spend another second in this city knowing her
father was here and Dore was waiting for him. She looked out at the
road. There were plenty of cars—she could probably line up a ride to
Pittsburgh soon enough. She stood out in the center of the road and
jabbed out her thumb.

She didn't get back to Pittsburgh until after two in the morning.
She had been lucky again, getting a ride for most of the way from a
middle-aged truck driver. He made her sit in the back behind a faded
pink curtain because, he said, it was illegal for him to pick up anyone and he had been docked for it once before. She didn't mind it
behind the curtain. There was a pillow, a blanket, and the steady
drone of the road to put her to sleep, deep and dark and dreamless.

He woke her up in front of a taxi stand and insisted on waiting
until she got another ride. It took her only two more rides to get into
the city, and then she used Dore's ten dollars for a cab, giving the
driver the entire bill for a $3.50 fare, a little surprised when he didn't
even thank her.

The lights were blazing in the house. Before Robin even stepped
onto the flagstone, the front door jerked open and Leslie strode down
the walk toward her. Robin froze in place. Leslie, silent, lifted one
hand and slapped Robin's face. Dizzy with fear, Robin stepped back.
Leslie had never struck her before, never, but here she was again,
moving forward, and Robin shut her eyes. But there were arms about
her, her mother's breath against her neck, the feverish warmth of
embrace. Two women hugging her in one day, Robin thought, confusing her, confusing time. "Let's get inside," Leslie said.

Leslie seesawed between anger and relief. One minute she was telling Robin to go get into a hot bath, that she would bring her in hot
cider, some aspirin; the next moment Leslie was grounding her for
three weeks, shouting question after question about where Robin had
been.

"I called every name I could remember, every name I could find in your room. I woke people up," Leslie said. "I was so nervous, I called the same names twice, three times—what did I care when people threatened me?" She brushed her hair from one shoulder. "Oh, God," she said. "I kept seeing you—I kept trying to feel you in my gut, to sense where you were, how you were, and all I felt was how very lost you were to me, and how terrified I was." She sat down. "Where were you?" she whispered.

Robin looked at her lap. She hated her mother, she loved her. "Philadelphia," Robin said.

"Philadelphia?"

Robin didn't even realize she was crying until she felt Leslie's body cushioned around her, rocking her, telling her that whatever it was, it was going to be all right, that she shouldn't be afraid to talk. The more she said that, the more hysterical Robin felt. Leslie smoothed Robin's hair. "It's okay, it's okay," she said. "You get a good night's sleep, and in the morning we'll talk."

Sunday morning, at the kitchen table, picking at the eggs Leslie had fixed for her, Robin made something up. She said she had impulsively bought a train ticket to Philadelphia to see a friend who had moved there. She had used the money she was saving for a leather jacket. She hadn't called because she thought she'd be back in time, and when she missed her train, she was afraid. That was why she had been crying, why she had been so wired.

Leslie, sipping coffee, shook her head. "How could you be so irresponsible? How could you do something so cruel? I was *scared.*"

"I'm not a baby," Robin said.

Leslie looked angrily over at her. "You could be ninety and it still wouldn't matter to me, I'd still be terrified and worried if you just up and left without even thinking enough of me to let me know." She pushed at her coffee cup. "You're so damned independent."

"I'm sorry," Robin said, but Leslie was getting up, clearing dishes, telling Robin she was grounded for a month. She turned toward her. "Go on," she said, "finish up those eggs."

All that day, Robin felt wounded. She carried Dore's phone number in her jeans pocket, pulling it out to look at it, stuffing it back into her pocket, unable to just tear it up. Sometimes she told herself it was a mistake. She didn't have the facts. Dore could have been lying. She might barely know Nick.

She wandered into Leslie's workroom and interrupted her to ask if Nick had ever lived in a trailer. Leslie burst into laughter. "A trailer?" she said, tickled. "Does your father look like the type to live in a trailer?" She couldn't get over it. She wanted to know where Robin had gotten such a wild thought.

"Oh, it was just something I was reading," Robin said, leaving the room.

She began watching Leslie with a new, critical eye. Leslie didn't brush her hair very often, and she sometimes wore blouses without buttons, even though she fussed at Robin's skewed hems. She wore stained, oversize T-shirts of Nick's to work, and heavy flannel gowns to bed. She almost never wore makeup, and when she did, it smeared because she kept rubbing and stroking it off while she sewed.

When the phone rang that night, Robin didn't rush to pick it up. Leslie grabbed it, and Robin saw how her mother's whole face changed, how she said Nick's name, curling up around the phone as if it were a lover.

Robin kept thinking that nothing her father ever did had anything to do with her—that was the problem. She was in bed when he finally got home, and she sat up, listening. She could smell the perfume Leslie had put on, she could hear Leslie's low laughter, but Nick's voice was low and serious—she couldn't make it out even though she got up and pressed her face against her door. "Oh, Lord," Leslie said. "Who do you think you are, making me miss you like this?"

Robin felt her heart hardening up inside of her, making her rigid. She wanted to walk right out into the living room in her T-shirt and socks and accuse him. She wanted to shout at her mother for not being prettier, for not being somehow better. She lay back in bed in a fever of reverie. She saw herself confronting Nick, shouting accusations, but then, suddenly, she saw Nick moving, on his own, uncontrolled by her imagination. She saw his face fading of feeling. She saw him neither denying nor affirming one single thing she said, only picking up the same two black leather bags he had brought into the house and taking them right outside again. "If you don't trust me, if that's the way you feel . . ." he said. She saw Leslie moving toward Nick, noticing her only enough to flash her a warning look of hatred. The car hadn't even had time to cool yet; the motor was ready to go, ready to take him back to Dore, back to anyplace that held no room for her.

Robin pulled the sheet slowly up over her head. She prayed. Not to her old guardian angels, not to Nick, but to Dore this time. She concentrated on Dore's face, her hair, the feel of her skin where Robin had touched her. Promise me, Robin transmitted, promise you won't take him totally, that you'll leave something for here. Promise it. Promise.

In the morning, Leslie had to wake her. Leslie's hair was clean, brushed down her back. She had on a red dress and blue clip-on earrings and she looked happy. "Sleepy jean," she said. "Let's go." She waited for Robin to rouse herself, then told her she hadn't said a word to Nick about the incident. She thought the whole matter was something the two of them could handle between themselves. "Like a conspiracy," she said. "Now scoot downstairs and say hello to your father."

Robin threw on a black corduroy dress, black tights and sneakers, and sprinted out the back door, combing her hair with her fingers, stopping only when the knots were too fierce for her. She turned only so that she could see Nick was actually there, before her head started hurting, and she blurted out that she was late, that if she mad-dashed it, she could catch the bus.

"I'll drive you," Nick said, but she was gone.

She avoided him as best she could, coming home right after school, barricading herself in her room with sandwiches and cookies, the warm, flat fizz of the canned Cokes she kept on her windowsill. She said she didn't feel well; she said she had to study. When she could, she stayed at the "Y," diving, trying riskier and riskier moves, staying submerged so long that the lifeguard came and poked the rescue pole down at her. She was lectured on safety, she was warned, but it only made her more reckless.

When she heard Nick approach at night, she bunched over her

desk, feigning sleep. He came in and gently lifted her from her chair, placed her on the bed, and pulled a light cover over her. She was so startled she couldn't breathe right. She lay paralyzed, waiting for him to go, but he just stayed there; she felt him so close she could have moved a half-inch and touched him with her shoulder. Go, leave, she willed, but when he finally did get up, when she heard his sigh, she felt like crying out for him to return.

Mornings, she got up an hour early. She never ate breakfast at home anymore, but stopped at a coffee shop a block away from school. She nursed tinny-tasting cocoa that came from a machine; she picked at greasy cheese Danish and talked to the waitress, the only other person there.

She didn't know how she felt when she came out of school one day to find Nick waiting for her, leaning against the car. "Hey, kiddo," he said, "long time no see." He was in a leather jacket and jeans. He wanted to know if he was embarrassing her, coming to school like this. He said he knew how kids felt about their parents when they got to be her age, but he figured this was the only way he was sure to see her.

He made her buckle her seat belt so she felt imprisoned, and then he drove a little; he said he wanted to talk to her.

"About what," she asked. She looked out at the street, unsnapping her buckle.

"Hey, hook that up," he said. "A vacation," he told her. "I thought we could go to a travel agency. It used to be my favorite thing in the world to do."

"I'm too old for a family vacation," Robin said.

"Too old for Hawaii?"

"How about Boston?" she said abruptly.

He turned right. "Too touristy this time of year. And anyway, that's no vacation for me. I go there all the time."

She didn't want the ice cream. She didn't want to get out at the travel agency. He pulled out folders to show her, but she just shrugged uneasily at them. He had fliers for Paris, for Egypt, for places so far away that no one could ever reach you; and finally, taking a bunch of them, he said they could go.

He waited until they were back in the car before he suddenly turned to her and asked her what was wrong. When she just shrugged, he pulled the car over to the side of the road. "You don't like me much lately, do you?" he asked.

She looked out the window, her eyes steely.

"Am I wrong?" he asked.

"Do you love mom?" she asked.

He was startled. "Why would you even think to ask something like that? Don't you think I do?"

She was so silent that when he sighed, she thought for a moment the sigh came from her. "Do you think I like to leave?" he asked. "Don't you think it's hard? Don't you think it's lonely?" He pulled out his wallet and showed her the plastic folders filled with her face and Leslie's. He pulled down the visor on the front window and showed her another picture of herself clipped up there.

He was buckling up his own face; she was afraid to ask him what he was thinking, afraid to say anything that might put her fear out into the open. You could give flesh and blood and bone to any thought just by giving it a voice; you could make all the dangers you ever worried about take on a life so strong you could never snuff it out. She swallowed.

"I'm just tired," she said. "School."

"Robin, listen to me—"

"I don't want to talk about it anymore," she said. "Really. I feel much better."

He looked at her doubtfully, then drove her home, the two of them in silence, and he didn't show up at her school again. He seemed to be waiting for something from her. He'd walk over to her when she was reading in the living room; he'd stand in her light until she looked up at him.

"So, what are you reading?" he asked. She told him, but he never seemed to be really listening; he seemed to be just looking at her, just taking her in.

He began leaving her alone again, although he still talked about family vacations. She found travel brochures scattered all over the house. Bright foldouts of Spanish beaches on top of the kitchen counter, pamphlets about Aruba by the shower. She heard Leslie proposing Florida one evening, telling him about a trip she had taken with her parents when she was just five, down for some tennis matches her mother had easily won, her father sweeping in second in the men's division. She said she remembered how yellow the sun was, she remembered the crocodiles that were teased for all the tourists. In the end, though, no plans were ever made about anything, and everything, for Robin, just seemed to be dangerously adrift.

TWELVE

        • • •

Robin began calling Dore after Nick left on his next business trip. He was going to Philadelphia. For a moment, watching him pack, Robin had this crazy fear that maybe there was another Dore waiting for him there; that maybe every place he had ever set foot in bred women who loved him with an ignorance so wild it frightened her.

"Let me come with you," she blurted, but he just shook his head. He said she'd be bored cooped up in the hotel, and anyway, she had midterms coming up, didn't she?

"I didn't say that," she said.

"Well, I saw the books," he said, folding a shirt. "I saw the exam schedule on top."

She was startled, uneasy. She walked to the car with him, following Leslie, who had draped her arm about his shoulders. Leslie held him for a bit, and then stepped away. "You rat, leaving when the weather's this nice," she said, managing a smile.

Robin didn't hug Nick goodbye. She stood there, aloof, watching him get into the car, and when Leslie turned, squaring her shoulders, striding back toward the house, Robin stayed out on the sidewalk, looking at the place where Nick had been just minutes before.

With Nick gone, the house emptied out. Leslie had started working every night now, designing dresses for a woman named Emma Sandstrom, who lived just a block away. Emma had a baby that she kept in a playpen in the center of the room, and almost immediately, the baby fell in love with Leslie. He brightened every time she came near him, his serious gray eyes following her as she fit fabric about Emma, as she reached for the new sketches of her design. When Leslie was finished for the evening, the two women would sit and talk over tea and coffee cake, and Leslie would linger because she liked the companionship.

Robin wandered alone in the house. She wanted Leslie to know about Dore, but she didn't want to tell her. She wanted to confront Nick, but she was terrified. Instead, she left what clues she could: postcards of trailers; magazine articles about marriages being saved or not because of infidelity; once, a whole clipping about a woman who raised pigs, an article Robin had torn out only because the woman's name was Dore. She left everything scattered across the dining-room table. She told herself it was in fate's hands, that she couldn't be responsible. She was young, she wasn't supposed to be shouldering pain like this.

Leslie came home humming, Emma's conversation still in her mind, feeling less alone. She passed through the dining room and, sniping at the mess Robin always left, gathered up the postcards and the clippings, the torn snippets of newsprint Robin had laid out for her. Sometimes she just put them in another place; sometimes she tossed them out. If she looked at any of them, she never told Robin.

Robin was so lonely, just sitting in the house, with her father gone, her mother down the block half the time, not able to voice anything to anybody. She had the phone next to her, her hand poised on the receiver, and she was thinking about Dore, about how easily she had let her in, how she had held her. "You call anytime," Dore had said. The call would show up on the phone bill, but Nick never even looked at the bills except to pay them, and Leslie, too, was careless. It would only be one number, one call. Robin counted to a hundred, and then slowly, slowly, she lifted the receiver, she dialed.

"Dore," she said. "This is Amy. You remember. I knocked on your door that day. I never even told you my name."

The first time, she was on the phone with Dore for a little over an hour. She didn't know what it was she wanted, only that she couldn't seem to hang up; she didn't want to close down Dore's voice and be left floundering in the wary quiet of the house. She didn't lie.

Not exactly. She told Dore she lived in Pennsylvania. She said she had run away because she had a father who was always away, a mother who was always there. She told Dore she had gotten her name from a friend who had lived in Boston for a while and then moved to California. She gave a description of this friend that could fit anyone—dark eyes, long brown hair—and a name common enough to forget: Mary Stone.

That first call, Dore didn't give any advice. But she listened, she was a presence humming over the wires. Robin wanted to ask Dore everything; she wanted to know everything about her life, and she wanted to know nothing, and she wasn't at all sure what she wanted to reveal herself. There was a whole series of terrifying *ifs*, and she hedged around them.

She asked Dore if she was happy, if she liked her life.

"Oh, sometimes," Dore said. "You know. I get lonely like everyone else."

"But you have someone," Robin said.

"Sometimes," Dore said. She was silent for a moment, and then she told Robin not to mind her, that she was just having a funny day and that was all.

Robin made up things just to stay on the phone. She talked about Rick, transforming who he was. The new Rick was in a rock band. He still adored her, even after the cruel way she had spurned him. He had written a song about her, "Birdie," after her name, Robin. "Isn't that something, having a song written about you?" Robin said. "He's gone now, though."

"Sometimes they come back," Dore said. "And you wait, I'll bet if he does, you'll appreciate him that much more for his absence." She mentioned the man she was seeing—Nick, she said his name, and hearing it made Robin twitch back from the phone. Dore said he had once been so close to her, he was just about the same as her husband.

"He was?" Robin said, chilled. "What happened?"

"I don't know. Everything. Nothing. Things." There was silence again, and then she asked, her voice brightening, "Just who is trying to help whom here?"

Robin began calling Dore more and more. She tried not to. She reminded herself that one lone call in a phone bill was one thing, a slew was another. She tried saving her allowance for pay phone calls, but there was no privacy, she couldn't cry when she was so exposed, she couldn't say how she felt; and worse, there were always people waiting to use the phone, tapping their feet and staring at her. She told herself she wasn't going to call anymore, she wasn't, but then she'd be so alone in the empty house, she'd feel her sorrow starting to surround her, and then her need to talk to Dore would be so strong it would blot out every other consideration, and she'd pick up the phone.

Dore asked her once how she could afford the calls. Did she want Dore to call her back? Did she want to call collect? "I work, I have money," Dore said.

But Robin was wary. She didn't know why, but it was somehow safer for Dore's number to be floating around in her family's bill than for her own to be on Dore's. She sometimes imagined that the grow-ing bond between herself and Dore couldn't help but loosen the bond between Dore and her father eventually, but it was a scheme that would work only if Dore didn't know who Robin was.

It cost her sometimes. Dore was so sympathetic, such a willing ear, it was sometimes tormenting to hold herself back, to have to skirt around the real pain instead of simply telling it in a great rush.

Still, she couldn't wait to talk to Dore. She rushed Leslie out to her night fittings, told her to stay as long as she wanted because she had a math exam and would be studying late.

Robin pulled pieces of her father's past from Dore, and when they cut her, when they made her feel ruined, she told Dore the pain was about something else. It was about Rick, it was about failing an exam in school, or sometimes it was just because her period was coming on and that was how she got. When Dore told her how long she had lived with Nick, how Nick had proposed marriage, Robin cried for ten minutes, and when she finally managed to get out a word, she blurted the most dramatic thing she could think of: She said she had tried to kill herself because she felt so alone. She remembered vague details about how you did such things—razors, pills; a girl at school had once become comatose because she had drunk quart after quart of vodka. Robin wouldn't say how she did it, but she told Dore her father had made her go for counseling and her mother had hidden all the scissors in the house and kept the aspirin in her boots in the hall closet, the second place Robin had looked.

She cried out her frustration and fear over the phone, and she let Dore comfort her. "You're not alone," Dore said. "I won't let you be," and then Robin cried some more. By the time she hung up, she felt parched, exhausted. She went to the sink and leaned into it, gulping water from the spigot. She got a Pepsi from the refrigerator and let the fizzy, silky flow of it burn her throat, cauterizing what tears she had left.

When Leslie came home, her spirits high, Robin was as distant as if she had been on another planet. It was a state that occurred more and more. Sometimes Robin was red-eyed, stormily raging about the house, barricading herself in her room. Sometimes she was dreamy-eyed and still. Now, though, she was frozen, sleepwalking through the dark dining room toward her room, gently closing her door without even saying hello.

It worried Leslie. She waited until she was sure Robin was in bed and sleeping before she began scavenging the house for clues to Robin's sudden new shift in behavior. She saw makeshift Ricks hiding out in the bushes, saw Robin's thumbs hitching a way to places where she might never be found. She looked behind the couch cushions for drugs, her fingers curling around stray pennies, pricking on a sewing needle. She sniffed the air for alcohol, for cigarettes that might belong to some boy she'd really rather not know. She stood in the center of every room and shut her eyes, trying to make her body into a kind of radar, trying to track whatever hidden signals might be around, but the only thing that happened was that she began noticing all the things that were wrong with such an old house—the funny way the boiler clicked on, the creak in the ceiling.

She went to check on Robin, who was sleeping fitfully, tangled in the sheets, a faint patina of sweat across her forehead. Then Leslie went downstairs to call Nick, waking him, whispering about Robin as if Robin were a secret she couldn't risk exposing.

"Wait, I can't hear you," Nick said, sleepy.

She spoke a little louder. She told him how Robin was sleeping, how she wandered the house. "Something's very wrong," she said.

Now he heard her perfectly. He wanted to know if Robin had a fever, if she had eaten lunch, eaten dinner. The details somehow calmed her, made her feel that he had control of the situation. He said he was going to drive home right now; that it was just as well to go now rather than wait until morning when the traffic would be terrible.

He got dressed. He woke the clerk downstairs so he could check out, and then he drove the six hours home.

He found Leslie asleep on the couch, and he carried her upstairs to bed, he kissed her, and then he went into Robin's room. All her covers were on the floor and she was curled up, shivering, mumbling something in her sleep. He knelt beside her, straining to hear what language she was speaking to him, what message. A snag of memory caught at him. In the home. Tony, the boy who slept next to him, a stocky, dark-haired boy who wet his bed every night, who woke shamed and miserable, bunching his wet sheets into a laundry bag, his wet pajamas, telling tales about spilling water in the bed, refusing to meet any pair of mocking eyes that might be affronting him.

The home tried everything. They told him he wouldn't be adopted, but that made Tony so nervous he began wetting his pants during the day. They made him go to counseling. They set alarms that were supposed to wake him up and remind him to go to the bathroom. They had him change his own linens in the dim hours before morning. Nick would wake up to the sounds of Tony's bare feet padding and clicking on the linoleum; he'd open his eyes just enough to see the trail of sheet. But Tony ended up using too much linen, costing the home too much.

Finally, one of the counselors came in to hypnotize him. He said you could do it while someone slept; you just watched for the REM sleep, when the eyelids started rolling, because that state was the same as a trance. Every night for two weeks, Nick heard someone whispering by Tony's bed, the voice low and insistent, and then suddenly Tony didn't wet the bed anymore. He got cocky and proud about it, and Nick could sleep through the night, riding on a crest of dream, escaping.

He leaned closer to Robin, studying her restless lids. "Robin," he whispered, and she stirred a little. "Lift one finger if you hear me," he said. He held his breath, saw her turn, and in the shadows he told himself he saw her finger twitch. He leaned closer. "Listen now," he said. "You'll keep yourself safe, no matter what." He watched her for a moment. "You hate black leather, you hate motorbikes and drugs." He rubbed his eyes; he tried to catalog all the dangers, but they kept multiplying, crowding into view. "You hate wine," he whispered. He slowly stood, his knees creaking. He moved back toward her for one moment, and then he whispered, "Sweet dreams," as if that, too, were a kind of command for her to willingly follow.

He was planning to watch her all the next day, studying her, but instead, he felt her gaze on him, long and hard and so insistent he had to get up and go into the backyard just to escape it. He tromped in the scrabby grass, waving aside the big black bumblebees that liked to hover around the bushes. He told himself he should get a badminton set, that maybe he could play it with her. Or croquet. He had clients whose kids loved croquet—but then again, what were they, kids of eight, twelve at most? Robin was a teenager, and he didn't know what to do about it.

He began taking her picture out of his wallet and holding it in his hand while he drove, sometimes talking to it as if she were right there beside him. He'd carry on whole conversations, taking her part as well as his own, until the constant pressure of his fingers started warping the picture, lining her face with years she hadn't lived through yet.

He hated it when she wore her hair a new way, butchering the front with bangs, straightening it once with Curl Gone. The Curl Gone made her hair so greasy, it took a week of nearly constant shampooing to get it back to normal. He hated it when she came home one day with a tiny fake diamond shimmering in one ear, an ear that two days later became so badly infected she needed two weeks of an expensive antibiotic. She admitted piercing the ear herself, using one of Leslie's sewing needles that she had sterilized in the blue flame of the kitchen stove. She said it hadn't hurt at all, that she had packed her ear in ice and held a potato against the earlobe so the needle would go through clean. She had been so proud of it all, so sure of herself, and it had made him furious. He wanted her in braids. He wanted to be a different father, flipping his baby up in the air on a bright sunny day.

For the first time, when he was at Dore's, Robin began itching her way across his mind. Dore was getting all these crazy phone calls from some girl named Amy, just another runaway who had shown up at her door. Dore always took the calls, she never said she had company, but he sometimes heard his name mentioned, so it didn't bother him; it soothed him into thinking he was still first in her mind.

When she finally hung up, usually after a half-hour, she didn't apologize. Instead, she was thoughtful. She curled up around him on her old sofa and told him story after story about this girl, trying to make him see her. But every word out of her mouth was a magnet, pulling him toward his own daughter, making him want to get up and call her to make sure she was all right. He didn't know how to sort things. He needed his family to be settled in Pittsburgh; he needed them to be his family. But here, now, right in front of him was Dore, unbuttoning his shirt, rubbing her nose against his chest, so that he forgot everything but the feel and smell and taste of her, the dizzying way she was stopping time, the sheer miracle of it.

Lines kept blurring. At sales meetings, he began noticing that some of the men who had started out as salesmen with him were now working desk jobs—editing the books he was selling, designing the jackets, and managing production. He didn't know them that well; he had never been to their homes, and had never thought to invite any of the other sales reps to his. But still he had small-talked with them, shared a beer after the meetings, and he had always felt they were somehow friends simply because they were all on the road.

Now Henry Robson, who used to joke to Nick that the one territory he really wanted was Paris, France, told Nick he was in PR. It was less money, he told Nick, but it made up in time at home. He had just gotten married, he said, and he had a baby son, a rough-and-tumble kid named Mike, whom he couldn't bear to be away from. "I'm home every goddamned night by six," he said. "I get to feed him and burp him, and I even get time with my wife." He shook his head at Nick; he wanted to know how Nick could still stand the road.

"I like it," Nick said.

Henry just looked at him for a moment. "But you have a family, too," he said, and then he mentioned an opening in production that Nick might be interested in.

Nick began noticing, too, that the new salesmen were all so young, some of them fresh out of college. They worked out with weights and ran around to after-hours clubs in strange cities. He didn't feel like talking to any of them; he didn't feel any connection.

He began to feel a little unsure. He doodled all the raises and bonuses he had been given in just one year; he wrote down all the buyers he knew who had been in the same stores since he first started selling. He began sitting through the sales meetings sunk against his chair. He stopped arguing about the books he didn't think he could sell, telling himself he was a kind of company unto himself, that he'd promote or bury books the way he wanted. He kept a yellow legal pad by his side and sketched out his plans, private strategies that pleased him.

Sometimes, watching Henry, he thought about what it would be like staying in one place all the time—coming home at six every night to a dinner cooking, to a table set with a white cloth, sterling at each place, maybe even a decanter of wine; being able to meet the woman he loved for lunch anytime he wanted, for sweet summer kisses, for the intoxications of afternoons in bed.

He started feeling so uneasy, so out of breath, that he had to excuse himself from the room. His memories were a raw tangle. He couldn't center on whom he really wanted to be with—wife and daughter, or Dore. And it was just the whole matter of staying in one place, the sheer, final terror of it, because when you chose to stand still, when you weren't the one doing the leaving, then you were the one giving someone else that chance—you were the one risking being left.

Dore found herself looking forward to Amy's calls. Sometimes she wouldn't go out at night until she was sure the phone wouldn't ring. Other times, she'd find herself rushing home to be near the phone, leaving a movie before the closing credits started to roll, irritating just about everyone in the theater as she bumped her way over knees and legs. Amy was the first of her kids to keep reconnecting, to seem actually to like her after the first flush of need had faded. Amy wasn't just telling Dore problems now; sometimes she talked about her life a little: how she loved to swim, and that the thing she liked best was diving, because it was dangerous—if you were a fraction off, you could break your neck, sprain your back, ruin yourself so you'd never in your life be able to do anything more strenuous than a dead man's float. Amy had lists of dangers she was sure could never touch her, including some she had already thwarted: hitching; Rick. There was only one danger she wasn't so sure of, and that was the one she refused to talk about.

Her mood switched on and off like electric lights. She'd talk about herself, about school, and Dore could feel her loosening up, becoming almost fluid enough to float through the wires if she chose to. Then she'd tentatively start asking Dore things, hushing down into silence to listen, and when she spoke again, her voice was wire-tight; the distance between them seemed to have expanded.

It was so odd to Dore. She had long ago stopped having any real confidants—not since Flora, really—and she liked being able to spill out as much of her life as she chose to Amy, but she learned to read Amy's silences as if they were braille, to know when to stop. She figured that something in her life was touching on one of Amy's wounds, that that was what was making her so silent, and that when Amy was finally willing to open up, the silences would stop.

Dore missed Amy when she didn't call. The girl touched her. All she had to do was say that she needed to talk to Dore, that Dore was important to her. Dore's whole being hinged around that word— need. It would warm her, and when the feeling started to wane, there was the next call, come to refuel her.

Amy's need made it all right that Dore was alone in the purpled fluorescent light of the supermarket, tumbling frozen TV dinners into her cart because it was lonely preparing meals just for herself. Amy's need made it all right for Dore to buy more paperback novels than she could read, rather than risk being alone in the house with just the TV for company.

It even made it easier when she was at the Suds'n Duds, and there amid her lace panties and tank tops she found a pair of Nick's jockey shorts, torn at the waistband, left in her tangle of clothing from the last time he had been with her. She had lifted the shorts to her cheek, not caring that the woman next to her was giving her a fishy stare, and at the moment when her desire turned to despair, she remembered Amy. She wanted to talk to her. She liked the feeling of being an authority on something, as if helping with someone else's pain might heal her own.

The connection with Amy made her want more connection with Nick. She had two people to miss now. She got tense; she brooded. Her dreams had Nick in them as well as Amy, and when she woke up alone in her bed, she felt there would never be enough to sustain her. When she saw Nick, all she could think about were the minutes, the seconds. She spaced his visits out by breakfasts and lunches. She glowered at his car as if it were her enemy, kicking the tires when she passed it. Sometimes it was hard to enjoy just being with him, because his impending departure kept crowding her pleasure.

And lately, too, he was different about her, he was sad. He watched her, frowning, and then gave her a half-smile and blamed his mood on work. At night sometimes she woke to find him sitting up watching her sleep, but he'd never tell her why. "Oh, your mouth was wide open," he teased. "I was watching the flies going in." She socked him with a pillow. "It was not," she said. Once, when she had a cold and had to sleep sitting up against a buttress of pillows instead of cradled in his arms, she woke up coughing and noticed him with surprise. He was sleeping on his back, his arms tenderly cradling his pillow as if it were her, held to his heart. She sat there, amazed, and told herself that a man who could miss her enough to fantasize her into a pillow just might be a man who could stay.

It was Amy who made her gather the courage to confront him. Amy kept saying she didn't feel love, she felt abandoned, and she didn't know what to do about it. "Sometimes you have to ask for what you need," Dore said.

"And what if you still don't get it," Amy asked.

Dore told her that you never knew if you didn't try—and as soon as she said that, she felt her nerves exposed.

She finally broached the subject to Nick one day when they were walking around Harvard Square, the two of them buying books and records. "We don't have to live here," she blurted out by the Harvard Coop. "We could move. I could teach anywhere. I could be a cashier in a supermarket. One of my students did it for a summer and ended up making more money per hour than I did."

Nick stopped walking and turned to her, his face miserable.

"I hate these halfway measures," she said.

He fingered the ends of her hair. "They stink, don't they," he agreed.

"You think that?" she said.

"Of course I do. I miss you. I love you. I'm just not sure what to do about it right now."

"Marry me," she said, and then burst into tears. A young mother with a baby passed by, her eyes averted. "I never wanted to marry you before, but now I do."

Nick put his arms about her and pressed her face along his shoulder where it fit. "Don't you love me the way you used to?" she asked. "I was your first love." She looked up at him; he looked like he was breaking apart. It made her words dry up inside of her. She placed her hands on either side of his face. "Is it no dice?" she asked.

"No, it's not that," he said. He looked toward the glass windows of the market, out toward the darkening streets, and she suddenly wasn't so sure she wanted to know what it was at all.

It wasn't a good three days. He just kept looking sadder and sadder; he seemed to be somehow contracting. She'd go out of the room for two minutes, and when she came back in, he looked caged. He was always at the windows, at the doors, always checking and re-checking the black itinerary notebook he carried, until she felt like ripping it from his hands and burning it.

He told her he loved her, said he just wanted more time being with her before they really thought about marriage, but she saw how sorrowful his face was, and she waited for the old signs of departure to show up. Always, when it grew time for him to leave, he'd start folding himself up as neatly as a suitcase; he'd start pulling away so that by the time he got into his car, it was as if he were already gone from her, as distant as a star she'd wish upon.

But when he left this time, things were different. She asked him to drive her to the Star Market at the far end of town, a store so dirty she was sure the food was diseased. She said she needed a special brand only they stocked, but really she didn't need a thing; she just wanted to ride with him, to see what the road might feel like as he was leaving her.

He seemed happy that she was coming, and said he'd bring her back home, but she told him she was going to walk over to the library from the store; she wasn't buying anything perishable and she could easily get a cab. "Come on, that's so dopey," he said, but she was so adamant, he finally just gave in.

He made a show of carrying her from her door to his car, almost as if she were a bride, and he had her scrunch in close to him so he could buckle the two of them up in his seat belt. He kept touching her, he told her he missed her already, but he drove fast, leaning toward the wheel.

In the parking lot, where all the young mothers were pushing food carts and baby strollers, Nick kissed Dore. He gave her cab money. "Are you sure you don't want me to wait?" he asked. "I have time. I just hate leaving you here."

She shook her head. She reminded him what a pain he was to shop for, how he was always buying things that ended up uneaten in the back of her shelf.

"Pickled plums," Nick said. "Get some goat cheese, too, and we can feast when I get back."

"It'll spoil," Dore said. "Your best bet is to stay."

He touched her knee, then unbuckled the belt and got out of the car with her, and there, where everyone could see, he held her and kissed her and stroked her hair back from her brow. She pushed her bangs back down, feeling too exposed, too vulnerable. She took off her glasses, rubbing her eyes. "Now I see you, now I don't," she said.

He wouldn't get back in the car until she had gone inside the market, and even then, through the dirty glass, she could see him leaning against the front of the car, watching her. He lifted one hand in a lonely little wave.

She wandered down one aisle, stepping over crumpled store coupons, ignoring the bags of cookies that had already been torn open and raided. She kept her jacket close around her, her hands drawn in so they wouldn't touch anything, and by the time she came back to the front of the market, Nick's car was gone. She stood perfectly still until a woman banged her cart against her. "Some people would like to get by," the woman said, maneuvering. Dore blinked at her, and then she turned and walked outside to the pay phone to call herself a cab back home.

She ate cookies for dinner, polished off a whole bottle of cheap burgundy by herself, and then curled up in bed, bunched about Nick's pillow so she wouldn't feel so abandoned. She should have told him to go fuck himself, to leave her alone. She should call him and plead with him to find another trailer they could move into and be happy. She lay there, waiting for something to go right, drifting, drunk, and when the phone rang, she knocked it to the floor. "Yeah," she said, plucking up the receiver, trying to sound tough.

"Dore? Dore?"

She sat up in bed. "Amy," she said. "I'm glad you called. Oh, God, I'm glad!"

"You are?" Amy paused. "You sound funny."

"I'm not funny, I'm fine," said Dore, and then she burst into tears. "You think only you have pain?" she cried. "You think just because I'm not fourteen anymore I know how to work out my life? Don't you think I wish I had someone I could call up any time I bloody well pleased?"

There was an edgy silence on the other end of the line.

"You can't take it? Fine. Then hang up, why don't you?" Dore swiped at her runny nose with one hand. "I listen to *you*," she said. She pressed the receiver between shoulder and ear and shucked off her shirt, blowing her nose into it. The room swam in front of her.

"I'm here," Amy said, faltering.

Dore sighed. She felt suddenly scared, as if she were emptying out. "Nick just left," she said. "I want to get married."

Amy's voice started to change. It got higher, smaller; it tightened. "You're getting married? You're marrying him? You can't do that, you can't—"

"I didn't say I was—" Dore started, but Amy was getting more and more agitated, telling Dore she couldn't do that to her, not in a million years, that this wasn't supposed to happen, not when she trusted her. "Wait," Dore broke in. She said it was all right, that a marriage didn't have to change a friendship. "Is that the problem?" Dore said. "Well, now you'll have two people to visit instead of just one." She felt like she was separating out, listening to another Dore talking about another life, a life that now seemed to have nothing to do with her. And then she realized what a fool she was, talking like she was going to get married, like she was married already, and she started crying again. Her tears silenced Amy. She was so drunk she couldn't think what she was saying, her words kept spilling out.

For the first time, she began telling Amy about Susan, about how she hadn't been such a hot mother, how she had loved Nick more than she had ever loved her daughter, and sometimes even thought she had become pregnant just to please him, because the whole idea of family was so damned important to him. It wasn't enough for him to have just her; if it *had* been, they could have made it after Susan died, they could have made it after anything.

"I helped you, though, didn't I?" Dore demanded. "That money I gave you when you were here, I bet it helped, didn't it? I would have put you up here as long as you liked. And all our talks over the phone—the way we're talking now." She pushed back her bangs, feeling an undercurrent—Nick's fingers in the same motion, out in the supermarket parking lot—and it made her whole body weaken. She sat up. "If I were your mother, I bet you never would have run away from home. I bet we would have always been close. We could have been real friends. Not just biology, not just relations."

"You had a baby," Amy said, her voice dazed, drifting.

"Had," Dore said.

"I have to get off the phone," Amy said quietly and then she hung up, leaving Dore only the surprising shock of silence, the dizzying, drunken curl of her thoughts. She settled herself down under the covers, around what she thought was Nick's pillow, and then, just as surely as she was missing Nick, she was missing Amy. She wanted the two of them to be missing her, too, noticing all that new and sudden need as though it were some marvelous hothouse flower that had just burst into bloom, miraculous and lovely, and fragile enough to remind them to take care.

THIRTEEN

• • •

Nick didn't want to choose. He had his life mapped out by the women in it, each one somehow placing him in time, bridging his way from one to the other. With Dore, he was in his past again, when everything was possible. With Leslie, he didn't have to worry about any possibilities, because things already were—he had his family, he had stability, he had a daughter who connected him to life. How could he give anything up? How could anyone?

He thought about marrying Dore, thought about her face, so soft and sleepy when she woke up in the morning, nuzzling against him; he thought how she ate her lunch, how she combed her hair with her fingers, and he yearned to be with her again, he did. But then he'd get home, and there would be Leslie with her hair fanned out around her, in one of his old shirts and her jeans, opening up to him for a moment before she slowly closed shut again, making him miss her as surely as he missed Dore. And there would be Robin, his own features subtly altered in her face. Her hair snapped and curled the way his did, but hers was fireworked with golds and reds. He saw her mirroring his walk, frowning and biting down on her bottom lip when she read, the same way he did, and it moved him so much it was all he could do to watch her in a kind of dumb wonder, a gratitude, as if she herself had chosen his characteristics as an act of love.

This time at home Robin trailed him. She wanted to go with him to the market for juice, she wanted to help bring up the lawn sprinkler from the basement, and he kept feeling her eyes on him, although she wouldn't look at him directly. He found her in his bedroom one evening, going through his things—his suitcase, his top drawer, the pockets of his suits, her face dark. "Hey—" he said.

"I needed some change," she said, flustered. "Do you have quarters?" She looked at the floor. "I needed change," she said again.

"Tens or twenties," he said, but she didn't make a funny face at him, didn't roll her eyes; she simply took the two dollars in quarters he managed to find, and then half an hour later, as he was walking by the den, he saw her foraging in his desk. As soon as she spotted him, she left, mumbling some excuse about needing a pen with black ink, not waiting for him to try to find one. He opened the drawers and tried to figure out what it was she had been looking for, or what it was she had found.

It wasn't just him, though. At dinner she stared at Leslie. "Is something wrong?" Leslie asked. "Are my jeans on backward?"

Robin had come to the table with pink lids and red lipstick, with lashes so mascaraed they looked black-and-blue. "This color would look good on you," she told Leslie, touching her eyelids. She had a tiny gold lipstick case in her hand; she showed it to Leslie.

"Not at the table, please," Leslie said, but she still twirled the color up and then twirled it back down again. "Oh, I'm not the makeup type," Leslie said.

"Sure you are," Robin said. "I could show you. She'd look just beautiful, wouldn't she?" She looked right at Nick.

"She looks beautiful now," Nick said, and Leslie turned to him, pleased and suddenly shy.

But Robin didn't let up. She went shopping and came home with a silky blue shirt for Leslie that she claimed was a belated birthday present. She brought back perfume samples in little glass vials she jammed in her pockets and rolled across Leslie's bureau for her to find. At night she went out to the library so Leslie and Nick could have the whole house alone; and when she came home, if they weren't in the same room—if Nick was reading in the kitchen while Leslie sewed upstairs—it made her crazy. She'd orchestrate things so they were all in the same room. She said there was a wonderful movie on TV; she made too much popcorn and needed help eating it. And then she stopped, watching the two of them until Leslie's hands would flutter automatically to her hair, her face, to wherever she assumed Robin was judging her, and Robin would avert her eyes.

She didn't really talk to Nick until the next week, when he was leaving for New York, and then she simply stood in front of him and asked him not to go.

"It's just three days," he said. He turned to get some clean socks. He was going to ask her what was the matter, but when he turned back around, she was gone.

She wasn't watching at the window for the car the morning he left. He used to think he'd be so relieved when she stopped doing that, but now it unsettled him, made him feel things weren't quite right.

As soon as Nick left, Robin began her steady retreat back into herself. It frightened Leslie. Sometimes when Leslie was working with a client, she'd excuse herself, leaving a hem half pinned, a sleeve hanging awkwardly on a bare arm, and go into the kitchen to call her daughter to see if she was all right. The line was always busy. She'd try again in ten minutes, in half an hour, until her client got exasperated. "Forget why you're here?" one woman sniped.

Leslie, standing there with the phone clenched in her hand, thought it a funny remark, because really, how nice it would be to forget, to stop worrying, to just get back to pulling forth a dress from a bolt of cloth, the only kind of magic she was ever able to do.

She came home and asked Robin why the line had been tied up like that, and Robin dipped her head so that her hair covered her face and said she was talking to some friend Leslie had never heard of, doing math homework over the phone. "Homework," Leslie said. She was certain it must be a boy again, but Robin was still so young, and if she was going to have any dates, Leslie wanted them to be with the proper sort of boy, a boy who would come to dinner and tease her into liking him, a boy who wouldn't meddle around with cars or emotions.

When the phone bill came, Leslie glanced casually at the amount, and then stopped short. It was so high. Nick kept a separate line for his business calls and was pretty strict about it, and she herself didn't call long-distance except for an occasional call to her folks. It had to be Robin. She trailed a finger down the list of phone numbers:

617-555-6788, over and over again. A half-hour. Twenty minutes. Once, two hours. She wondered how many other calls to that number had been made from the home of a friend, whose parents might be angered at the size of their bill. She knew the area code was Boston from all the calls she had made to Nick, and for a moment she felt a stubborn flash of sympathy for Robin, a bond built out of telephone wires and the endless neediness of loving. She looked at the dates of the calls, days when Nick was out of town, in other cities. It made her feel so strange. Her husband and her daughter's boyfriend might have been in the same city—a boyfriend, that must be it—and she couldn't imagine how Robin had met such a boy.

She didn't know what to do. She'd have to confront Robin with the bill, but she knew Robin would just pay it off with allowance money and wouldn't give Leslie any information at all about anything. Leslie thought maybe she'd call the number, just to see who answered. Maybe she could pick something up from the boy's voice. She had a sudden nervous feeling that it might be Rick again, transplanted, dangerous in new ways. And if it was someone perfectly proper, perfectly nice? Well, she didn't want to interfere with Robin, she just wanted to know what was going on. She yearned to somehow be a part of it.

She called on a night when Nick was in Philadelphia and Robin was swimming at the "Y."

The line rang only once, and then a woman's voice said, "Yes?" Leslie felt foolish. She rubbed at her eyes, and then the woman said, "Amy, is that you, honey?" and the voice was so kind, it made Leslie want to speak.

She didn't give her full name, not at first. She politely explained about the phone bill, all those calls to that number. "I think it's probably my daughter, Robin, who's calling, and I think it might have something to do with a boy." She felt more and more awkward, more and more guilty, too. "Uh, do you have a son?" Leslie asked.

There was silence on the other end, and Leslie thought, Why, this woman didn't know what her son was up to. Or maybe she did know—maybe she got calls like this all the time.

"Listen," the woman finally said, "I don't have a son, and no one named Robin has been calling me."

"No son?" Leslie said. "But I don't get it then. The numbers are right here, for an hour at a time. She must be calling you—she has to be."

There was silence again, thickening through the wires, and then the woman cleared her throat. She said she didn't know if she should even be talking about this, but there was this one girl who called her, but her name was Amy. "I can't tell you what we talk about, it's all in confidence." The woman laughed a little. "I guess I'm kind of like a psychiatrist sometimes."

"I'm kind of like a mother," Leslie said, her voice tight.

"All right, all right," Dore sighed. She told her what she could. She sketched in Robin's features, the hair, the stubborn strong voice, the way she had just shown up on her doorstep.

"It's got to be Robin," Leslie said, "but why would she come to you? How would she know?" She bit down on her lip. "What did she say to you?"

"Nothing so terrible, she just wanted to talk," Dore said. "I'm sorry—it was personal. I can't betray a confidence. I feel funny telling you what I'm telling you now, except if you're her mother—"

"I *am* her mother."

"Maybe," Dore said.

"She's never even been to Boston," Leslie said. "Her father gets there on business sometimes, he's due there in a few days, but Nick's never taken her with him, although I remember she did want to go."

"Nick?" Something snaked up along Dore's spine.

"My husband sells books," Leslie said. "He's out of town a lot. I don't know, I think it upsets her. No, I know it does." She curled the phone cord about her hand.

"Excuse me, what did you say your whole name was?" Dore asked, keeping her breath quiet, and as soon as she heard Leslie say Austen, something ruptured inside of her and she had to sit down.

"And your name?" Leslie asked, but then something happened to the phone—it gave an odd click and there was a dial tone. Leslie called back, but the line was busy, and when she called the operator to check on it, she was told the phone was off the hook. It made her a little angry. But she had a number now, she could call back. These calls weren't about a boy, she thought. They were about something else, something she would have to get from the one person who could storytell it to her, from Robin.

Dore didn't know what she was doing. The whole world seemed to be moving in slow motion except for her, and she was moving in small, brilliant panics, she was all bone. She watched the phone, and when it rang, the sound crawled up along her spine. She was half-certain that if she dared to touch the receiver, her own pain might electrocute her.

She walked. She tried to go into neighborhoods that were unfamiliar, that seemed as lost to her as her own self. She kept her head down, ignoring people if they smiled at her, if they excused themselves past her. She scowled at the dogs lazily loping past her. I'm a stranger in a strange land, she thought. She wished she were getting on a plane and just leaving. For the first time, she felt exactly the way her students probably did, looking for safe haven; for a hand to hold back the fever that raged away inside of you; for a rational, calm voice that knew just what you should do next.

Amy, she thought. Betrayer. She thought the girl had loved her a little. She thought they had a real connection. But all those questions, all those calls—they took on a different meaning now. Who knew how she had found out? Who knew how careless Nick was? But there it was. Amy, a lying little heart, small and hurting as a cramp, pulling her life and her past from her for nothing at all.

Oh, Lord, she used to think how Nick might like Amy, how maybe Amy could be their bridge to another child of their own. What a fool she was. And Nick, sad and silent, gutless at giving. "He's not worth you," her mother used to say about boys she disapproved of. "He's hardly your kind." She'd said it about the butcher when Dore was seventeen. She'd said it about Nick when she found out they were living in a trailer court, a time when Dore's heart had kept expanding because she was so happy. Why had she kept thinking he'd change, be different?

She thought suddenly, What if she never had anyone else to love in her life, anyone else to love her back? It was difficult, being a teacher. She heard the talk in the teacher's room, the stories, the fix-ups that didn't quite take, the lives going nowhere, the kids in your classes always the same age, year after year, while you just got older and older. Whom did you meet teaching kids all day long? Divorced, unhappy parents trailing into the PTA twice a year. Other teachers, most of them women.

It was a fluke, her meeting Nick. She remembered the other teachers talking about it, joking about how they were all planning to pretend they'd misplaced their glasses, even when their vision was so perfect they could spot a kid chewing gum a mile away. They all wanted a catch like Nick. Oh, yes, what a catch! Tumbling right out of her hands, taking pieces of her right along with him.

It was fate, all fate and all timing. One minute more and she never would have met Nick at all, her life would have wound its way into something different. One minute less and Susan might still be alive. In another few minutes, she wouldn't have been home to get that call from Leslie, she would have been at the market, buying wine, squeezing fruit. She wondered what would have happened then—whether Nick would have divorced Leslie and married her; whether he ever would have admitted that she wasn't his first-and-always. Maybe things would have just stretched out along the same path until she got fed up.

Married. How could he be married to someone who wasn't her? She tried to frame a picture of Leslie in her mind, but the only face she could conjure up alongside Nick's was her own. Maybe Leslie would be the lucky one, maybe she'd never even realize whom she had been talking to, or maybe it wouldn't even matter. An old girlfriend always mattered less than a wife, didn't she?

She crouched in bed, miserable. She remembered Leslie mentioning Pittsburgh, and she called Information and got the number, planning to confront Nick. But the first time she called, Amy—Robin—answered, and, stunned, Dore hung up.

She tried calling him at work, and in the end he just showed up. "I thought I'd surprise you," he said.

She bolted back. "Don't you try talking to me!" she cried.

"What did I do?"

"It's what you *didn't* do." She decided she couldn't speak, and she was too angry to stay still, so she went outside and started walking. Nick walked along with her, a little in front of her, so she'd have to see him just by looking where she was going.

"Talk to me," he said. "Speak."

"Leslie called me," she blurted, and as soon as she had that name in her mouth, it was as if she had bitten down on rusty tin. "Your daughter, Amy—Robin—was *here*," she cried.

He froze in the middle of the sunny sidewalk, his face changing. "Here?" he said. He washed one hand over his face, looking at the sky, the walk, anywhere but her. "Dore—"

"Shut up," she said. "You have a *wife*. You have a *daughter*. You have what I'm supposed to have, what I'm supposed to *be*, and you think you have any right to come here and talk to me?"

"I have a right," he said, grabbing her arm. "What did they tell you?"

"I hate you," said Dore. "I'm right here and you're talking about someone else. You're so anxious to know, you ask them."

"I love you," he said, his voice fierce. "I loved you the day I saw you struggling in that hall. I loved you when you shut me out with nine million students, when it was all I could do to get you to look at me, let alone talk, and I love you now." He pulled her roughly in front of him. "You *listen*," he said. "I was fucked up, I was wrong. I don't know why I didn't tell you—I was afraid of what you'd think, I was afraid you'd disappear. I'll marry you now. I don't care about anything, just don't leave, just don't."

"You didn't want to give any of it up, did you?" said Dore. "You didn't want to marry me at all. It was just a daydream, like winning the lottery."

"Jesus, I *love* you," said Nick. "How many more times do I have to say it?"

"What about your wife? You love her? What about your daughter?" She yanked herself free. "I'm second-best to you, and you're crazy." She swiped at him.

"*Listen* to me," Nick said; but she broke free, she shouted at him that she never wanted to see him or his family again, that he had better not come around, because she would call the cops, she would create a scandal that would bruise more lives than her own. He called her name, he came toward her, his face miserable, and she started running, staring straight ahead so she wouldn't have to notice whether or not he was following her, wouldn't have to face the possibility that he wasn't.

She wasn't sure where she was going. She heard his steps, his voice, scraped from his throat, but she kept taking shortcuts on him, sprinting across lawns, through bushes, into alleys he knew nothing about, and then she entered a neighborhood that was unfamiliar, and when she glanced back, he was gone. Sometimes a car would beep at her, but mostly she felt as if she were running hidden, and she stopped only when her side stitched up on her, and she leaned against a pole.

When someone touched her, she jerked up, her hand raised to strike, but it wasn't Nick, it was a man in black sweats, asking her if she was okay. "You're nuts to run in boots," he said. He made her breathe in and out deeply. He said he got cramps all the time when he didn't pay attention to how he ran, and then he introduced himself. His name was Ray and he taught anthropology at B.U. and he said she ought to rest. He knew this coffee shop. She didn't know why, but she let him take her, and when she was sitting in the booth, exhausted, when she managed to look up into a strange, bright face, she thought only that it wasn't Nick's. And she knew suddenly that Nick's face would be one she would miss every morning and every evening of her life from now on, and there would never, ever, be anything she could do about it.

Nick sat on Dore's front stoop, sure she would come back if he stayed there long enough. She'd be exhausted, her pain would be dulled, and he'd be able to talk to her. Her love might refuel—everything might be all right.

He was losing everything. He didn't have his family the way he used to, he didn't have his work the way he used to, and now he didn't seem to have Dore. He thought about Robin being with Dore, and it chilled him. He couldn't imagine how she had known, why she had kept calling, and what he was going to do about any of it.

The afternoon light was dying. Men and women were coming home with briefcases, stepping over him. He got up. He thought about leaving Dore a note, but he couldn't find a pencil, and, too, he kept having visions of Robin finding his words on Dore's mailbox. He traced his hand on her mailbox, on her name that she had handwritten, and then on impulse he dug the name out and put it in his pocket like a lucky charm. He had thought that once—he had thought nothing could go wrong as long as she was in his life, as long as *someone* was. He remembered his dizzy relief whenever he came back to Pittsburgh and there was Leslie, among her pins and her patterns, getting up to fling her arms about him. And he thought about Robin, how he wanted her frozen in time.

He suddenly thought of this one boy from the home. Mike, who had actually lived with foster parents for so long that everyone was certain he'd be adopted. After he'd been gone two years, they all stopped talking about him; they let him fade into memory, into a kind of dull hope that what had befallen him might befall anyone. And then, one day, he was returned to the home, driven up by a cheerful, tanned couple who said nothing was wrong, he was a won-derful boy, but they had simply changed their minds about having a boy around.

Mike kept running away, running back to the people he insisted were his family, and each time they brought him back, until finally they called the school and told them to pick him up because they didn't want to waste the gasoline. Mike had stopped running after that. The kids had befriended him, but Nick remembered how he had never been able to look at Mike without feeling a deepening chill, without craving warmth.

He walked down the block to his car. He felt a terrible, dangerous tide moving in toward him, tugging, pulling him back toward what he was, what he had always been, an orphan, belonging to no one.

Robin, terrified, stayed up in her room, the door shut. She had come home to find Leslie with the phone bill fanned in one hand, her face terrible. "I spoke to your Dore," Leslie spat out, saying the name as if she knew everything connected to it. Robin hadn't even thought to lie. She had just sat there on the couch opposite Leslie, spilling out the story, crying, half in fear, half in relief, and when she finally looked at Leslie, Leslie's face was bleached of color and her hands were shaking.

Leslie got up slowly. She acted as if she didn't even see Robin anymore. As she walked, her fingers seemed to read the tables, the walls, and when she got to the door, she quietly stepped out.

Robin didn't move. She sat on the couch for over three hours, trying to figure out how she should be positioned when Leslie came back in. Should she be slumped over and miserable? Should she be erect and stoic? Should she even be still sitting right where Leslie had left her?

When Leslie finally did walk through the front door, Robin bolted upright. "What's the matter with me?" Leslie said quietly. "I'm your mother. Didn't you care how I might feel? I don't understand. Just who were you trying to protect?" She was so still, it frightened Robin.

"You know what?" Leslie said. "I went and called her from a pay phone outside. I didn't want to call her where you could hear, where you might get hurt. Isn't that funny? She didn't want to talk to me, but she didn't hang up, either. I kept thinking she was lying—maybe she was some crazy client who just had a crush, who made up a life with your father." Leslie straightened. "She slipped out a few de-tails—things no one else could know unless they were close. She said—" Leslie's voice cracked. "She said, 'How's Robin taking this?' And that's when I did to her what she did to me before. That's when I hung up." Leslie looked at Robin. "She has my husband," she said. "But I swear to God, she isn't getting my daughter."

Leslie had to call three locksmiths before she found one who would come over right away. He was just a young kid in jeans, and he told her he was really a writer, that he just did enough lock jobs to keep himself going. He tried flirting with Robin, who got flustered, and then Leslie marched him to the back to start him on the dead bolts. She changed front and back door locks; she put in window locks, too, and would have installed a whole alarm system except it would have taken much too long and cost too much. When he was finally finished, she made Robin come with her to try out the keys.

She called the phone company and told them she was getting obscene phone calls and had to have a new, unlisted number imme-diately. She said she wanted the new number under her name and wanted no one, under any circumstances, to have access to it, no matter what they said, no matter how much they might beg and say it was an emergency.

Nick was expected home past midnight that evening, and Leslie grew increasingly nervous. She wasn't sure he couldn't get in if he really wanted to. The locksmith had told her stories about thieves swinging like chimps from window to window, about iron bars being sawed. Rick might do anything. Oh, the house was hers, but he could still call the police and make her open the door. He could take Robin. Then again, he might not show up at all. He could have found out that she knew from Dore, and he could just count that as a finish, leaving her standing in the darkness by the window, night after night. That way he'd never know how hard she had tried to keep him away.

But at three, she heard his car. She couldn't bring herself to actually look out the window at him. She didn't want to see his face, his body; she didn't want his scent loosening her anger. She heard his steps coming up the walk, his key jamming in the lock, not fitting. The bell, when it rang, hurt her ears. She listened to it, over and over, not sure what to do, and then she heard him calling her name. It seemed to scorch from his throat—he cried it like a cat—and when she turned away from the door, her arms cradling her ribs, she saw Robin poised in the light on the stairs, in a thin cotton night-gown.

He shouted her name. She could almost feel the lights switching on about the neighborhood, the faces staring out. Then he shouted Robin's name, and without turning, Leslie shouted back, "I know everything." There was silence, then his steps fading back down, the car turning on, and Leslie locked eyes with Robin, who slowly turned from her, who went back into her room and shut the door, leaving Leslie alone in her locked house, in her darkness.

All the next day, they both stayed in the house. When Leslie spoke to Robin, her voice was so soft, Robin wasn't sure it was her mother's voice at all. For a while, Nick kept driving by the house, sometimes parking, sometimes getting out to try the door Leslie refused to answer. Robin watched him from her window. He ate hamburgers out of white paper bags that he basketball-tossed into the back seat; he smoked whole packs of cigarettes; and once, he said something to a neighbor passing by, and they both stopped talking to look over at the house. He even sent a few telegrams that Leslie was at first fooled into opening. "Forgive me," they said. "Let me talk to you, let me explain. You're my wife." Leslie began refusing them, but they still came.

He left finally, the car disappearing for one day and then another, and it was Robin who got furious. She was angry with Leslie for not somehow being able to fix things, for not softening enough to give Nick his chance to explain, to lie even, to do whatever he could to bring things back to where they'd been. And, too, she was angry with Nick for the seeming ease with which he gave up, for the way the car just glided out of her sight, and for the way he sent every single one of those telegrams to Leslie, and none of them, not one, to her.

Leslie might not have spoken to Nick, but she did have conversations with him in her mind. She asked him why he had done this, why he hadn't told her about his past. And when he answered, she could see him so clearly, feel his breath right on her neck, but the answers he gave her were blurry, the language garbled. It was a while before she realized it was she who was blurring things, she who was stubbornly refusing to hear what she most wanted.

Leslie refused to talk about anything that had to do with Nick, but she did things that showed how she felt. She came home one day and started gathering up all of Nick's things—his clothing, his papers, the endless little gifts she had given him just for loving her—and she gave them to Goodwill, keeping only one old blue flannel shirt that she sometimes slept in when she was feeling most lost. She knew how he was about his possessions—his *things*—but she didn't care. She wanted him to know what she had done, to know that he wasn't the only one who could give away what he wasn't supposed to, what he had no right to let go. And she watched Robin's reaction, almost daring her to object, to say one word, but all Robin did was turn her white, baffled face away and go back upstairs to her room.

Leslie took her wedding band to sell, and the thin gold chain she had never liked because it made her feel like Sammy Davis, Jr., the same chain she had never once taken off because it had been an anniversary present from Nick and he had taken such shy pleasure in it—and in her. She had a few more gold pieces, a few silver ones, and she walked into the first store downtown that bought metals. The man at the desk told her airily that gold wasn't doing so hot right now, that in his opinion she'd be better off waiting. When she insisted, he just shook his head. "It's your funeral, lady," he said.

He gave her just twelve dollars for everything, for pieces that were each worth four or five times that much, and as soon as Leslie felt the press of bills in her hands, she started crying. "Look, maybe I can get you four more, five tops," the clerk said, a little startled, but Leslie pushed her way outside, struggling free of the pull of a present she was doing her best to turn into a past.

She was going to do everything differently. She turned the bedroom into her sewing room; she spent four days cleaning out the sewing room, and she slept in there. She threw out everything Nick had ever given her, and she thanked God that the house had always been hers. She pierced her left ear and wore a tiny green stone in it. She stepped up her business and learned to keep dry-eyed with her clients because her tears made them suddenly remember that they had to be home early, or had to go into the other room and make a phone call. When she walked at night, she called out to the neighbors who had always watched her. She was suddenly invited up onto cool front porches, offered limeade and packaged cookies. She found out about their lives, their families—all the details she had never cared about before and only half-heard now. It was just the sound of all those voices, the caress of the cadence, that lulled her into a kind of comfort.

She and Robin, though, moved like ghosts past each other. Robin never said one thing, just looked at Leslie hard-eyed when she thought Leslie wasn't noticing. The more Robin pushed out of the house, the more Leslie wanted her home. She wouldn't drive her to the "Y" to swim nights—she said there was something wrong with the car. She wouldn't let her study at a friend's because she wasn't feeling well and might need Robin to run to Walnut Street and pick up a prescription. When Robin reminded her that they delivered, Leslie told her to watch that mouth of hers, to stop being so fresh.

Leslie couldn't help it, she couldn't make herself stop. She'd see Robin leaning along the front window and all she could think was that Robin was waiting for Nick as if he were some white knight come to deliver her out of this castle, and she would feel herself growing afraid. Every car that passed by could be Nick daring to take his daughter, daring to take another thing from her.

She made up elaborate dinners with all of the four basic food groups represented. She bought tea for Robin, international coffees for herself. Swiss Vienna Malt. Ginger Java. Apricot Java. She thought she was going crazy. Once, feeling Robin's stare on her, she stared back. "How was I any different?" Her own voice sounded strange to her, foreign.

"What?" said Robin.

"I see how it is," Leslie said. "I know what time the men around here get home, what time they go out again to their clubs or their bowling, to bluegrass bars for half the night. I'm at their houses, listening to the women waiting for their husbands to call, to come home, to just drop by. They spend more time alone than I ever did. Really. And when Nick was home," she said, "he was *home*. He was happy."

Robin stood up from the table, taking her cup.

"Stay," Leslie said. "Talk to me a little, why don't you."

Robin balanced her cup. "I don't have anything to say."

"Turn the dishwasher on, then," Leslie said.

That evening Leslie sat in the living room by herself, braiding and unbraiding her hair, thinking about tornadoes, about Danny being saved only to be sparked into oblivion by a live wire. These days, she felt the air thinning out, felt the ground blistering, giving way. You couldn't count on anything, she thought, and you couldn't escape.

She went to bed with pillows at her ears to muffle the sounds, and when in the morning she thought she heard hornets, she decided the thing to do was try to take some control, try to make herself unbendable, a strip of steel. She forced herself to get up, to start. She walked past Robin's room, the door still shut, and went downstairs. She got out the Yellow Pages and slapped them onto the kitchen table. Still in Nick's blue flannel shirt, she flipped the pages, and when her fingers found the columns and columns of lawyers, she started crying, her sobs ragged, torn from her, because it hadn't taken any time at all for her to get to this place, because it was almost natural, and, mostly, because now there wasn't any reason at all not to pick out one of those numbers and go ahead and dial it.

FOURTEEN

• • •

At first Nick stayed in a Pittsburgh hotel. When that got too expensive, and too lonely, he sublet a small furnished one-bedroom over in Squirrel Hill, on a densely shaded street just ten minutes from his family. He brought almost nothing of his own into the apartment. He didn't want to feel that this stay had any sort of permanence to it, that this was anything at all like how things were going to be.

He called Dore, but she never picked up the phone. He sent her letters that came back in the mail still sealed, and then he stopped putting a return address on them and they didn't come back at all. It was easier that way—he could at least imagine her reading them. He drove by Leslie's house and parked, watching the lights inside dim and brighten and then fade back toward black. He rang her bell, and he wrote her letters, too, with his new address, his new phone number firmly inked across the top. He slept with the phone crooked in his arm, willing it to ring, willing a voice to wake him from his night.

He was trying to park the car one morning when a man in a black suit approached him and called him, questioningly, by name. "Yes," said Nick, waiting, and then the man politely handed him an envelope and turned to leave. As soon as Nick ripped open the envelope, he saw the legal writing and knew what it meant. He stuffed it back into the envelope so he wouldn't have to read any more.

He tried to call Leslie all afternoon, and finally he called the lawyer whose name was on the papers. He told the lawyer there must be

some mistake. "No mistake," the lawyer said. "Do you have counsel
of your own?"

"Counsel? I don't need counsel," Nick said.

"Good," the lawyer said pleasantly, "then she'll be able to get the
divorce by default."

Nick hung up. He looked at the papers again. She wasn't asking
him for anything; all she wanted was to keep what was hers—the
house, her business, and she wanted custody of Robin, though Robin
could visit him whenever she wanted.

He thought suddenly that Robin would never want to visit him,
not now, and then he thought of going away for a while, letting
things quiet down before he tried to patch them back into place.

He didn't know where to go. At first he thought of all the places
where his clients were, and he circled those points on the map.
Then gradually he began to realize that his job was now part of the
problem. He didn't feel like talking to his clients anymore. He didn't
like it when they asked about his family, and he didn't want to ask
about theirs. Selling didn't interest him the way it used to, either.
Suddenly, he didn't know how to tell a buyer what he should do, not
even in a matter as simple as reordering a book that had sold out. He
didn't know how to be friendly when he felt terrible. As soon as he
walked into a store, all he could think about was getting out again.

He had vacation time coming up, three weeks of it, and he had
enough money saved to take even more. Nothing was final. Nothing. He'd call it a leave of absence, that was all, a kind of hibernation of the soul. He wired the people he had sublet the apartment
from, telling them he had to leave, giving them two months' extra
rent and a promise to sublet the sublet. He sent postcards to both
Dore and Leslie, scribbling on both sides so they would read his
words despite themselves. He wrote, "GOING AWAY—I LOVE YOU,
NICK." He called and called, using up the time he should have spent
packing, always keeping the phone close.

He sublet the sublet easily, and then took a day and drove to
Robin's school. He walked right in to the principal's office, the same
easy way he had when she was little and he had wanted to take her
on an all-day outing. He wasn't sure what he was going to do, how
he was going to act. He saw himself just driving and driving with
her, the two of them loose and easy in the front seat, breezing their

way out to Arizona, to Mexico. Sometimes he saw Leslie in the back
seat, quietly talking to Dore. Oh, God, his family.

The principal was a tired-looking blonde. She pumped Nick's
hand. "I like to see parents taking an interest," she informed him
cheerfully. "Especially fathers." She kept talking about Robin, about
what potential there was if the girl would just buckle down a bit. She
had to ask a computer where Robin was right now, and then she
called out to an overweight boy in jeans and a green flannel shirt
who was stapling fliers together. "I need you to play messenger,
Bob," she said.

"Beats this," Bob said. "I'm getting staples in my fingers."

She scribbled him a pass. She wrote down where Robin was and
told him it would behoove him not to dawdle because she knew
exactly how long it should take him to get back. When she turned
back to Nick, Nick saw Bob give her a Nazi salute and then smartly
goose-step away.

Nick waited nearly half an hour before Robin showed up. Her face
seemed to be flying off in all directions when she saw him. He
couldn't make out any one expression, just a melding and shifting of
many. He took her over to the side of the hall, touching her shoulder. Her eyes were very hard and bright. "I knew you'd come to see
me," she said.

"I'm going away," he said, and then she stiffened; she strode from
him, pushing her way out the front doors and into the street.

The principal looked warily at Nick. "I'll take care of it," Nick
said.

He went outside and got in the car and drove, looking for her. He
was staring so hard at the sidewalks, at the alleys, that he didn't even
see the cab swerving toward him, not until he heard the horn, until
he heard the other driver shouting at him to goddamned watch.

Watch—that was what he had been doing, what he did. He pulled
the car over to the side and looked blindly out at the empty road.

Dore's line was disconnected. Leslie stayed on the phone with her
lawyer or with her friend Emma, talking out her past, crying sometimes. Robin sat out in the back and could hear her. Leslie said how
unfair it was—now that he didn't have her, now that things were
ruined, he was acting just the way she had always hoped. Being

sweet. Sending cards and letters, all that sugar through the mail, calling, parking his car out front—oh, not anymore, but before the divorce papers, he did. It was as if he knew the secrets to pull her back, only now she had to shut herself off from them, now she couldn't let herself think they meant anything other than a soggy heart trying to heal itself whatever way it could. When Leslie talked about Robin, she lowered her voice so Robin couldn't hear. They never spoke about Nick between them, and never mentioned Dore.

Robin felt completely alone, attached to nothing. For months she kept expecting Nick to show up at her school again. She wore her best blouses, her most adult skirts. He'd have to court her, she told herself. He'd have to be the one to do the proving, because she was going to be aloof and snooty at first; she was going to be untouchable. She waited for him. She got passes and left class so she could parade past the long open windows by the road, where he might drive by and see her. She was tense, expectant. On her fifteenth birthday, she stood out in front of the house and waited for the mailman, sure there would at least be a card, and when there wasn't, she told herself it must have gotten lost in the mail.

Nick never showed up. He never called. He wasn't one of the drivers who honked at her. She kept calling Dore's disconnected number; she kept calling Information to see if there was a new one. She missed talking to Dore. At night, Leslie would grab a jacket and stride purposefully out of the house, and Robin would just wander around her room. She couldn't bear it, not knowing if Nick was with Dore, if they were going to get married, circling back to a past before she had even existed.

She kept to herself at school. She was in the tenth grade then, and she spent a lot of time in the science lab doing experiments. It was quiet and orderly in there; she could do the same experiment over and over, and every single time she'd come up with the same answer. It comforted her. It made her feel there was some stability in her life, and she began showing up so often, the science teacher gave her a permanent pass.

She liked him. "Legs," the kids called him, because his name was Douglas Nylon. He was new that year, young and funny, and he wore thick Coke-bottle glasses and his hair slicked back. He was a good teacher. He brought in plants that smelled like rotting meat and that he said were pollinated by flies; he brought in a pitcher plant that dosed insect victims with a narcotic before it began the business of devouring them. He let the kids call him Douglas, until one day the principal came by and heard that, and the next day Douglas cleared his throat and told the class they had to call him Mr. Nylon from now on. He said he didn't quite see the point, but he had always been one who liked to play by the rules.

A few kids didn't believe him. They called him Douglas, and he looked right through them. There were gibes about it. "Playing by the rules," someone snorted. "Kissing ass is more like it." But Robin found herself taking sudden new note of him, a man who walked an unbendable path, a man who could be trusted.

She started watching him. He wouldn't accept a paper if it was ten minutes late, because those were his rules. He wouldn't let someone into class late, either—he said you were either interested or you weren't, and if you weren't, why were you taking his class? She began to look forward to the jokes he always cracked while he handed back their papers, to the same expression of annoyance that flickered in his eyes when the bell rang. She knew what to expect with him— he made her feel safe.

She was alone in the lab one day, trying to clone carrots, when she started crying. She happened to look up and she saw Douglas passing, and she dipped her head again, and he continued to walk. She quickly sluiced back her tears and tried to concentrate on her tiny furls of carrot, but in a minute he was back, slapping a chocolate bar against the table. "Come on, it'll make you feel happy," he said.

"Sugar's junk," she said.

"Junk? Who the hell told you that?" He sat down beside her. "Chocolate has the exact same chemicals that your body manufactures when it's in love." He tried to get a glimpse of her face. "It'll make you feel better," he said. He lifted up the bar. "I'll flunk you if you don't."

"You will not," she said, but she took part of the candy.

"So, you want to talk about it?" he asked.

She shook her head.

"Okay," he said easily. He got up, patting her on the shoulder, leaving her the rest of the chocolate, and went on down the hall.

She watched him, taking another bite, rolling the sweetness on her tongue, trying to make it last.

She didn't know how it happened. It wasn't like her old crushes, the moony falling until a boy would like her back, his attention like a signpost to his flaws—the crook in a nose, the cowlick marring a part. Douglas wasn't like the ones she usually was drawn to, the wild ones in leather and torn denims, the ones who couldn't pronounce the names of the books she kept taking from her purse so she could read while she waited for a sundae, while she waited for her bus stop, while she walked so slowly she could have been standing still. Douglas wasn't a boy at all.

Something was snapping on and off inside of her, carrying her. She didn't wake up remembering Nick wasn't there anymore, because she was rushing to shower and dress and get to school the same time the janitor did. She was dressing as neatly as she could so she could sweet-talk him into letting her in early, so she could be at the lab doing experiments before Douglas arrived.

She sat in the lab, her heart thudding, working on her carrot clones, waiting for him, and then as soon as he walked in, she felt riddled with doubt. His belly stuck out. His shirts were so terrible they pained her to look at them. Engineer shirts, short-sleeved striped cottons tucked into red plastic belts. He wore penny loafers that he actually put pennies into. She'd juxtapose him against the boys in her class and feel herself withering, tell herself this was nuts. But then, when she was in another class, the desire would hit her, and she'd have to excuse herself to go into the ladies' room and fill up a sink with cold water and gently dip her face down into it.

More and more, he was in the lab mornings when she got there. He praised her experiments, said he was delighted that she was buckling down so well, and then he told her about his life. He said he had grown up in a family of five girls, all of them wanting to be nuns, talking about heaven and Jesus. One of his sisters even had a color picture of the pope she had taken from the Sunday supplement and played with it the way she would a doll, giving it sips of imaginary tea from a cup, folding a blanket up to its chin.

"I was the bad boy," Douglas told Robin. "I stole packs of gum from the store, I skipped classes, I swore, and I slept with my hands under the covers." He laughed and Robin blushed. He told her that only one of his sisters had become a nun, and she had lasted less than a year before she fell in love with another nun and dropped out of the cloister with her. One of his sisters had a drinking problem, one dabbled in drugs; the others, he said, were fine, though no one ever went to church. "Except me," he said. "Sometimes on Christmas, I like to go. I turned out to be the Goody Two-Shoes of the family, I guess. What can I say?"

She didn't care what it was he said, only that he keep on talking to her. The silences were hellish for her. She'd go home and try to plan out conversations she might have with him, writing down possible topics of conversation, the rejoinders he might make. All she usually needed was one line to start him off, a piece of thought about learning to take photos, about learning to dance, and then he would be racing out words, telling her about the time he spent a whole weekend just photographing sneakers, about the time he was the only male in a ballet class of sixteen-year-old girls.

He was curious about her own family, but she was sure he could never love a girl who was somehow involved in her father's infidelity, so she lied. She said her mother designed dresses for *Vogue*, that she was planning a whole exclusive line for Robin now. She said her father was away on business again, but he sent her first-edition books airmail, every stop he made.

"It must get lonely, I'll bet," said Douglas, watching her.

"Oh, not so," said Robin. "We're an extremely close family."

When school was out, she'd hang around and watch his car leaving, and then she'd cab over to his neighborhood and see if he came out. He never did. When she came back home, Leslie would be all over her, wanting to know where she had been, why she hadn't called. "Why are you doing this to me right now?" Leslie asked.

"I'm not doing anything," Robin said.

"That's right," Leslie said. "No one's done anything at all around here."

"Well, *you* sure haven't," Robin said, and Leslie turned to her, steely-eyed. "You wait until you know a little more, until you get a little smarter, before you dare to say something like that to me," Leslie said.

Leslie went upstairs to sew, and when Robin passed by, she saw that her mother's shoulders were crumpled. It frightened Robin a little, made her feel as if she were floating, as if there were nothing to ground her.

She was crying in the lab again one day when Douglas came in. He sat quietly beside her, and as soon as he touched her, she blurted out that she was in love with him. He took it very seriously. He told her it was natural for a student to feel that way about a teacher, especially when they were friends, but he had to tell her that nothing like that would never happen. "I'm your teacher," he said.

"No, you're not," she said. "You're more."

"Look, it's totally unethical, first of all—"

"That makes me love you more, saying that," she said.

He got up, pacing. "No, it's impossible," he said. He grabbed up his books and told her he had to go, that maybe she had better go, too. She tried to follow him, but he was gone.

He acted differently toward her after that. Sometimes he wouldn't call on her in class, even when she was the only one with her hand up, and he wouldn't give her any more passes to the lab, even when she begged him, when she said her carrot clones would die if she didn't attend to them. He must have spoken to the janitors, too, because they wouldn't let her into the school before anyone else anymore, no matter how she teased and smiled, no matter how high she rolled her skirts.

She didn't know what to do. She wrote him letters in purple ink on white parchment, love poems and songs. She drew on the envelopes and mailed them to his home. "You could never do anything wrong," she wrote him. "You could never be less than I imagine."

She knew he got the letters, because suddenly he seemed to be looking at her differently. His eyes seemed sad, his face a little haunted, and sometimes she'd look up from her work to find him staring at her.

She walked home from school. The walk calmed her—it stretched out the day before she had to go back in the house and see the look on Leslie's face, the misery because she couldn't help missing Nick.

Robin was taking the long way home when she heard a car beep. She turned, half expecting her father, and there was Douglas, a red baseball cap pulled over his brow. He was unsmiling, but he leaned over and opened the door of his battered blue VW for her.

"Okay," he said, "so ethical isn't working. Maybe we need some new rules of conduct here."

She got into the car and he drove, keeping his eyes on the road, not saying anything until he came to a small, deserted parking lot, and then he stopped the car and turned to her. He said he didn't know what was the matter with him, that this whole thing was crazy, that he should be ashamed of himself.

"Ashamed about what?" Robin asked, but he shook his head and kept on talking. He told her he had never really been in love with anyone before, that women his age didn't take to him for long. "I was sure what you felt would just wear off. I mean, Jesus, you're my student, you're just a *kid.*" He tugged at the brim of his cap. "But you were so *there,* so around me all the time, and at first I just felt flattered.

"When I started to feel something else, I tamped it down, I told myself I was being an idiot. It was a crush, just a crush, the same silly thing you had for me, only for me it was worse, because I was the teacher and it shouldn't have been there at all.

"I was sure it would pass, I was sure, but, God, Robin, it *didn't.* It just got worse. I'd come home and I'd be thinking about you while I graded papers. I'd dream about you at night, and when I saw you in school, I thought my heart would stop because I had to make myself turn away, had to pretend I didn't care when inside I was dying. And then those letters, and—" He stopped, looking at her. "You over-whelm me," he told her. "I never in a million years would believe I'm sitting here telling you this, but I'm falling in love."

"I'm already in love," Robin said, and she tentatively touched his face.

They began seeing each other, plotting their meetings as carefully as an experiment, making sure nothing could go wrong. He still ig-nored her at school—he told her it wouldn't do to show her special favor; that he'd rather not call on her at all rather than risk someone seeing the look flooding his face when he did. No more labwork outside of class, no more walking down the corridor together. In-stead, she was to act cool toward him, do her schoolwork, and keep her eyes focused on experiments, not on him.

After school, she was to walk home the long way, taking the bus four stops out of Pittsburgh into Dormont, a small working-class town where no one knew them, where she could meet him at Rita's Coffee Shop at the corner. He bought her hamburgers and fries; he held her hand under the table the whole time he was telling her how mad this all was, that he should have his head examined, falling in love with a fifteen-year-old girl.

She kept asking him what she had done to make him love her, and when he said, "Well, you just kept at me, you were so open," she felt triumphant. She came home, her eyes sparking, and studied Leslie. "You look like the cat who swallowed the canary," Leslie said, suspicious. "What makes you so special?"

Waiting for the bus back, Douglas would draw Robin under a tree and kiss her, and the whole bus ride back, she'd feel something twitching up inside of her, yearning back toward him.

He still acted like her teacher, like he was in control. He told her she should wear her skirts a little longer, that she should part her hair on the side, and not the center, because it was more dramatic, more striking. He talked a lot about making love to her, about how important it was to do it properly since it would be her first time and she was so young. He was going to take care of everything; he had already had a great deal of experience, and he gave Robin money to get herself fitted for a diaphragm.

"I know secrets no one else knows," he said. He told her he had learned about concentration from the Chinese man who did his shirts, who loaned him books on Zen; that he had learned about lovemaking from the Chinese man's wife, who took him into the back room while her husband pressed other people's suit jackets. "We did it sitting on chairs, we did it breathing on the same beats, we did it without moving," he recited.

Robin didn't know what he was talking about, she had no one to compare him to as far as lovemaking was concerned, she had only her belief in him, her absolute trust.

"We'll plan it out," he told her. "We'll prepare it and do it right. We can get wine, some cheese, all the foods you're supposed to have. You'll see, it'll be so special."

But the first time he made love to her was in a park in Dormont. She had on a long black coat and blue jeans. Her diaphragm was at his place because she couldn't risk keeping it at home. He suddenly stopped talking and lifted up her coat and undid her jeans. He tried to enter her, but the angle was wrong; when he was facing her, he couldn't push himself in. "You should have worn a skirt," he said.

She looked up and saw two joggers going by, but she didn't care—she was almost glad to have them see her. And then he turned her around, and came into her from behind, making her cry out in surprise. He was quickly finished, and then he turned her toward him again and swooped her up, her jeans still unzipped, and carried her over to a bench. He did up her jeans for her and nuzzled her neck. "You won't get pregnant, I came outside of you," he said, stroking her hair back. "You're all right," he said. "You're fine."

Making love with him was always like that—quick, sudden. The one time she suggested they try some of the Chinese ways, his brow furrowed in annoyance. "And where are we going to get chairs in the woods?" he asked. He wouldn't let her come to his house; he said it was just too dangerous, there was too much chance of being caught. Still, he told her he loved her. He talked about going away together, because he wanted her all to himself; he was jealous of the boys at school. "I see how they look at you."

"They do not," she said. "They never do."

"Yes," he said. "It's only a matter of time before you leave me. Sweet little fifteen and big fool me."

She was charmed. "Me leave you," she repeated, astounded.

In the end, it was his love, he said, that made him resign. He knew of a teaching job out in California; he had already written to them, and he wanted to take her out there with him.

"Leave here?" she said.

"I love you. I want you to really be with me. All the time, not just in bits and pieces, not this skulking around. Don't you understand—this is for *you*. We can't be together here."

He told her he would marry her in a minute if he could. He had spent four hours in the law library checking the statutes of every single state, but the only way a fifteen-year-old could get married was if she had parental consent.

"I could never get that," Robin said.

"But we could live like we were married, couldn't we?" Douglas asked. "No one would suspect we weren't. We can buy wedding bands and wear them. You'll call yourself Mrs. Nylon, I'll call you my wife. We'll go out to California where no one knows us and we'll be man and wife in our eyes and in everyone else's. It'll be no less of a bond. And the second you hit eighteen, we'll get married for real."

"You'll marry me at eighteen?" Robin asked.

"I told you, I'd marry you now if I could. I love you. I can't think straight anymore. All I see is you, and I need you to come with me. Please, please, say yes."

"I don't know—" said Robin, torn.

"Listen, I'll take the responsibility," Douglas said. "I'll take care of everything. Nothing's wrong if there's this much love involved. Think about it, Robin, just think. Who else loves you as much as I do, as much as I will for all the days of my life? We'll be each other's family, each other's everything on earth."

Robin's heart was racing. "I'm coming," she said, and she threw her arms about him.

He had all these plans. She could finish school out there, they could have a garden. He told her the thing to do was to fade into the background, to act as if nothing unusual were going on.

So Robin began coming home right after school. It was easier being with Leslie knowing she was already starting to be gone. She sat out in the sunny backyard while Leslie tugged up dandelions. She went with her to do the grocery shopping, idly wheeling the cart while Leslie tumbled cereal and broccoli into it. Leslie, touched, bought a bolt of pale blue silk and made a blouse for Robin. "Something for special," she said, and Robin, dreamy, saw herself in a VW a little darker than the blouse, riding toward her future.

There were stories about why Douglas Nylon resigned, rumors about drugs, about his going off to write a play. The school immediately hired a young woman called Dr. Kubler, who came to class in a starchy white doctor's jacket, her glasses suspended about her neck on a red beaded chain. She didn't allow any talking in class.

"I miss Nylon," a girl whispered to Robin.

"I miss him, too," Robin said.

She didn't think about Nick showing up anymore; she didn't keep trying Dore's disconnected number in hopes it would be answered; and Leslie's arms about her didn't seem too dangerously confining. She was filled with Douglas. She felt a part of something other than her own family—and, oh, yes, she was loved. How could you doubt it with a man who was giving up everything for you, a man willing to quit the job he loved and drive across the country just so he could have you, a man who was going to marry you and be with you every second, who'd never drive off and leave you, who'd never be with anyone else?

She didn't pack anything. She took her purse and her leather jacket and left the house the day Leslie was home ranting about the divorce papers that couldn't be signed because no one could find Nick. Leslie was thrashing dishes in the sink. She called out to Robin that she could help out in the house once in a while, that it was her home, too.

Robin, half-listening, opened the front door and stepped out onto the walk, toward the bus that would take her to her future, to Douglas.

FIFTEEN

• • •

Nick drove. It was funny not working, not having to meet appointments, not having to do anything but drive. He wasn't interested in forgetting. He pressed himself to remember everything, to make the past so real it might breathe back into life again.

He sped on the highway and unrolled his life like a movie. He saw himself standing in a long white school corridor, watching Dore stumble toward him; he remembered the shape of her breasts, how pale her skin was, so that even when she managed to get something of a tan, she still looked completely untouched by the sun. He saw himself in the back of a cab, holding Leslie, while Robin struggled to get born. And he saw Robin, a toddler, teething on his itinerary book, so that when he took it from her, there were her teeth marks in the leather. He replayed scene after scene as he moved from state to state, and when it got to be too much, when it got too real, he pulled over to the side of the road and rested his head in his hands.

For a while, out of habit, he wrote in his itinerary book. He wrote down the time he made, the Kentucky Fried Chickens where he ate, the Hardy Beef Boys where he got indigestion, and, more imporant, he kept detailed accounts of when he had tried to call Leslie, and when he had tried Dore. At night, sleeping in the too soft bed of some cheap hotel, or sometimes in the back seat of the car with his legs cramped about him, he leafed back through the book, and seeing the names made him relax a little, made him feel as if he were still a part of them. In every new city, he stopped and bought postcards. He wrote "I MISS YOU," "I'M SO SORRY," "I LOVE YOU." Anyone could tell where he was just by the postmark. Anyone could follow.

He was in Michigan when he finally reached Leslie, but she was cold on the phone. She wanted to know who he thought he was calling her. She said after they were divorced she might talk to him, but not now.

"What, I'll be safe then?" he asked.

"I'm hanging up," she said.

"Let me talk to Robin," he begged, but she said Robin didn't want to talk to him any more than she did, and in any case Robin wasn't home, and then she hung up.

He was still in Michigan when he decided he wanted a lawyer. He wanted to give support money to Robin, and he also wanted to be sure he had visitation rights in writing. He called Pittsburgh, and wired a retainer to the first lawyer he called, who told Nick to call him regularly to see what was going on. Nick stayed in Michigan a few weeks, long enough for his lawyer to tell him that Leslie's lawyer said she was adamant about not taking a dime from Nick, and that as far as visitation went, Robin wouldn't discuss it. "I knew it," Nick said glumly, but his lawyer told him to give it time. "It's not like she's some little kid you can just whisk away. Visitation rights or not, if she doesn't want to see you, you can't make her."

The last thing Nick did before he left Michigan was open a bank account for Robin. He told the bank he'd be mailing in money, but he wanted all the statements mailed to his daughter. She'd open those statements just because they looked official and adult, just because they were from a bank and not from him, and she'd see the money growing into something, she'd somehow know that he was taking care of her, and that was a kind of love, wasn't it? That surely counted for something.

He drove. He stopped in Madison, hot and hungry, missing everything he had left so much that he couldn't seem to breathe right. He was planning to stay only a day or so, long enough to check in with his lawyer, to relax, but then he started walking around, and he fell in love with the lake and the boats, with the bats idly whirling around the gold dome of the capitol building, and he thought he'd stop his traveling right then and there. He rented a whole two-story house on Miffland Street for less money than it would have cost him anywhere else, and he moved in immediately, filling it with a few pieces of used furniture, a new bed, and lots of books.

He couldn't stand not doing anything, but he didn't want to take on too much responsibility. He kept telling himself that any moment he might have to leave to reclaim his old life, any second the phone might ring and it might be Dore telling him it had all been a mistake. He took a job clerking at a place called Brini's, a small bookshop owned by an old man named Jack Scarzinni, who clearly thought Nick was nuts to take a job so beneath him, a job reserved for college kids who needed book money and date money and that was about all. But Jack was also smart enough to know he'd be getting intelligent company by hiring Nick; he'd be getting another man with whom to while away the slow afternoons over a good game of chess.

Jack told Nick he had started the store himself, over fifty years ago, naming it after his wife, Brini. Brini had spent half her life worrying about how she would ever manage to run the place herself if Jack upped and died on her. "She was so crazy that way," Jack told Nick. "She wouldn't let me have an ice cream in peace because she was sure I'd have a heart attack. She wouldn't let me carry anything heavy—she'd try to heave it up herself."

In the end, though, it was Brini who keeled over and died one summer day when the mercury had climbed to 104°. She was only thirty-eight, and no one could figure out why she died, even after the autopsy. "I never forgave her," Jack said. "Lying to me like that, pretending that I was going to be the one to do the leaving. I'd never have left her. Never."

Nick liked Jack and he liked working at Brini's. He kept the stock in order, he worked the register, and when the salesmen came in, he went into the back and kept to himself.

One evening he phoned his home office in Philadelphia and told his boss he needed more time. "This is getting tiresome," his boss said, but he gave him the time anyway.

It startled Nick when he began recognizing the customers who came into Brini's, when they started recognizing him. And then people in his neighborhood began to be familiar, too. The woman next door waved to him mornings. Once, she brought him some brownies she had baked herself. "Too many rots the kids' teeth," she told him. But just the same, whenever he found himself looking forward to going to work, to coming home to a neighbor who waved to him, he told himself it was all only temporary; he straightened up and started planning his next letter to Dore, his next payment into Robin's bank account, his next call to Leslie.

Dore stopped expecting anything from anybody. She got herself an unlisted number and a new job teaching high-school English. At night she lay in bed with a book and a glass of wine. Time didn't seem to be doing anything. She was in a kind of vacuum, which was all right for her, because she knew that as soon as she saw any kind of movement, the pain would start up again, and she would remember just what she had lost, just what she no longer had any chance of having.

It surprised her when she came home one day to find a man waiting for her. It took her a moment to recognize Ray, the man who had taken her to the coffee shop that night when she had been running from Nick.

"How did you find me?" she asked him.

He grinned. He told her he had looked her up in an old phone book. When he dialed the number, he found it had been changed to an unlisted one, but he had taken a chance that her address was still the same. "So come have another coffee with me," he said; and simply because she was lonely, she said fine.

He began coming around. She told him the truth—that she didn't care whether he came around or not, that she didn't have anything to offer him right now. "Oh, I don't think that's so true," he said. He came over every Friday; he was polite and unpushy. He brought her comic books and daisies, gifts so cheap, or so silly, that she couldn't possibly find any reason to refuse them. He treated her hostile moods as nothing more than squalls, which would blow over any moment if he just stuck around and waited.

"This is never going to work out," she told him. "So don't think that it is. I don't want a relationship. I can't even handle a friend." She wouldn't let him call her during the week, and when she found herself thinking about him, she got her jacket and took a walk. Sometimes she thought about hiring a detective to check up on him and make sure he didn't have a wife in the background, another woman he liked to bring comic books to. But that would have meant that she cared enough to worry, so she dropped the idea.

She slept with him sometimes when she was the most lonely, when she was missing Nick, but she would never let him stay at her place, and she wouldn't go to his. She made him go to hotels with her, the two of them driving in separate cars. He always stood outside with her before she drove away again, and when she bent to open her car door, he gently placed his hand just on top of her head so she wouldn't bump it when she got in. The gesture touched her so much, she had to bite down on her lower lip to keep from crying. As soon as he removed his hand from her head, she missed it, she wanted it back.

Nick was getting ready to leave for Brini's, making coffee, overcooking some brown eggs in a skillet, when the phone rang. It startled him. No one ever called him, except for an occasional wrong number, and then he always had to suppress his instinct to engage the voice in conversation. He lifted up the receiver and there was Leslie's voice, washing over him like cool water, taking his breath.

"Is she there?" Leslie blurted.

Nick sat down, sighing. Oh, Dore, he thought. To think of her as actually here, in the other room, humming as she corrected papers, always grading on how hard she thought the student tried rather than on the actual quality of the work. "If an A student can get an A without even thinking about it, what good is it?" she used to say. She wanted to see originality. She wanted to see risk. Risk—he had shown that.

"I haven't heard from her since when," he said.

"Oh, God, neither have I," Leslie said, and burst into tears, surprising him so much, he stood up. It was hard to understand her; she was tumbling out words, saying something about the police being rude to her, about wanting him to help with money so she could hire a detective, and then, in a snag of conversation, he heard Robin's name, and he realized just who it was that was missing.

He felt something crumpling inside of him, an implosion. Robin unsafe. "I'll find her," he said.

"I wouldn't call you except I don't know what to do anymore. The cops told me to wait another week or so, can you imagine? A week or so, they said. Kids come back, they said."

"It's all right," Nick said. "You don't have to do anything. I'll take care of it. I'll look for her myself. I'll even hire someone and I'll call you every week. Every single week."

"You'll let me know?" Leslie said, crying. "You'll find her and send her home?" She snuffled. "She hates me. I never did anything to her, and she hates me—"

"No one hates you," he said. "And I'll find her. I'll call you next Monday. At six. Don't worry."

He hung up in a confusion of feelings. First was the deep, raw edge of panic about Robin, the visions of her wandering about in a shabby subway, foraging in dumpsters for something to eat, or, worse, in the arms of some man who had plans. He refused to think of her as anything but alive. "Robin!" he said, as if his voice might position her into place until he could get her.

He felt helpless, but he felt elated, too, because now he had the right to call Leslie every week. Now she would willingly talk to him, and if he found Robin, if he sent her home, Leslie might be glad enough to actually see him. He'd have the right to contact Dore, too, because Robin had been close to her and might go there. It brought him a kind of twisted joy.

He wasn't sure where to start. How did you go about looking for someone who might not want to be found? He took out ads addressed to her, begging her to call him. He put them in papers he thought kids read—the bulletin-board back pages of the *Village Voice*, the *Boston Phoenix*, weeklies in Berkeley. He splurged and took out ads offering rewards for information about her, but all he got were crank responses. He got letters offering other young girls—girls who could use their tongues as instruments, girls who would do whatever he asked as long as he paid attention to their price rates.

Finally, he went to a detective named Rory Clarkson, who frowned at him and said that Nick would have to let him handle it alone—that if Robin didn't want to be found and Nick went out looking for her, he'd only end up pushing her farther into hiding. He told Nick that while finding his daughter might be a piece of cake, it might be difficult to get her to return home. "But you leave it to me," Clarkson said.

Nick did what he could. He sent Dore a card at her old address, figuring it would be forwarded to her. He got back a plain white postcard, mailed from Vermont; she wrote that she was sorry about Robin, but she hadn't heard anything. She said if Robin showed up, she would send her home, since Robin obviously didn't belong with her. Seeing Dore's writing lit up something inside of Nick.

He waited. He went to work, but he didn't tell Jack anything about why he looked so exhausted, why other times he was so wired he couldn't sit still. Jack, who believed everyone was entitled to keep his wounds private, never pressed Nick for explanations. Instead, he did what he could to change Nick's moods in other ways. He let him take over ordering all the stock, and when Nick gave him a suspicious look, Jack told him to just keep his spine in joint, that he was giving him the job because he himself was too lazy to fuss with the forms anymore. And anyway, Nick knew the customers as well as he did, and knew the stock even better, since he was the one who took care of all the shelving and returns these days. It did help Nick. He was somehow nourished by the extra work, the responsibility. He'd work long hours, interrupted only when Jack took him for something to eat at Rennabaum's Drugstore, where, Jack claimed, they served the tastiest liver and onions in the whole town.

Every Monday, Nick called Leslie, but when he hung up, he always felt dislocated, strange. He had comforted her, and she needed him—she actually thought he could find Robin—but the whole time he was having nightmares about Robin floating facedown in the Atlantic. He'd wake, confusing the salt of his own sweat with the ocean. He saw Robin in every ragamuffin kid begging spare change on the street. He gave them all dollar bills, ignoring their sly smiles, because they could be Robin. And yet, there was something else, too, something he couldn't explain. He had this feeling that Robin was somehow orchestrating all of this—that she, among all of them, was really the only one who knew what she was doing, the only one who had any sort of control.

Robin thought that the closer she and Douglas got to California, the more she would shed her family like an extra coat she didn't need in the sun, and the more bound together she'd feel to Douglas. She kept twisting the gold wedding band he had hastily bought her, kept glancing over at his gold ring, but he was harried. He didn't speak to her much. He wanted to put as much distance between them and Pennsylvania as possible, but the traffic was terrible, and every time a police car passed, he seemed to stiffen.

His mood didn't lift until the next day, and then he parked the car and took her with him to buy some bread and cheese and a bottle of wine, and that night, he drove the car to a park where they could watch the sky. They toasted each other with the wine.

"Look at you, I can't believe you're mine," he said. "You wait, as soon as we can, we'll have a real wedding. I'll buy you a whole new ring. An expensive one."

"I don't need a new ring," said Robin, stroking hers.

He bent to kiss her. "You know what? I *feel* married to you. I *am* married to you. I can't help it. I keep thinking of you as my wife, as Mrs. Nylon. I love you so much," he said, and his eyes were shining, and so starry that Robin shivered.

He sped toward California. Robin stared dreamily out the window and twirled her wedding band about her finger. Everywhere they stopped, she looked for opportunities to announce herself as Mrs. Douglas Nylon, a name with none of her family in it. She got out library cards she wouldn't be in town long enough to use; she made dinner reservations she would call to cancel a half-hour later. She called Douglas "my husband" to anyone who would listen. "My husband loves apples," she informed a vendor on the street. "My husband already has today's *Times*," she told a boy hawking papers. "Okay, okay," Douglas said, extricating his hand from hers. "Enough's enough."

She began annoying him on the ride. She kept buying books at every place they stopped, paperback classics she'd read while he was driving. "You're making me dizzy," he informed her. "How can you read when we're moving?" She just looked at him for a moment and then returned to her book. She read in restaurants when they stopped for hamburgers; she read before they stretched out in the car as best they could to try to sleep. And when he woke up in the morning, cramped, his legs hurting, she was contentedly reading, unaware of him or the muggy smell of the car, of the long, tedious stretch of highway ahead of them.

And she read so fast. She'd run into drugstores to find a book and then two hours later she'd be carefully placing it in back among the growing pile, and reaching for another. She told him she always read quickly, but he didn't believe her—he said she must be skimming, she must be losing half of what she read, and he wanted to quiz her. He picked up *Bleak House*, which she had read in one day, and held it up. "All right, tell me the theme," he said.

"I will not," she said. "Leave me alone." She plucked up *The Sun Also Rises*, and contentedly, she began reading, leaving him to maneuver and drive.

When they finally got to California, they rented a tiny studio apartment an hour north of San Francisco. It was really too small for two people, although Robin kept saying how cozy it was. They bought a pull-out sofa that took up so much space when it was pulled out that you had to walk right over it to get to the bathroom. The plaster was chipping off in the corners, and no matter how much Robin cleaned, there was always dust. She set up the books she had piled in the car, and she waited for a married routine to start.

It didn't take Douglas long to find a job teaching at the local high school, but he didn't like it. The kids were spoiled. They didn't listen to him and they made constant fun of his accent, of his pale skin. When he walked into the room, the kids hummed "Casper the Friendly Ghost."

"So who wants skin cancer?" Douglas said, and even as he spoke, a girl in the back was adjusting her strap over a tan line, a guy was checking his supply of zinc oxide in his pack. They weren't interested in science, he told Robin, unless it had to do with setting up home labs to make designer drugs. They didn't even read unless the book had already been made into a movie.

He was startled when Robin refused to go back to high school. "Why should I?" she asked. "I have responsibilities." She had all these ideas of how a married woman starting out acted, and not one of them had anything to do with Leslie. She went out and got a part-time job waitressing at the local Arby's, and on her way home she'd stop and buy one of those women's magazines so she could figure out a recipe for dinner. She carried *Ladies' Home Journal* and *Woman's Day* under her arm, unbagged, so everyone could see.

Douglas didn't like it that sometimes when he left school he'd find Robin waiting outside for him, looking younger than some of his students. He didn't like coming home to a five-course dinner he didn't feel like eating because it was just too hot outside. She wanted to make love all the time. She kept her hands on him even when he was sitting outside at night, trying to get cool because they couldn't afford anything better than a fan, and all that did was stir up the dust. "Isn't this wonderful?" Robin said, leaning her head against his shoulder, shyly taking his hand, but all he could think about was the clean, quiet lab in Pittsburgh, the air-conditioning in his old apartment.

They kept to themselves. Robin didn't mind; she liked it that she seemed to be the center for him, that he never even wanted to go out with anyone else. He didn't tell her that he turned down invitations from other teachers because he was afraid they would judge him. He felt as if he were waiting for Robin to turn eighteen so they could get married, so he could feel respectable. On her sixteenth birthday, even though it was just the two of them, he wouldn't let her put any candles on her cake because he didn't want to be reminded.

It was easy enough to go from spending time just with her to spending time by himself, easy enough to hang out alone without her asking him fifty times if he loved her, without her always touching him, always watching him, her eyes so needy he felt as if she were drinking him right down. He'd come home and she'd be silently waiting for him on the porch, and then he'd see how beautiful she was and his insides would rush into water; he'd remember how he had felt about her before, how her innocence and her need had intoxicated him then. He'd sit down beside her and take her head in his hands and kiss her nose. "You'll never leave me, will you?" she said. "Never, ever."

He sighed. "No, never."

"You'll always love me," she said. "You'll always take care of me."

"Always," he said, his mouth dry.

"You'll always need me," she said, and this time he stretched up; he told her they should go inside and get something nice and cool to drink.

She wouldn't let herself get lonely, wouldn't let herself think one single thing could be wrong. She never worried that Nick or Leslie would show up. She knew she was bound to Douglas now and had nothing to do with either of them. She worked at making herself and Douglas as much of a family as she could. She thought families should have dogs, something she had never been allowed because Leslie didn't like them, and she went down to the Animal Rescue League and picked out a small yellow mutt. Douglas gave her a look when he saw the dog, but because it made her so happy, because it took some of the focus away from him, he agreed they should keep it. "Next, we need a baby," she said, wrapping her arms about his neck. "Like we need a hole in our brains," he told her, but he nuzzled her neck and suddenly wanted her so much, he dipped her down to the floor.

She named the dog Toby. It thrilled her to come home and see the dog prancing around waiting for her—she swore he barked out her name. Toby followed her around, adoring. He slept at her feet at night, and when she woke, hot, and padded into the bathroom to lie on the cool white tiles, she'd wake to find the dog there with her. She found herself thinking about the dog all the time. She stole treats for him at Arby's, long strips of lean roast beef, hamburger meat. When she took her lunch break, she'd walk home in her uniform with a sandwich and share it with the dog, one hand ruffling up the yellow fur on his back. When she had to leave to get back to work, Toby whined and tried to leave with her.

"I'll be back," she soothed. "I'll always be back."

She and the dog would go and meet Douglas after school; they'd shadow him to the beach and to the market. "Can't I have some time to myself?" he asked. "Give me a kiss," she told him. She was upset when he was late, and she worried when he came home silent, when he didn't want to tell her about his day. "You're shutting me out of your life," she said, but he shook his head; he said the problem was more that she was taking over his life. Wounded, she drew back; she went to take Toby for a walk.

She told herself their life was stabilizing. She tracked the months they were together in the studio, chalking up six months, then a year, then a little more. There were long periods when he seemed less than delighted with her, true, but there were also stretches when he surprised her with flowers, when he tumbled her to the floor to make love. And when she turned seventeen, he seemed visibly happier—he even let her put candles on the cake he bought for her.

"One more year and we'll be home free," he told her, and she relaxed, because it was future talk.

She was sure what they needed to really cement their life together was a baby. If she got pregnant now, it could be born by the time they married for real. But when she broached the subject to him, he laughed. "You're the baby around here," he told her. She didn't tell him when she started coming to bed without her diaphragm. She made a show of going into the bathroom, where she daubed a swirl of Ortho cream about her vagina where he would taste it, so he would never suspect.

In the spring, the weather started changing. It was earthquake season, people said. Robin blamed the weather for the way Douglas was acting again—his distancing himself from her, his silence. She asked one of the other waitresses at Arby's, who claimed to be an expert on earthquakes, if the weather could do things to people. The girl laughed. "Oh, sure," she said. "It makes my cat crazy." She told Robin to get some bottled water to keep in the house, to hit the ground if she felt a tremor.

"Oh, stop scaring her," Robin's boss said. "Look at her—she's blue around the gills already."

"I am like fun," Robin said, but she went into the small employee bathroom and studied her reflection.

She began feeling nauseated in the mornings, as if she were seasick. The dog padded after her, concerned, rubbing up against her bare legs until she shivered. She missed one period and then another, and then she went to the free clinic over on Horatio Street and waited three hours to see a doctor. The doctor looked at her wedding band, but he didn't really believe she was married, because she was so young. He said he wanted her to tell him the truth. He kept smiling, sympathetic, waiting, and before she left he gave her pamphlets—"Abortion, the Right Choice" and "Giving Your Baby Up for Adoption." "You think about it," he told her, but she crumpled the pamphlets in her hand and stuffed them into the trash on her way out.

She knew Douglas. He'd do what was right. He'd let her have the baby and he'd love it because that was what fathers were supposed to do. The thing that worried her lately, though, was whether or not he'd love *her*. He had gotten even more distant. Angry when she called him at work to ask if he wanted string beans or limas for dinner, to tell him she missed him in just the two hours he had been gone. "God, can't you do anything by yourself?" he asked her when she trailed him on his walks, when she wanted to come with him to the tennis courts and watch him hit balls. At night he turned from her when she woke him up wanting to make love. She stroked his penis, but he said he needed his sleep. Uneasy, she touched his belly. "Just tell me what you want," she whispered.

"Maybe what I want is just something you don't have," he said, punching down his pillow. "I gotta sleep," he said, rolling from her, leaving her reaching her hands out into the darkness for the dog, for whatever comfort she could find.

She told herself there was plenty of time to tell him about the baby. She fought her unease by concentrating on the life inside of her, by letting the baby carry her through her days. She talked to it the same way she talked to the dog, so that whenever she was telling the baby how pretty California was, describing the sky and the trees, the dog would perk up his ears and bark happily. She developed a habit of keeping one hand on her stomach, so that her boss began asking her if she had eaten something that didn't agree with her.

"No," she said, smiling, secretive, "I'm okay."

"Well, cut that out, then," he told her. "It isn't good for business to have you always looking like you got a funny taste in your mouth."

It was two days later when the dog started whining and carrying on. "We ought to just get rid of him," Douglas said, brushing dog hair off his jacket, heading for the door.

"Oh, we should not," said Robin, stooping to try to pet the dog, who cowered from her, bunching himself up under the table. She left him a dish of hamburger meat to tempt him, a clean bowl of water, and then she went to work, and when she came home, she couldn't find him anywhere.

"Hey, Toby!" she called, clapping her hands. She checked the loose back window the dog sometimes used to get out of the house. She checked under the beds. She went into the kitchen again to make herself a cup of tea, to calm herself down. She was just about to pour herself a second cup when the whole apartment suddenly started to vibrate.

Robin grabbed the edge of the table, but it shook in her hand; it rattled the teacup and saucer right off the edge so they smashed into pieces, so the tea slid and stained the floor. She crouched down, terrified, beneath the table, holding on to the legs, trying to re-member what you were supposed to do, and around her the cups rattled and fell from the shelves, the paperback books she had amassed rained down from on top of the dresser, from the cabinets. When she dared to glance up and saw the stove shivering in place, she started crying. She tried to place her hands on her stomach, to comfort the baby, to comfort herself, but she couldn't feel anything inside of her, and for the first time she didn't feel she was any child of danger at all, she didn't feel safe or reckless, she didn't feel any-thing but absolutely and terrifyingly alone. She started crying harder, dipping her body as low to the floor as she could, and then, almost as soon as the tremor started, it stopped.

She wouldn't get up from under the table. Gradually, she heard voices outside, steps in the building, and nervous spurts of laughter. Slowly, she started to unpeel herself and stood up.

She looked around the studio, keeping one hand braced along the wall. Other than the smashed plates and glasses, there wasn't much damage. If you didn't know what had happened, you might just have thought there had been a fight going on, people throwing things out of rage.

She made herself move to the phone to call Douglas. She made the principal call him out of class, and as soon as she heard his voice, she started crying again. "Hey, hey," Douglas said. "Come on, it was just a tremor." He told her they hadn't even stopped class for it. He tried to cheer her up by telling her how all his students made fun of it, how they called it a "tourist quake" meant to impress anyone not smart enough to know it was nothing at all.

"I don't care about that," she said. "Come home."

She didn't clean up anything. She wanted him to see how terrible it had been for her. She sat quietly under the table, and when she remembered, she got up and called for the dog.

Douglas didn't come home until four, his usual time, and as soon as he saw her face, and the apartment, he took her in his arms and rocked her; he made her come and sit on the sofa bed with him.

"Listen, I just couldn't leave. I had to take over another class, and then I had to give a test."

"But I asked you," she said.

He was silent for a minute, and then he looked at her and told her that was the trouble, she was always asking, and he couldn't keep answering her the way she wanted. She was too young and he was too tired of it. "I think we should get you back home," he said.

"No," she said, "you don't think that one bit."

"I do," he said. "I must have been crazy running away with a student, thinking it would work. And now that we're out here, I see how things are, I see how they'll get."

"You love me," she said. "I know you do."

He put his head in his hands, pushed his hair back with his fingers. When he looked up at her, his face was crumpled. "Look at you," he said. "You should have a high-school diploma. You should be thinking about college."

"You don't know," she said. "You don't know at all." She stood up, suddenly fueled by anger. She plucked up her sweater from the floor, still damp from the tea that had spilled across it. "Who says?" she said. He started telling her something about the rent being paid up for the whole month, about his staying someplace else, but she concentrated on the sound the lock made as she opened it, on the sudden sharp slam of the door against him.

There was a note when she got back home, wrapped about $250 in cash. "Go home, Robin," it said. There was an address, too, one of the cheaper hotels in the city and a phone number. He didn't come back, but the dog did, two days later, wagging his tail. He wouldn't eat the food she set out for him. "Traitor," she said, thinking he must have let someone else feed him, must have let someone else wrap their arms about his neck and hold him close. She cleaned the studio. She left the sofa bed open all the time for the dog to sleep on, and she began working later hours so she wouldn't have to come home and see just how alone she was.

She began to be scared about having a baby, about having to take care of it and raise it. She wished she could get back one of those pamphlets about adoption, about abortion. Douglas would hate her for doing either; he wouldn't think it right. She kept walking the dog past the clinic, kept thinking how simple it would be to go in again, to have someone tell her exactly what it was she should do, and how she should go about doing it. She thought about the doctor she had seen before, how he had smiled at her, and finally, on one of her walks, she stitched up her courage and walked hesitantly toward the door.

Just as she reached it, a woman sprang up in front of her, jabbing a pamphlet at her. Robin took it automatically, reaching one hand for the door. "Read it," the woman said, unsmiling. "You take yourself a good long look." Robin glanced at the pamphlet. On the front was a color picture of a baby, swaddled in a bloody towel, stuffed into a trashcan. "Abortion is murder," the woman told Robin. She lifted up one hand, perhaps to make a point, and the dog gave a sudden wild bark, making her step back, alarmed, giving Robin time to turn around and bolt.

She and the dog ran all the way home. He thought it was a game and didn't want to stop when they finally got there, but kept frisking about her, yapping, tugging at her shorts, until she burst into tears. She sat down on the front steps. She didn't know what she was supposed to do.

She stopped talking to the baby out of terror. She wouldn't look down at her stomach, wouldn't place her hand there. "Glad to see that habit stop," her boss informed her. I'm seventeen, she told herself. I'm seventeen. And all the while her jeans were getting tighter and tighter, her shirts didn't look right anymore, and at night she dreamed she was giving birth to wild animals, to insects with red, glittering eyes, insects that stung her as soon as they fluttered from her, divesting her of any motherhood she might have felt.

Sometimes she thought about calling Douglas, asking him what she should do, what was right. And, too, she missed having him in the studio. Without him, there didn't seem to be a good enough reason to sweep the dust from the corners, to clean the grease from a plate. She showed up at the school one day, but when she saw him walking out, he was taking the arm of a woman who was old enough to be a teacher. She had curly black hair, a green plaid dress that covered her knees, and she was telling Douglas something, leaning toward him, and he was laughing and laughing, delighted. He reached up one hand to brush at something in her hair, and Robin felt her heart cramp. She turned away.

She didn't know when it was she started thinking about Dore again. At night sometimes she'd concoct conversations in her head where Dore would tell her exactly what to do, where Dore would hand her a palmful of green herbs that could rid her of a baby in such a way that it would seem the baby had never really been at all.

She called information and got a whole series of numbers in Boston that might be Dore's, and then there was one the operator said she couldn't give her because it was unlisted.

"That's the number I need," Robin said. She begged the operator to call Dore for her. "It's an emergency," she begged. "Just give her my number then," Robin said. "Let her call me."

The operator paused. "We're not supposed to do that," she said. "But then, I've always been a fool, so why break the pattern now? You hang on."

Robin was startled when she heard Dore's voice on the wire, cool, detached. "Your parents are looking for you," Dore said. "Don't you think you should contact them?"

Robin started crying. The dog, curled beside her, looked up expectantly and then curved himself closer to her. "I contacted you," Robin said.

"Why?" asked Dore. "To torment me?"

"I never did that," Robin said.

"Oh, please," Dore said, her voice edging. "And what was that fake name? What was the spying for your mother?" She paused. "I thought we were friends," she said. "No, that's not right. I thought we were more than that—that we were . . . special."

"If you had known who I was, you wouldn't have talked to me," Robin said. "I was afraid. You were the only one who listened to me, the only one who was there."

There was silence for a moment. "I *was* there," Dore said. "Sometimes I even kept the phone by the bed because I worried about you at night—I wanted to be sure to get the call if it was you. Every time I went shopping, every time I picked up a sweater, I'd think about how you would look wearing it, how it would get you to smile, how it would make us closer." She sighed, and when she spoke again, her voice was so soft that Robin had to press the receiver close against her ear to hear. "What is it?" Dore asked. "What's wrong?"

"I want to come there," Robin said. "To stay with you. I could keep house for you, do errands."

Dore laughed. "You haven't seen my place recently, have you?"

Robin was about to blurt out that she was pregnant when Dore interrupted her. "I used to think about your living with me," Dore said. "If you knew how I rearranged my apartment in my head, how I planned it so there'd be an extra room for you, an extra place at the table. I planned *meals* for you. I made you an orphan, just so you could be my daughter, just so Nick and I could adopt you and all be together. God."

"I could be your daughter," Robin said.

"No," said Dore. "All we'd be is just two outcasts from the past, that's all. And anyway, if I were your mother, you know what I'd be doing right now? Letting you go. Pushing you out into the world on your own."

"I've been out in the world," Robin said. "And it stinks. Please. You helped me before—"

"Did I?" Dore said, surprised, thoughtful. "I guess I did. I really did, didn't I?" She was silent again, and in the silence Robin heard another voice, a man's voice. "You look like a girl who could use some cookies," he said, and then his voice dropped down and Dore's voice wove into it, and then Dore came back to the phone.

"Who was that?" asked Robin.

"Not Nick," Dore said. "That's all you and I have to know. He's not Nick."

"Are you happy?" Robin asked.

"Of all my kids, you were the only one who ever asked me questions like that," Dore said. "I think that's why you got to me the way you did." She paused. "Listen, you can't call me up anymore. It isn't fair. It just stirs up old pain. You need to get on with your life, the same way I do, and to do that, you just have to let go of the past. You can't keep trying to replay it, even the good parts."

"You hate me," Robin said.

"Who said I hate you?" Dore said. "Oh, maybe. For a little while. But then I let go of it. I forced myself to forget everything I knew or felt about you and your family. It was like going insane for a while, but I'm okay now. I have a life, I have a beginning going toward a center again. And then this call . . . I don't know, it touched me, I guess, like you can't imagine, your calling me now when you don't have to, not really, when there's no longer any connection for me with your family, when all this call has to do with is me.

"Oh, Lord, this is starting to hurt a little, and I really want to hang up before it starts to hurt a lot. Robin, the last thing I can do for you is tell you to go home where you belong. Call your mother. Call Nick, Robin." There was a pause. "Isn't that funny?" she said. "That's the first time I ever called you by your real name. Robin," she said, and then she hung up, gently, leaving Robin with the phone cradled in her hand, the dog, rolling away from her in his untroubled dog sleep.

Lost, lost, she thought. Every time she stepped outside the studio, she was sure she wouldn't be able to find her way back, sure that something terrible was just waiting to happen. She tried to stay with what was familiar. The place where she worked, the streets she knew, the café down the block, so close to her apartment that she could see her whole front window from any of the tables.

She was sitting at the café one day sipping iced tea, feeding bits of her pastry to the dog, who had settled under the shade of the table. *The Great Gatsby* was cracked open in front of her. A man suddenly sat down opposite her, waiting. She glanced warily at him. He was older than she was, older than her father, with white hair and a blue sportcoat. "I'd like to be alone," she said politely.

"Your parents are looking for you," he said. "Most people would have given up after two years, but not them." He paused for a moment. "Now, doesn't that tell you something?"

She tensed for a moment, before she remembered to keep her face impassive, to give it the curious bland stare of a stranger caught in a misunderstanding, blameless.

"You've got the wrong person," she said.

He shrugged and then pulled out a card and handed it to her. "Detective," she said. "Well, anyone can get those printed up. I could get one for myself if I wanted."

"Robin," he said. "Your parents gave me pictures of you. They gave me the fingerprints taken when you were a baby because your father was worried you'd get stolen. I asked a whole lot of the right questions to trail you here."

"That's not my name," she said. She held up the gold band she hadn't been able to take from her finger. "Mrs. Douglas Nylon," she said.

He sighed, fidgeting for something in his pocket, pulling out a stubby yellow pencil, a scrap of paper. "I'm not a cop," he said. "As much as I'd like to, I can't force you to go home." He scribbled something on the paper.

He handed her the paper. "It's your father's new address and phone number," he said. "So you can call if you like, at least to let him know you're okay." He put the pencil back in his pocket. "*I'm* going to tell them you're okay. Why should they worry, right?"

Robin stood up, tugging on the dog's leash. "You don't even know if I'm Robin," she said. "Do you?"

"You took the phone number," he said, and she flushed, turning from him.

Robin sat in the muddle of the studio fingering the piece of paper the detective had given her. He must have been Leslie's idea, she thought, her mother's surrogate, trailing, spying, a kind of carrion bird feeding on bits of her life. She was furious with Leslie, furious with Nick, too, but for different, more confusing reasons. If he was so concerned about her, why hadn't he ever shown it before? It was like him, too, to send a detective—to send anyone but himself. She bunched up the paper and threw it against the wall, and then, later, she got up and smoothed it out, folded it in half, like a small, closed mouth, and put it into her purse.

She had to decide what to do. She couldn't afford to pay for the studio herself, and she couldn't ask Douglas for money—she couldn't continue that tie. And then, too, she was sick. She'd been having night fevers. She'd wake up in a damp tangle of sheets, her head on fire. She'd stumble to the freezer and chip out some ice into a plastic bag and put it to her head. She'd fall back into bed, exhausted, and in the morning the sheets would be soaked from the ice and her sweat. "You don't look too good," her boss had told her. "Go home. You're scaring the people with money." He was trying to be nice, but still, she burst into tears. She had to be calmed down until she finally let herself be put into a cab home, where she immediately fell asleep.

The dog kept away from her, which was the thing that scared her the most. And she began to be frightened about the baby again. Maybe the baby was making her sick, maybe God was punishing her for some terrible defect. Or maybe her sickness was killing the baby. The next day she went to the library and looked up pictures of fetuses. What was inside her looked no larger than an insect. She closed the books, dizzy. She couldn't have a baby. Not at seventeen. She couldn't be pregnant. She was afraid to go back to the clinic and she didn't have enough money for a proper doctor in a clean white office. She couldn't go home to Leslie, and Dore wouldn't have her.

She took out the piece of paper and looked at Nick's address in dazed wonder. Madison. What was he doing there? She could show up on his doorstep and he'd have to take her in. She thought about the whole scenario, and even as she felt her anger freshening, getting sharper, there was something else, too—an undercurrent of longing relief at having someone else telling her what she should do, someone else knowing what was right, taking control.

SIXTEEN

• • •

Nick never expected Robin to appear. When he thought of her, he thought of a phone call in the small hours of the night, and the voice he heard was always the detective's, not hers, telling him where she was, how she was, and where she was going. She wouldn't want to see him. At first, when Clarkson was narrowing her whereabouts down from state to state, Nick had planned to go down there. He thought he could charm her back to him by making dinner reservations for two, by sending her tickets to the ballet and showing up himself. But she was never in one state for very long, according to the detective, and then, when he thought about the reservations, he began to think of himself waiting for her at an empty table while his stomach kicked and growled. He saw himself watching a ballet with an empty seat beside him, not letting anyone from the cheaper seats move down into it, even during the last ten minutes, because there was still a chance she might show up. He always thought of seeing her, but he never thought of it as long-term—he never thought he had the right. He'd take her to dinner and then put her on a plane back to Leslie, back where she belonged.

He sometimes wrote letters to her, but he didn't really know what to say to her, and he didn't know where to mail them, and it usually ended up making him feel that much more alone.

His one comfort was Madison. He was surprised at the way he was falling in love with the town, the way he was beginning to feel as if he had finally found the place where he belonged. He loved the

241

muggy, still heat of the summer; the bats by the capitol dome and in his attic; the foamy detergent frothing at the edge of one of the lakes. He knew his neighbors and they liked him well enough to invite him to dinner, to come by with tins of home-baked chocolate cookies or potted red geraniums for his windows because they looked too bare. He was kidded about being fixed up, he was told about four sisters, each of them prettier than the next, but no one pushed, no one asked about the photographs of three different women in his house, and when he got strange and silent, they let him be.

The bookstore, too, gave him more pleasure than he could have imagined. Jack, who had been threatening to retire for years, finally decided enough might be enough. He was going to get a couple of dogs, maybe a cat, and just stay home. He told Nick not to worry, that his job was as secure as any man could ever hope for, and that the new owner was a man he'd respect as much as Jack did. "I'll be around to visit," Jack told him. The day he left, Nick took him out to dinner at L'Héritage, an expensive new French restaurant, and when he handed Jack his present, a leather-bound blank book, Jack handed him a sealed white envelope. "What's this, my walking papers?" Nick asked, and then he unfolded the paper and saw that the shop had been deeded over to him. "Who else was I going to leave it to?" Jack said. "My cat?"

Nick closed the shop for two weeks so he could take down all the books, dust the shelves, and put things in the order he wanted. He bought a few cheap, comfortable chairs so people could sit down and read if they wanted. He bought a small stereo so he could play Vivaldi and Bach while people browsed. He turned it on as soon as he opened the shop mornings, flooding the rooms with sound, stopping his routine to conduct or to just stand still and listen to some passage of eerie beauty. He didn't change the name of the shop, and he didn't do anything to the floors or the walls other than to rewax and repaint. And only sometimes at night did he wake, panicking, realizing that he owned something named for a woman who had been more loved than most people could even imagine; that he loved the shop, too, and that now it had a claim on him: Now he would have to stay in one place—he couldn't run.

He was home from work, exhausted, wanting only to make himself some supper and go to sleep, when the bell rang. He smoothed down the rumples in his shirt, and then he opened the door, and there was Robin, her skin yellow, a big, dirty-looking dog growling beside her.

"I'm pregnant," she said defiantly.

He made her come inside; he backed away from her, half-afraid that if he turned for one moment, she might disappear again. He wanted to touch her, to grasp her to him, but when he moved, she flinched.

He made her sit on the couch, but she wouldn't tell him where she had been, by whom she was pregnant, or how she had found him. He felt a quick buckling of irritation at the detective, who should have known, who should have called.

"You look terrible," he said.

"I know how I look," she said.

He stooped down toward her. He wanted to place his forehead against hers to see if she had fever, the way he used to watch Leslie do so many times when Robin was little. Later, when Robin was older, when she insisted on a thermometer because it was more adult, he had seen what that had done to Leslie's face. She'd go and get it, but not before she dipped down and felt her daughter's head anyway, pretending to be very clinical about it. It was as much of a hug as Robin allowed in those days, so Leslie was always feeling her head, as much as she could get away with.

Nick hesitated, then put his hand out and touched Robin's forehead. "Hot," he said.

He brought her herb tea. "Listen, we've got to get you well first," he said.

She blinked at him. "First?" she asked, but she slumped back against the couch, and after a time she slept.

He sat by her, just watching, just making sure she was really there, and when she woke up, she seemed dazed. She kept looking around.

He fixed up the spare room for her. He made her a supper she barely touched. Sometimes the mad flutter of the bats trapped in the attic above her would wake her and he'd make a show of getting the broom and going upstairs to swat at them, but he never really did, because he knew it would just make them crazier. He'd stand outside the small musty attic for a few minutes and bang the broom around, just loud enough so Robin could hear it. When he came downstairs, she lifted herself up on one elbow and sleepily thanked him. Later, he took the broom and went up to the attic again, just so he could come back down and collect the look washing across her face.

She was asleep for the night when he called Leslie to tell her Robin was really there, Robin was really okay. "I can catch the next plane," Leslie said, and he felt himself brighten, but then she stopped herself. "Oh, God, who am I kidding?" she said. "She'd hate that. If she knew I was coming, she'd be gone before I even got there." Leslie sighed. "Listen, will you tell her for me that I love her? Tell her you called me, and tell her . . . tell her it's okay if she doesn't want to call me back right now."

"It's not okay," Nick said.

"Tell her anyway," Leslie said.

She wanted to know how Robin was, where she had been—all the details that Nick didn't know. He told her Robin would probably open up once she felt a little better, and that he would call the detective. He didn't tell her Robin was pregnant.

"I'd love to see you," Nick said, but when Leslie spoke, her voice was bitter.

"Do you think for one moment that I would be calling you if it weren't for Robin?" Leslie said. "I want her home, but I wish what happened with Robin would happen to you. I wish you would disappear. I wish you would stop being real."

"I loved you," Nick said. "I love you."

"What do you know about it?" Leslie said, and then she hung up.

Nick sat down. It wasn't over with her. Not yet. She'd call him as long as Robin was here. He was the bridge she needed to travel to get to her daughter. It might still be all right.

He went to check on Robin, who was still sleeping, and then he came back into the kitchen, made himself coffee, and sat down to think. He wanted to call Dore. He had had her number for a while now. The detective had jotted it down when he had gone to ask her questions about Robin, and he had passed it along to Nick, whose sole reason for not dialing it the second it was in his hands was knowing just how much Dore would resent him for intruding upon her, for spying. But it was different now. Robin was here with him. And he somehow wanted Dore to know that. As soon as she answered, he said, "Robin's here, she's fine," so she wouldn't hang up on him.

"She's safe then," Dore said, relieved,

"Would you like to see her?" Nick asked.

Dore was silent for a moment. "That's not very fair," she said. "You think that I wouldn't? That I wouldn't mind seeing you, either? What I want and what I'm going to do are two different things." She was silent again.

"You could come anytime," Nick said. "You could risk it."

"You know how some people believe in reincarnation?" Dore said. "Some of my kids do. They have all these crazy Edgar Cayce books and they try to hypnotize each other in study hall so they can get back into whatever past lives they're sure they've had." She laughed, and Nick laughed, too.

"Well," she said, "sometimes I feel as though I've been reincarnated three times just in this one stupid life—that I've had three lives, all of them different, and all of them defined by you. One before I met you; one when we were living in the trailer, when we were happy; and now I'm starting my third life, without you. And you can't mesh different lives—that's how come people supposedly forget who they were in the past. It's a safety valve, it protects you."

"Dore," Nick said, "we're not talking about kids' theories—"

"I know what we're talking about," Dore said. "And it hurts. I don't know how you got my number, but please, please, don't call anymore. I'm glad you called about Robin, because I would have worried, but I don't want to hear any more about you. I'm in another life now. I'm getting as happy as I can again."

"My phone number is 608-775-6681. Madison, Wisconsin," Nick said.

"Goodbye, Nick," she said, very gently, and she hung up.

He felt lost in the sudden still of the house, and he automatically picked up the receiver and dialed Rory Clarkson. He told the detective that Robin has shown up at his doorstep. Clarkson didn't seem surprised. He said he'd found her two days ago and decided to give her a few days to go home on her own. He'd had a hunch she would, seeing how things were with her.

"What things?" Nick asked.

Clarkson said he'd found Robin in California, living with her old science teacher, a man named Douglas Nylon. The two had split up and she was clearly scared. "I gave her your number, and she took it."

"You should have called me the second you saw her. You should have let me know," Nick said. "What the hell kind of a detective are you?"

"I guess not yours any longer," Clarkson said. He told Nick he'd mail out the report right away, and if Nick ever needed him again, he knew how to get in touch.

"I won't need you," Nick said.

He felt empty. He went to sit down beside Robin. She was here, but she wasn't, not really, and he had this overwhelming feeling that he had lost everything he possibly could. He reached out and took Robin's hand, and she woke, startled. She roughly pulled her hand from his. He didn't care. He reached for her hand again; he told her how glad he was that she was there.

"Why?" she asked.

"How about love for a reason?"

She sat up, kicking the blanket from her. "As soon as I'm okay, I'm leaving," she said, her eyes serious.

"Fine," he said. "I'll help you get well."

She didn't talk to him much. Not at first. She never berated him for hiring a detective to follow her; she never asked if he was calling Leslie with news of her, if he had called Dore. And because of that, he in turn never approached her with what he knew about her running away, her California life. He gave her her secrecy, her distance, out of a kind of respect, and, too, because he didn't feel he had any right to pry.

She was suspicious about him. She stiffened when the phone rang. When the paperboy came to the door, she went into a back room. She couldn't help going through the mail, sifting through Nick's bills and sweepstakes offers, peering anxiously at the names she didn't know.

When she finally approached him about helping her find a free clinic because she needed to do something about the baby, he shook his head. "We'll get you a private doctor," he said.

"I don't have that kind of money," she said, so seriously he almost laughed.

"I do," he said.

She dug her hands into the pockets of her jeans, swaying on the heels of her sneakers, and then suddenly she started to cry. "I don't want to have this baby," she said. "I do and I don't. I do and I *can't,*" she said, and this time, when he touched her, she let herself lean against him.

"I know how it is," he told her, and then she pulled away, averting her face.

At night he sat up, just listening to her soft prowling about her room, the scrape of furniture being moved, the opening and closing of the sticking drawers. He kept thinking about her. She couldn't sleep either. It would be easy enough to walk past her room on some pretext, needing water, wanting a cool shower because the house was so hot. He could knock on her door and tell her he was making iced coffee and would she like some? He could knock just because he was her father. He sat up straighter in bed, but he didn't get up. He kept thinking, thinking. His baby having a baby. His baby losing a baby, choosing to lose it. It made him half-mad, and sometimes, very late at night, just before the sun shimmered into the sky, it made him see Susan, reborn in the shadows just under his door, always disappearing into mist as soon as he stretched out his hand.

He thought about Robin's California life. He tried to piece it together. What the hell kind of a man was this Douglas Nylon, leaving Robin to struggle with this on her own? What the hell kind of father? He felt like phoning him and yelling. He thought of all the ways you could harm someone—the curses, the mad violence you might do. He could see him in jail if he wanted to put Robin through that, if he wanted to risk her running away. And then he thought, well, who was he to talk? Who was he to judge anyone?

He never slept until the noises from Robin's room stopped, and even then he drifted, and in the morning, when the alarm bolted him awake, he sometimes felt as if he were still dreaming.

It took him only two days to set up an appointment with a doctor for Robin. He thought a woman might make her more comfortable, but he didn't know whom to get, whom to even ask for referrals. He didn't want to tell his daughter's business to his neighbors or his staff; he didn't want her to feel her privacy was invaded. So he went to the library one morning while Robin slept and he leafed through the reference books on doctors. He picked out the ones affiliated with hospitals, the ones who had gone to the best schools, the ones who were young. When he finally narrowed his choice to Elizabeth Nagle, it wasn't just because of her credentials, but because she listed that she coached tennis, and it reminded him of Leslie's mother, and he saw it as a good omen.

He drove Robin to Dr. Nagle's office for her first visit, prepared for a battle about his coming into the waiting room with her. But she didn't fight him. She stood outside in the sun, scared, blinking, waiting for him to follow.

He felt funny in the waiting room. It was painted bright pink, and taped all over the walls were crayoned drawings by children, self-portraits that an adult hand had carefully signed each child's name to. There were other women in the room: one swelling with child, her hands folded over her stomach; another woman, long and lean, nipping kisses at the man seated beside her. Everyone looked up at Nick and Robin. Robin, in blue jeans and dirty white sneakers, self-consciously flinched down into one of the red leatherette chairs.

It didn't take long. Elizabeth Nagle came out herself to greet each patient, her pale brown hair in a lank ponytail, a white doctor's coat thrown over a brilliant red jumpsuit. She called Robin Mrs. Nylon, which made Robin start. Dr. Nagle acted as if having a pregnant seventeen-year-old in her office was perfectly normal, and when Robin stood up, Dr. Nagle gently placed one hand on her shoulder. "We'll just do some talking today, do a quick exam," the doctor said. Robin turned back to look at Nick, her eyes haunted, before she disappeared behind the door with the doctor, and it was all he could do not to get up and follow her.

She came back out fifteen minutes later, her eyes red, the doctor behind her. She wouldn't talk to him in the car; she kept looking down at her hands, lifting them to bite her nails. She wouldn't tell him anything. He stopped at the first Dairy Queen he saw, telling her that he didn't know about her, but he certainly needed one. But when he came back carrying two chocolate double-dipped cones, she took one look at them and started crying. He didn't know what to do with the ice cream; he hadn't really wanted one anyway, so he just dropped them into the trashcan and got back into the car and sat beside her.

"It's alive and I can't have it," she cried, and then abruptly drew herself up. "Millions of girls have abortions," she said stiffly. She started talking about how simple a procedure it was—it could be done right in the office. He'd have to come with her, though, be-cause she might need help getting home.

"Of course I will," he said.

"You hate me," she said. "You think I'm disgusting." Her voice was so flat, he turned to stare at her, astounded.

"That's what you're supposed to think about *me*," he said, and then she looked at him for a moment before turning toward the win-dow, lifting her face up to the breeze.

She was told not to eat, and to count on spending some time at the doctor's office, one hour just lying down so she could be moni-tored after the procedure. The appointment was in the morning, and she dressed up for it, in a new blue dress, in black heels she could barely walk in, her hair twisted into a knot and fastened with a silver clip. Nick, in blue jeans and an old black sweater, not wanting to take the time to shave that morning, felt grubby beside her. "You look very lovely," he told her.

"I just want to look old," she said.

Nick sat in the empty waiting room and tried not to think about what was happening to Robin. He thought about birth. He remem-bered Dore telling him how her mother had given birth to her one sulky, shiny, hot summer day while her father was at a baseball game, and even though they had had him paged, he hadn't shown up at the hospital until late that evening, when Dore's mother was asleep. He remembered Leslie telling him how one time her mother, in a rage, blamed Leslie's birth for the athritis that robbed her of her tennis career, and then felt so guilty she went out and bought Leslie a fresh box of Crayolas with a built-in sharpener and three new col-oring books. He remembered Susan's birth; he remembered Robin's, how hard it had rained that day; and then he remembered Helen nuzzling his boyish hair when he was small, telling him his birth had been a privilege.

It seemed like hours before he was allowed to go in and see Robin. "She's just fine," Dr. Nagle told Nick. "Though I'd make sure she takes it easy this week."

Robin was lying on an examining table, a light blue blanket over her, her hair coming undone from the silver clip, and when she saw him, she sat up. "I thought you had gone," she said. "I kept hearing the door."

He sat down beside her, taking her hand.

"I kept thinking and thinking," Robin said. "The whole time they were doing it, I kept thinking how I'd have to get myself up and get on the road and start hitching someplace, only I didn't know where else I could go anymore, who I could go to." She lay back against the pillow. "I'm no child of danger anymore, am I?" she said.

"Who wants you to be?" said Nick.

He sat with her that hour, while a nurse whisked in and out, cuffing Robin's forearm for pressure, bringing her something red and sweet to sip, and then eventually he helped Robin get up, he had her lean on him.

The dog was crazy at the door when he spotted Robin. He had chewed up three books and the toes of Nick's favorite cowboy boots, but rather than being the least bit ashamed, he had left his damage in the center of the living room. "It's lobotomy time for dogs," Nick warned, but the dog cheerfully ignored him and wagged his tail at Robin. "You good boy," she said.

He set Robin up on the couch downstairs because she said she didn't want to feel isolated. He rolled in the small black-and-white TV so she could watch the old movies that ran through the afternoons. He set up a small bookcase for her, filled with new books from his store. She wasn't supposed to be in bed very long. He knew some women who had an abortion in the morning and went to a film that evening, but Robin stayed prone on the couch for three days, and then four, until he began to worry. He kept asking her if she was all right, if he should drive her back to the doctor's. "I'm fine," she said, but she didn't get up, she just lay back against the pillows, staring moodily out at the night, her hands on her belly.

He began noticing how tense she sometimes got when he went out to the back with the plastic bags of garbage, when he went upstairs to shower; how she didn't seem to relax until he was back in the room with her. Sometimes her eyes were red and she'd shield them with one hand and blame it on all the books she was reading. He had the groceries delivered and tried to run his bookshop by phone, always promising to be in the next day.

In the evening, he let the dog out into the backyard. It was fenced with white picket, and the dog could run wildly without bothering the neighbors. Nick made grilled cheese sandwiches for Robin and himself, and they ate together. He waited for her to talk to him, but she was silent. After a while her silence began to make him uncomfortable, so he began to talk.

At first he thought he was just going to tell her some stories, the way he had when she was little. He thought he'd talk about the shop, about growing up in the home, maybe tell her how he had met Leslie, how he remembered her as a baby. He didn't know what it was—maybe the strangeness of having his daughter in the house with him, without Leslie, without Dore in the distance. Maybe it was just Robin's stubborn refusal to reveal her own life that made him want to reveal his.

He found himself talking. At first about places—about his first year in New York City, his slanted, grimy floor, the roaches, the way he used to like to sit out on his fire escape nights with a book and a transistor radio and a bottle of wine because he thought it was such a New York City thing to do, because for a moment, before he remembered who and what he was, it made him feel he belonged to the city, that it was all right for him to be there.

He told her how he used to sit on the steps of the Forty-second Street library at lunchtime amid the throngs, just hoping to meet someone. Sometimes on the streets he'd pretend to be lost so he could stop the first friendly face he saw and ask directions, make some contact. He told Robin how he had once lied on the subway, how he had told this perfectly nice old woman that his young wife had died in a farm accident and he had moved from Iowa to New York chiefly because there wasn't a chance of seeing a cornfield there. The woman had told him that it was all right. "My own husband ran off with my best friend when I was twenty-three years old. I was crazy in love, and I'd told my best friend every secret, everything. That, to me, is worse."

He told Robin about the trailer park—what it was like to live in a home that swayed when it got too windy, where you could hear the sounds of a family fight from halfway down the block.

Robin never took her eyes from him while he talked, and she began asking questions. But then the dog started barking, wanting to be let in, and Nick had to get up.

In all, Robin was on the couch for a week, and each night, he'd let the dog out, serve her a dinner she rarely did more than pick at, and then tell her stories. He told her about Leslie—how he had met her, how she had worried that Robin as a baby didn't like her.

"She worried about that?" Robin asked.

"Well, you weren't a cuddly baby with her," Nick said. "She took it personally."

And then he began talking about Dore—how he had met her that day in the school hall, how she had been his first love, his first friend, his first everything. He stopped, yearning back toward the past, when everything was possible.

"I know the Susan story," Robin said, her voice low. "Dore told it to me."

He looked over at her. "Well, now I'll tell you," he said. "It's my story to tell, too."

He told her about Susan, about a baby so beautiful that people would stop him just to take a look at her, a baby so precious he had to interview twenty girls before he found one he could trust to baby-sit. "She was me," he said, and then he told how he was robbed of his daughter by a thing as simple as a single breath; how in a way it had robbed him of Dore, too. "I used to watch you sleep," he told Robin. "And every breath you took just made me worry about the next."

"You left me to go back to Dore," Robin said. "I saw you. I hitched to Boston to surprise you, to be with you. I had it figured out how happy you'd be to see me, where we'd go for dinner." She sat up. "I *saw* you."

"It had nothing to do with how I felt about you," Nick said.

"How *did* you feel about me?" she cried. "You tell me how. You were with Dore and I was home with Leslie, and you were leaving us both, you were leaving *me.*"

"Who told you that?" he said. "If I were with Dore, or by myself

for the rest of my life, I'd still never leave you. I'd make sure I saw
you, that I spent time with you—"

"You were *never* with me!" Robin cried. "You were on the road,
you were at the office, you were anywhere and everywhere except
with me!" She was furious. "Leslie will never take you back," she
said. "Dore won't either."

For a moment, Nick felt something giving way inside of him, and
then he sat up a little straighter. "I know what I have and what I
don't have," he said. "You don't have to do any reminding."

She sighed, some of the anger leaving her, making her body
looser.

"You know what?" Nick said. "Any minute, you could leave me,
too. Don't think I don't know that. And don't you think I don't love
you."

Outside, the dog was barking frantically, and Nick stood up to let
him in. "I'm not going anywhere," he said to Robin. "But tomorrow
I'm going to work. I just want you to know in case you wake up late
and don't see me, that's all."

"So go to work," she said.

She was sleeping when he got up the next morning. He went to
open the bookshop, and every time he went to phone her, something came up: a new salesman wanting to deal directly with Nick; a
wrong shipment; a customer trying to resell some books he had
stolen from the shop. By the time Nick closed up, he was exhausted.
He stopped at the grocery and bought a frozen pizza and two ready-
made salads, forcing himself to believe she still might be home.

By the time he got to the front door, he could smell something
cooking inside, he could hear the dog's short, angry barks. She
opened the door in the same blue dress she had worn to the doctor's,
a wood spoon fisted in one hand. "I made dinner," she said. "I was
bored, that's why." She made him sit at the table while she set down
platters of cheese and bread, then brought out pasta in a strange
green sauce that tasted delicious. She insisted on feeding the dog
scraps from her plate.

They never discussed her staying or not staying, but every day he
woke up expecting to find her gone, and every day she was there, the

dog on her bed. She began showing up at the shop. He introduced her to the staff and let her sit in one of the chairs reading book after book. After a few days, Nick told her to make herself useful. He showed her how to unpack the books, how to check invoices and manage the stock. Once, he heard her talking to a customer, recommending books, and it made him smile.

He began to get used to her being in the shop. She never walked over with him, and she never showed up at the same time. She spent her lunch hour going home to walk and feed the dog, but she always came back. In the evening, she usually waited for Nick to close the shop, and then the two of them would walk home together, stopping at the Quick-Check to pick up something for dinner.

She was the only one of his whole staff who actually liked working the cash register, who didn't feel the need to tell every person who approached her with a few dollars and a paperback that she was really a student at the university, that she was really writing a novel due out in the fall. She didn't mind people asking her how old she was, and she wasn't afraid to confront someone she suspected of shoplifting. One afternoon she even washed out both display windows, picking out the dead flies and dusting off each book.

At the end of her first week of work, Nick handed her a check. She was baffled. "You work, you get paid," he said.

She blushed a little. She said he didn't have to do that; it wasn't as if he had really hired her. "I don't even know how long I'll be here," Robin pointed out.

He said as long as she was there, she could have the job. He watched her. He was always waiting for her to leave, and every morning he was grateful to see her at his breakfast table, rubbing her eyes, stroking the dog's rough fur.

There were pieces of her all over his house now. Pastel stockings dripping from the shower, powdered eye shadows and tubes of lipstick across her bureau. She liked heavy dime-store perfumes—Lily of the Valley, Gardenia—and because the fragrance was so strong, he could catch her scent almost as soon as she walked in. She didn't ask permission to do anything, and the only thing she refused to do was answer the phone or the door. She'd flinch as soon as she heard the ringing; she'd go and get Nick out of the shower, or from the backyard garden. She tried to talk him into getting an answering machine; she said the great thing was you always knew who was calling and you never had to speak to anyone at all if you didn't want to.

"I hate answering machines," Nick said.

She drove him crazy with the phone. He'd try to call her when he knew he was going to be late, and he never could tell if she was just ignoring the rings, or had gone out to walk the dog, or if she had left and was already standing out on the highway, her thumb jabbed out, headed for nowhere he could ever find. He made up this signal for her to know that it was him calling her. Two rings, hang up, two more rings, and she was to pick up on the third.

Sometimes, though, when he was home and picked up the phone, she would stand quietly against the long white expanse of wall and listen to him. When it was just a client, she'd turn away and go upstairs. When it was Leslie, she'd stand perfectly still until Nick had hung up. He waited for her to ask something, but she never did. He'd tell her that Leslie had sent her love, that Leslie missed her, that Leslie wished Robin would call. Robin would nod and then turn away, her face hidden from him.

At dinner one night, Nick talked about Leslie. He did it casually, as he was spooning green beans onto his plate, and he watched Robin, trying to gauge her reaction.

"What do you tell her about me?" Robin asked, picking at her food. "What do you say?"

"I say you're doing fine here. I say you seem happy. Is that wrong?"

"What else?"

"Listen," Nick said, "your life is your life to tell or to keep secret. She knows you went to California."

"The rest?" Robin asked. "Did you tell her the rest?"

"That's for you to tell if you want," Nick said. "It's your business."

Robin relaxed into her chair. "She hired a detective on me," she said.

"No," Nick said. "I did."

Robin gave him a sharp look. She was silent for a moment, and then she said, "She drove you away. She drove us both right out of the house, only I didn't have any Dore to run to the way you did."

Nick rested his head in his hands, rubbing at his forehead. "You think that's what happened?" he said quietly. "You think it's that simple? She didn't drive anybody away, least of all me."

"I can't eat this dinner," Robin said, pushing her plate away, stiffly getting up.

Robin watched the Madison teenagers sometimes, and she yearned. She wanted to be fifteen again. Really fifteen. Feeling like a kid, whispering secrets to a girlfriend or moonily smiling up at some boy she liked. She didn't want to know anymore what it was like to live with someone like you were married to him, what it was like to have been pregnant, to have had an abortion. She didn't want to know what it was going to be like to have an ex, how to live with a baby that was made up of nothing more than memory and pain, a baby that would never get any bigger than the small hopes it once generated, hopes that had died right along with it. And she didn't want to know anymore how pain could amplify, how you could suddenly find out that all the roads you had ever waited and waited to travel were dusty and dirty ones, seeded with dangers you were unprepared to face.

None of it would leave her alone. She couldn't stop thinking about the baby she had lost, about almost having been a mother. She kept away from the children's book sections at Brini's; she froze when a mother pushed a stroller through the door. The doctor had told her she was doing the right thing, that there could always be other babies, when she was ready, when she was prepared. And Nick, who made such a big deal about family, had supported her. She unconsciously took up her old habit of touching her belly, the way she had when she was newly pregnant and working at Arby's, and when she realized what she was doing, she angrily jerked her hands away.

She wanted a different kind of comfort than what Nick was giving her. She dreamed about Dore holding her, rocking her as if she were six years old and everything could be healed in a hug. She remembered Dore's hand soothing her brow; she remembered Dore before Dore had refused to see or talk to her anymore. She remembered feeling mothered.

Mothered. When she had been pregnant, she had told herself how unlike Leslie she was going to be. She had listed the ways to herself like a litany: She would never pit the baby against Douglas; she would never grow cool and then warm, but would be as constant as the stars. But when she started ticking off all the good things she would do, memories about her mother cropped up despite herself: the way Leslie had let her climb into the big bed and cuddle when she was frightened; the songs Leslie sang to her; the time Leslie taught her to drive. And then Robin's whole mood would change. She'd find herself missing her mother; she'd feel unsure and lonely and lost to herself and to everyone.

Now Leslie's calls softened something inside of her. She sometimes felt like taking the phone and crying; she sometimes wanted to tell Leslie about losing her baby, about losing Douglas.

But her confusion, her anger, got in her way. How did she know that Leslie wasn't calling her just to have a good excuse to talk to Nick? Maybe Leslie was wearing down—maybe being alone in the house was making her want Nick back, no matter where his heart really was. How could she know that she wasn't somehow being used? How could she believe that it was just herself that Leslie wanted now, herself without Nick? I'm here, not you, she thought, as if her mother were her rival.

She kept track of her mother's calls, jealous of the way any ring of the phone would make Nick look optimistic. But she noticed that Nick never stayed on the phone with Leslie very long. He said hello, he started to tell her something, and then he was cut off. "All right," he said flustered. "All *right.*" He held the phone out to Robin, and when she shook her head, stubborn, he tried to talk to Leslie again, but it was always useless. "She wants to talk to you," Nick said. "Not to me."

"Yeah, right," said Robin, doubtful.

And then, one week, the phone didn't ring at all, and she hated how deserted she suddenly felt, hated the panicky edge forming along her heart. "Well, you never want to speak with her," Nick said. "What do you expect?"

"Nothing," Robin said. "Suits me fine." But she didn't feel good at all. Not speaking to Leslie, but knowing that Leslie wanted to speak to her, was a different matter than this silence. And she knew what she expected, all right—that now that her mother didn't seem to want Nick anymore, there was really no reason for her to want Robin, either.

SEVENTEEN

• • •

But Leslie did call again. She had had a bad case of the flu, she told Nick, and it had been all she could do to drag herself from the sweaty tangle of sheets to the bathroom. She had unplugged her phone, and all the clocks, too, because even the slightest noise hurt her. She wanted to talk to Robin.

"Flu," Nick said, and Robin tentatively took the phone. Nick left the room almost instantly, and Robin sat on the kitchen stool, tense, waiting.

"Hello, angel," Leslie said. She didn't demand that Robin come home. She didn't mention that legally, she could force it. It wouldn't count if Robin wouldn't come on her own, willing to stay. She didn't pry into Robin's life with Douglas, she didn't say that the only thing that was keeping her from pressing charges against him was wanting to protect Robin from any more turmoil. And if she knew about the abortion, she kept silent on that subject, too. She said nothing about Nick at all. Instead, she asked about the dog she heard barking in the background, and she asked how Robin was. Only once did her voice break. "I wish you'd think about coming home," Leslie said. "You could just visit." When Robin was silent, Leslie sighed. "Well, thanks for talking to me, honey," she said. "I love you."

When she hung up, Robin burst into confused tears.

Robin began taking Leslie's calls, telling herself it was just an experiment, that she'd talk with Leslie only as long as she felt Leslie

258

was really interested in her. She was always a little guarded, always listened intently to what Nick said when he was on the phone with Leslie, and every time Leslie said she loved her, Robin stiffened, suspicious.

Leslie was always loving on the phone, though, and she always thanked Robin for speaking to her. Yet as soon as they hung up, Robin felt restless and miserable and unsure. She took the dog out and sprinted through the streets, trying to get so tired she wouldn't feel anything but the ache of her muscles. She knew Nick watched her when she came into the house. He always tried to make her feel better by taking her to the movies or out for ice cream. He never told her that sometimes late at night Leslie would call and weep, wanting to know what was really going on with Robin.

"She's not coming home, is she?" Leslie said. "I get dressed up every day, half expecting her to show up, wanting to look great for her. It isn't fair. It isn't even like having visitation privileges." She was silent for a moment, then said, "You want her there, don't you? This is just how you like things," and she hung up.

Before the loss, the grief, could touch him, he saw Robin walking past the back window, dancing a stick in her hand for the dog to wildly leap at, and he went out to the backyard, too. "That dog couldn't catch his own shadow," he said, grinning.

"Can too," Robin said, laughing, coming over to stand by him, so close he could smell the clean shampoo scent of her hair, feel the rough wool of her shirt. She put one arm about him, just for a moment, and he leaned down and kissed the top of her head. "Toby!" she cried, moving away, tossing the stick in an arc.

Oh, she was so there sometimes, so around him. She could run the shop by herself; he could take the whole afternoon off just to browse in the other stores, to see what the competition was doing, and when he came back, there would be money in the register that hadn't been there before. She was starting to cook a little more, too, and because she didn't believe him when he said the food was good, he ate three helpings and asked for the recipes. He liked it, seeing her, knowing she was in the house, and every time he called Leslie, he felt as if he were proving something to her. He wanted Leslie to visit, just so she could see how good he was with Robin now, and how at home Robin was.

The summer had started turning, cooling toward fall, when Robin turned restless. At first Nick thought it just had to do with the university students pouring back into town, filling up the spaces she liked empty—the banks by the river, the silent parks. They came in station wagons, their parents awkward and boisterous beside them, balancing stereo systems and sets of skis, carrying guitars and computers. They were packed into airport limos, spilling out in front of the sleek steel high-rise dorms, the shabby student housing. They didn't get their textbooks from a place like Brini's, but they came to buy the books they wanted for pleasure, and they hung out. He saw how Robin watched them, how she'd shelve books a bit closer to any one group just so she could hear what they were saying. Once, he found her leafing through a course catalog, but when she saw him watching her, she was embarrassed she put it away.

"You want to go back to school?" he asked her.

She just shrugged. "I don't know," she said. "Maybe."

"You want me to contact the school board for you?" he asked.

The more he talked about it, the more excited he got, but the more she withdrew. He said she could always go to night school if she wanted, that maybe she could just take her SAT and if she scored high enough, she could go right on to college. "I don't know," Robin said. "I don't know what I want."

I know, he felt like saying—I know what you want. But instead he just roughed her hair, just told her tonight was his turn to cook supper, and it would be ready in an hour.

She was moody a lot. One day in the bookshop she suddenly smelled this kind of piny scent, the same kind Douglas used to douse over his face mornings because he had read in some magazine that pine was the masculine scent of the Eighties. Her whole body had turned inside out when she smelled the pine. She was terrified to turn around, and even when she finally did, and saw a middle-aged woman in a blue dress, she still couldn't stop the seasickness swelling inside of her. Whenever she thought of California, on the hottest summer days in Madison—California heat—she thought of Douglas; she'd practically see him, talking to his students, maybe catching the eye of someone else who was the way she had once been, young and yearning and hopelessly, helplessly dazzled by love itself.

She began calling Leslie herself, and one night she called when

Leslie couldn't keep herself from crying. She had just gotten home from a late-night movie, sitting beside a couple who were kissing and nuzzling, practically moving their passion right into her seat, and it had made her feel so alone and miserable that she had angrily stood up, pushing past them, not caring that her popcorn drizzled across them. "Hey—" the guy had said angrily, standing, white kernels falling from his lap. "Hey up your ass," Leslie said, and then she came home and there was Robin on the phone and she couldn't contain how much she needed her.

"I miss you," she wept. "Tell me how I was a bad mother and I'll be better. Tell me what I did. Tell me how you can possibly blame me for Nick. I know you do, I feel it." She sighed. "Everyone I know is somewhere else," she said wearily. For a moment she managed to gather up some of her old undauntable cool. "Look, you can stay in a hotel if you think it will make you feel better, if you think it's somehow—I don't know—safer. I'll even pay for it."

"I miss you, too," Robin blurted.

"You do?" Leslie was quiet for a moment. "You were the absolute loveliest thing about my life with Nick," she said. "I'd look at you and I'd think, why, you were him and me. Even after everything happened, I'd still look at you, and it was like I was looking at the memory of how happy I had been, and then I was looking at this separate, unique person that I had actually carried and talked to, that I had promised everything to.

"You know, when I was carrying you, I used to read all these books about parenting. I'd read them all the way through, right up to the chapters on adolescents, on young adults. It was always so sad, so odd to get to that chapter, to have all that growth abruptly stop, like your child's life ended when she hit eighteen, like you were supposed to just disappear.

"Anyway, I read them, I swore to myself that when you turned eighteen—when you turned sixteen—I wasn't going to be the kind of clutchy mother they warned about—I wasn't going to hold you back from anything. I did some things right. I never made you clothing identical to mine, though I certainly could have. I had clients who used to offer me all sorts of money to do it for them and their daughters, but I wouldn't. I couldn't. It was just one of my principles.

"Oh, I was so determined not to cling, never. But the thing was, I never *had* you, I never did, so how could I let you go? How could I be magnanimous about any of it?" Leslie started to cry again. "I'm your mother. I don't care what the books say, I can't be your friend. Not if I stood on my head. I love you. Can't you just come home to try it out, to test the waters? You're going to be living on your own soon enough, lost in all that space after the chapters of those child-care books end." She stopped for a moment. "You can be with me, can't you? You can come home. And, baby, I promise, you can go back to your father if you want."

"You hate him," Robin said.

Leslie sighed. "No, I don't hate him. Not really. How can you hate someone you loved, someone you lived with? And anyway, it doesn't matter what I feel—it doesn't have to have anything to do with what you feel."

"I don't have Douglas anymore," Robin said. She started to say something about the baby, about the abortion, about how she couldn't even walk past the doctor's street anymore. She folded inward around the pain. "Like mother, like daughter," she said.

"No, it isn't like that at all," Leslie said. "My pain is my pain and don't you take it from me." Her voice softened a little. "And yours is yours," she said. "Listen, you think on it. Call it a visit, a trial run, whatever you want."

Robin was torn. She kept thinking about going home, about how it would be to live in the house again, to stay in her old room, with her old things, to be surrounded by all the trappings of her old self. She could *feel* fifteen again, couldn't she? And she kept thinking about Leslie, and the more she thought about her, the more she missed her mother. She could try to go home, couldn't she? She could look at it as just the next step in her experiment with Leslie, working things out, a day at a time if she wanted.

She was scared, though, to tell Nick she wanted to go home. She was afraid that all she had to do was say that she wanted to be someplace else—even for a while—and he'd withdraw, he'd change. She could go to Pittsburgh, but what if she wanted to come back to him as soon as she set foot in Leslie's house? What if she hitched all the way back to Madison and found the house sold, empty—found Brini's suddenly renamed something trashy and foreign, remodeled with white Formica shelves, the display windows thick again with dead flies? What if she were never able to find Nick again?

She kept her fear lodged inside of her, hard as a nut, until one night, choking, she burst into tears.

"What is it?" Nick asked, alarmed, moving to her, making her flinch away from him, knowing if he so much as touched her, she'd never get the words out, never be able to risk saying anything. When she stammered it all out, he stiffened. He was the one to step back. "For good?" he asked.

"No, not for good," Robin said, sluicing back her tears. "Just for a while. Just for now. I . . . I miss her."

He was so still, so silent, it made her afraid. "I'm going to start missing *you* as soon as I leave," she said.

"Good," he said. "I want you to miss me. Then you won't be able to help yourself, you'll have to come back."

She looked up at him. "Is it all right?"

He touched the side of her face. "Why wouldn't it be?" he said, and then he drew her to him, he rocked her, and let her weep in his arms.

When Robin left, she left as if it were just a vacation, with no permanence attached. She cleaned up her room, but only a little. She left her old sheets rumpled on the bed, her paperbacks scattered on the dresser, their pages open and laid facedown because she never could manage to find a bookmark, their spines hopelessly cracked. She left her favorite denim shirt in the closet, her beaded belt that said TEPEE TOWN across the back. She also planned to leave the dog.

She told herself the dog had a whole green backyard to play in, and that he'd be company for Nick, but really she wanted the dog there so Nick would remember her every time he filled the dog's water dish, every time he let Toby in and out the back door. There was also the fact that Nick wouldn't be able to leave Madison without telling her, because the dog was still hers and she would have to be the one to decide what to do about him. When she cried now, she told Nick, fiercely, that she was crying because she had to leave the dog, because Leslie didn't like pets.

"Don't you leave that mangy thing with me," Nick said.

"Why not?" she asked, startled.

"He's a one-person mutt," Nick said. "And anyway, if I'm going to have to miss one of you, I might as well miss both."

So she made plans to take the dog, but still, she continued to leave pieces of herself all over the house. Books and clothing, a splash of perfume on the hallway rug. He knew perfectly well she didn't have to leave one thing for him to fill with her presence, but he never stopped her—he'd take as much of her as she'd leave him.

When Nick called Leslie, it surprised him that she thought he had been the one to prod and encourage Robin to go back to her. She kept thanking him, laughing and talking, full of plans. "I love you for this," she said. She said that now she would be the one to call with progress reports, and that he was free to call Robin anytime he liked—it would be all right; they could all be civilized. "She can visit you anytime she likes. Anytime," said Leslie.

Nick kept silent. He didn't tell her that he hadn't done one bit of pushing; that if anything, he had begun to think of Robin as truly and miraculously his.

He was the one now to sit in the kitchen when Leslie called, the one to listen while Robin now did the talking, her voice low and halting. "I will," she kept saying, and he wondered, I will what? He listened to her reciting back the plane reservations Leslie had made and paid for, the time schedules, but he kept his feelings against his chest, tried to casually sip his coffee, to nod happily at Robin when she shyly looked over at him.

When she got off the phone, she sat beside him, she started to say something, and then stopped, biting down on the corner of her lip. "Listen, I could go for a good stiff ice cream," she said. "Want to walk to the student union with me?"

He didn't want ice cream, didn't want to have to get up and stretch his legs into movement, but he wanted to be with her as much as he could now, so he stood. He went with her and got two scoops of ice cream he never even tasted before he threw it, melting, into the trash.

The night Robin left, she made Nick promise to disappear. She didn't want him driving her to the airport; she didn't want him around when her cab came. "No goodbying," she said. "That isn't what this is about." She didn't want to think about his standing there in one place while she was moving on to another. She wanted Nick to go out, and when he came back, when she wasn't there, he could imagine she'd just slipped out to the market for something for their dinner, he could imagine her returning any moment.

So he gave her that last gift. He walked all over the city, forcing himself not to think, not to look at his watch and measure out the minutes, thinking this is when she'd catch her cab, this is when she'd get her boarding pass, this is when she'd be in the plane. He walked to the capitol, and then to the student union, and then into the suburbs, dark and silent with night.

At one point, he stopped at the Regency, the old movie theater that he and Robin used to frequent. It never seemed to show anything but the cheapest kinds of horror movies, and although he preferred the foreign films and classics the student co-ops showed for a buck, he'd come here every time the movie changed because his daughter loved to be scared, and because she liked him to go with her. They didn't change the movies very often, and the film that was now playing—*Night of the Famished Dead*—was the last film he had seen with Robin. Splashed across the poster in front was a warning: You couldn't get in without a special vomit bag the usher would hand you; and once the film started, you couldn't leave lest you reveal one terrifying second of the plot. He remembered the usher had completely forgotten the vomit bags—Robin had had to remind him. The movie hadn't been scary at all, but Robin had brought home both vomit bags and kept them in her top drawer.

He touched the poster, remembering, and then he walked on. Past the woods where the botany students were always collecting leaves and muttering the names of the shrubs and trees to themselves, past the center of town, and over toward the lake. All the time he kept reciting to himself, like some secret litany, These are my boundaries—this is what I can own.

He kept walking, faster and faster, and when he got closer to the lake, the wind sprang up and stung the tears from his eyes. He thought about the fall here, turning into winter. "Nine o'clock nights," they called them here. Nights when it got too cold to go out, when the wind was so strong it had once pushed a small girl into the path of a car. It had been in the papers—last year, he remembered—and although the girl had only been scratched up a bit, the whole thing scared people so they stayed close to the trees when they walked, or kept a grip along the chain link fences. It had made the college kids giddy in their boldness, and sometimes they would link arms and play snake in the wind, winding in and out. There were warnings for people with respiratory ailments to stay indoors. You could sometimes see people trudging in the snow, white surgical masks warming the air they breathed, insulating them.

It made him think of Pittsburgh, one terrible summer when there had been some sort of failure at one of the mills. The home had put surgical masks on all the babies. They had tried to put them on the boys, but the kids wrenched them off, angry at being asked to take on another thing that would make them different from other children.

Nick thought suddenly that maybe winter would be good—maybe a cold, bony freeze might slow down feeling, might stun pain itself into a kind of woozy hibernation. There was hope in thinking that. Abruptly, he stopped walking. He was exhausted. He turned, toward the home he owned, the home he had shared with his daughter, and moved toward it.

EIGHTEEN

• • •

L eslie had spent three whole hours at the brightly lit Giant Eagle trying to decide what foods she should buy for Robin's homecoming. She wheeled her cart up and down every aisle, tumbling in boxes of pastel ice cream, plastic bags of cookies, soda pop and luncheon meats. It wasn't until she was at the counter, and paying for all the food, watching its steady slide down the conveyer belt, that she felt suddenly depressed. Look at it. It was all the kinds of food an eleven-year-old kid ate, but foods Robin at eleven never touched, let alone asked for. Every item passing her now seemed like just another part of her that Robin could reject.

There were four brown bags, and she struggled home with them, unloaded them. Then she cleaned the house, debating the logic of keeping Robin's room exactly the way it had been left, or changing it, buying a new spread, new curtains. In the end, she did nothing to it at all, not even dust.

She kept telling herself, this was a girl who had been living with a man, who had done God knew what else. She wasn't an ordinary kid anymore. She sat down, dreaming, realizing that what she really wanted returned to her was a baby, who clung to her skirts, who sucked at her breasts, who cried out for her in the endless deep quiet of the night. She wanted a runny nose to swab dry; the effortless pilings of laundry; the hand that reached out to hold hers; the damp, open mouth that cried when she wasn't there. Oh, Lord, she thought, fool that I am.

267

She sat out on the front stoop to wait for Robin. Robin had told her not to come out to the airport, that she'd take a limo, and Leslie knew her well enough not to argue. When the cab drove up, Leslie stood, her heart expanding so she thought her chest would break open. Then Robin stepped out, looking ragtaggled and tired, a dog beside her, growling low in his throat as Leslie slowly walked toward them, willing her face to stay calm. It was Robin who was suddenly crying, who wrapped both arms about her, and this time Leslie was careful to be the one to release her grip first, to step back, and to beam.

"And just who is this?" she asked, narrowing her eyes at the dog.

"He's with me," Robin said. "Toby, good boy, sit."

"Well, I guess he's with me, too, then," Leslie said. She lifted one hand and gently petted the dog's head. "How much?" she said to the cabdriver, but Robin was already fanning bills into his hand, and Leslie thought suddenly, Now it begins.

It wasn't what either one of them expected. At first they were careful about each other, almost too polite. Robin spent a lot of time in her room. She put on the clothes she had left behind, but they didn't feel comfortable, didn't seem to quite fit anymore. She tried playing her old albums, but halfway through, the music would begin to irritate her and she'd shut it off.

She didn't know what to do with herself a lot of the time, and she hung around Leslie, who never mentioned what had happened in the past, who acted as if a time warp had occurred, as if Robin had just stepped out one day to go to the market, and here it was ten minutes later and she was home. She said "I love you" a lot to Robin, and Robin tried to trust it, tried to relax. She didn't see how Leslie sometimes sat up nights by herself, rocking in the chair that her own mother used to rock her in when she was a baby. Leslie never let Robin know how much she wished Robin would be the one to say "I love you," to surprise her with it. And she never for one moment let Robin see that every time she looked at her daughter, she saw something of Nick, and it hurt.

Robin called Nick every week, walking down to Walnut Street and using the pay phone at the Gazebo coffee shop. She had to shout over the din and squeeze close to the phone so people could jam in and out. It was hard talking to Nick. As soon as she heard his voice, she felt as if she had made the wrong decision, as if she should get on a plane and go back to Madison.

She didn't like hearing that he had hired a "temp" to take over her duties at Brini's, even when he assured her that the new person wasn't a fifth as good as she had been. He told her everyone at the shop missed her, that the salesmen asked for her every time they came in, that the bats in the attic were cranky without her.

"Oh, they are not," said Robin, pleased.

"I miss you," Nick said. "I love you," and she pulled in a breath. He kept asking her questions she couldn't answer: How was she doing with Leslie? What did it feel like to be back in Pittsburgh? She couldn't bring herself to hang up, and would have just stayed on the phone, feeding quarters into the slots, if two boys hadn't started jostling her impatiently.

As soon as she gave up the phone, she felt the pull of Madison leaving her; she saw the Gazebo, she remembered Leslie, and she went to buy a cheesecake—blueberry, the kind Leslie liked. Then she walked home, hoping Leslie was there, feeling good because she had such a hope.

Leslie was indeed home, sewing. She stopped to smile at Robin and got up to fix something for the dog, who still eyed her suspiciously. "Goodness," Leslie said, "it's tuna in springwater, better than most dogs get."

Robin held out the cheesecake. "Just what I want," Leslie said, beaming.

What Robin began to want was to go back to school. She kept thinking how nice it would be to have her days planned out for her, to have fixed schedules and rules, boundaries you couldn't cross. Still, she hedged: She was going to be eighteen in a few months; she'd stick out; she wouldn't be accepted. She would have given the whole idea up, but she kept yearning.

When she broached the idea to Leslie, Leslie looked up at her. "I think that's great," she said, "but you left in your sophomore year— they might want you to repeat that whole grade."

"I can't go back to that school!" Robin cried, alarmed.

270   CAROLINE LEAVITT

"Listen," Leslie said, "that half-finished coat lying right in the next room belongs to a client who's on the school board. She'll know what programs are available for you. Adult education—whatever you want. I can call her right now."

When Robin nodded, Leslie smiled, buoyant. There were still things she could do for Robin. She called her client, and when she hung up she had the names of three different programs. High School Equivalency—GED, they called it. Robin wouldn't have to set foot in a traditional classroom if she didn't want to.

Leslie set it up for her—a program at a private school, classes of ten adults, every day from ten to three. Three Rivers Institute, it was called, and it was right across the street from Kaufmann's, so Robin could poke around and shop afterward, buy herself some little thing as a reward.

"Is it all right?" Leslie demanded.

"It's fine," Robin said, and she turned, so Leslie couldn't see how scared she suddenly felt.

She practiced feeling confident. She stared at her face in the mirror, willing the fear away. Whenever she talked to Nick, she made him remind her of how well she had helped him run the store. "No one dared to steal a thing when you were around," Nick said. "The terror of Brini's." Then he told her he loved her, he missed her, and that made her feel better, too.

Robin dressed in one of Leslie's blue wool dresses and took the bus to Three Rivers. As soon as she walked in, she felt like turning around and walking out. It was really just one big room, with gray, peeling linoleum and white walls, a series of wood tables pushed together in front of a long blackboard. People were already sitting, talking, and none of them looked anything like Robin. There were two women in their fifties, both in print dresses, passing a lipstick. There were a few men in shirts and ties, and there was one boy, who looked younger than Robin, in torn jeans, who stared angrily at the floor. Robin sat down at the end of an empty table, looking at her bitten nails. This was not being fifteen again; this was not where she had left off.

The classes were terrible. The teacher was an impatient woman, not much older than Robin, and she talked too fast. The material was endless—a series of twenty-five pamphlets on grammar, arithmetic, and reading comprehension. Robin didn't see why she had to learn the things she knew already, why she had to wait and wait for someone else to figure out what the subject of a sentence was, what the verb was. She shot up her hand so many times, the teacher sarcastically suggested that Robin give others a chance. "We all know how smart you are," she said, which set something boiling in Robin. By the time they moved on to the arithmetic, which was really nothing more than word problems with addition and subtraction, Robin felt ill.

At the end of the class, she got up and asked the teacher if she could just take the GED test cold. She said she was sure she could pass it—that she probably could have passed it back in third grade.

The teacher gave Robin a long, cool look. "So you think you can pass it, do you?" she said. "Well, you need sixteen hours of this class before I'll even allow you to look at the test. Now, have you had sixteen hours?"

Robin wouldn't ever have more than the three hours she had managed to tolerate that day. She came home and took off Leslie's dress. Then she made a careful list of all the high schools in Pittsburgh and asked Leslie if she would call them to see if they would let her attend.

There were problems. Zoning restrictions. If Robin wanted to attend a certain school, she'd have to live near it. Leslie would never be able to bring herself to give up the house that had been handed down to her, the one thing she always felt was really hers, and it would cost too much for Robin to have her own apartment. Besides, none of the schools much liked the idea of a student living on her own in an apartment; they said it set a poor example for the others.

In the end, Robin realized that if she wanted her high-school education now, she would have to go back to her old school. It made her dizzy. She tried to talk to Leslie about it, but Leslie told her that it was her decision, and that whatever she decided was perfectly fine. She talked to Nick, who said only how proud he was that she even wanted to go back to school, and that he knew how difficult a thing like that could be.

Panicky with impatience, she was about to hang up when he started telling her how he had made it through his own high-school years. He had made it a point to dress differently, with his black sweater, his sunglasses, and his cigarettes. He had prided himself on the fact that he didn't fit in at the home, that he was different. "Unique," he called it.

She listened to him, and realized that she could do that, too. She could swagger her way through school without letting any of it wound her where she was still tender. She could be her father's daughter.

Robin was eighteen when she finally reentered her sophomore year. She asked Leslie to design her some clothes, something very different. Leslie was delighted. She hadn't made anything for Robin since Robin was a baby, and it touched her that Robin had asked. It made it very important to her that what she designed be wonderful. It also gave her a chance to show Robin what she could do. Robin would see how the owners of the fabric stores fell all over Leslie as soon as she walked in, how they saved the imported silks, the special linens for her because they knew what she could do with them.

Leslie spent hours taking Robin's measurements, drawing sketches for her. Robin would peer down at the drawings. "I can't tell . . ." she said. But Leslie held up one hand. "I can," she said.

Leslie stayed up nights sewing. Sometimes she'd wake Robin to come downstairs and try something on. She'd hold her breath just watching her girl touch the fabrics. She'd make her stand very still while she draped on extra pieces, while she tucked in the cloth with her fingertips, making the fit right.

The clothes were unusual. Fluid jersey dresses; pants that draped and tied and snapped; everything in the deep, dark colors Leslie always thought were more provocative than brights. Leslie tried to be cool, to steel herself for Robin's reaction. She doesn't like them, she thought, watching Robin squint, feeling her own mouth start to tremble. She hates them.

Robin wrapped her arms about herself and then tentatively reached out and touched each dress, each skirt. "Oh, God," she whispered to Leslie, and when she looked up her face was bright. "These are fantastic."

"What did I tell you?" Leslie said.

She was so pleased, so proud, that all week, whenever Robin was out of the house, she'd go into Robin's room and just look at the things she had designed for her, she'd see how they were hung in the closet, and then she'd feel giddy with a pleasure that lasted all day.

Robin took a city bus rather than the school bus to school. She didn't want more contact than she would be forced to endure. When she got off the bus, two blocks from the school, she walked with her head very high. Like a dancer. Like Nick striding into Marks, she thought suddenly, remembering the stories he had told her.

Even if she weren't who she was, she would have stood out in school. No one else was wearing clothing like hers, no one else had the kind of shoes Leslie had ferreted out from the wholesale theatrical shops she liked to frequent. The other kids were in frayed jeans and T-shirts and high-top Converse All Stars. Robin walked down the hallways and felt the stares, heard the whispers. She didn't recognize a single face—her old class was gone, and this new crop was strange to her. But even so, they somehow seemed to know her. She'd see groups of kids nodding to one another as she passed. Once, she saw a girl actually pointing her out, and heard her say clearly, "Mr. Nylon," and then, "That's the one—that's her," and the others huddled around to hear the rest.

Robin had thought at first that if she tried to be friendly, that might ease things, but she hadn't realized that an eighteen-year-old sophomore would be such an anomaly. The three years' difference might have been twenty, and her experiences seemed to doom her to solitude. She might as well have been a Martian for all she had in common with the others. She overheard conversations. Kids worried about whether to call up and hang up on a boy they liked, whether to pretend to have lost a class ring rather than have to give it back. They discussed in detail who was putting out and with whom and how; who would let you; and who had birth-control pills to pass out as casually as sticks of gum. It all made Robin feel so old, so distant from everything, because none of that meant anything to her anymore. All of it seemed just like memory.

It was different with her teachers. Most were kind, welcoming her back as if she had been on vacation and praising her for trying so hard. Only one teacher gave her any sort of grief. His name was Robert Engles. He taught math, but he had Robin for study hall every day at three. He had been a friend of Douglas's. They'd palled around after school and played softball in Schenley Park, and once or twice, Douglas had told Robin, they had double-dated. Robert was always going from woman to woman, Douglas said; he liked having three-month relationships that never went any farther than Friday night dates and Saturday breakfasts.

He hadn't known that Douglas was seeing Robin—he hadn't even suspected Douglas liked her, let alone that he would run off with her. But no one in the school believed that he hadn't known what was going on, so they made him share some of the blame, some of the stigma. The principal had called him in to question him, to remind him what effect scandal had on tenure. And now, there was Robin, that girl in his study hall, back here where Douglas couldn't be anymore. He treated her as though she were taking up someone else's rightful place, as indeed he thought she was. He sniped at her when he caught her dreaming. "This is study hall. So study," he said. He didn't have to mention Douglas; his disdainful look was enough to make her feel small.

No one really talked to her. She knew she had a reputation. Some of the boys followed her. One or two asked her out, their stance defiant, and when she refused, they whispered things under their breath at her. She began taking her time leaving her classes, going out into the hallway only when the few kids there were rushing to class and had no time to stop to stare at her. She ate her lunch in the girls' bathroom or in empty classrooms, hiding from the school monitors.

It was funny to have homework to do again, to have this routine, but she found she liked it. It felt safe and stable. She'd come home and Leslie would have a snack waiting and all kinds of funny stories and gossip to tell her. The two of them would sit at the table and talk and eat until Leslie went back to work and Robin started her studying. She sat at the kitchen table, spreading out her math books, her biology texts, and all the time she felt as if she were practicing what it was like to be fifteen years old again, as if enough practicing might help her to get it right. She could hear Leslie sewing in the other room, and it comforted her.

Sometimes in the middle of her studying, she'd write to Nick. She told him about school, said she missed him. It was funny how just the writing made her feel reconnected to him.

He sent her letters, and as soon as they flopped in through the mail slot, she saw how Leslie's face changed. She left the letters open on the hall table, one of her hairs across them, and went out for a while. But when she came back, the letters were always right where she had left them, her hair still in place on top of them.

When Nick called, Leslie never said more than "Hello, how are you?" before passing the phone quickly to Robin. She'd get moody; she'd get her jacket and go for one of her walks, and later she'd just come over to Robin and put both arms around her, cradling her for a moment, rocking, before she released her with a quick, grateful kiss.

One night, Robin was finishing an English paper on Jane Austen when the phone rang. She picked it up automatically, sure it was Leslie, who had said when she would call, and there, across the wires, was Douglas.

"What do you want?" she asked guardedly.

"I just want to talk to you. I had to risk it. I'm allowed to be interested, aren't I?"

Robin hesitated. "You talk first," she said.

So he did, telling her about his teaching job in California, his new apartment that actually had its own outdoor pool and a communal vegetable garden. "I'm cauliflowered out these days," he told her, laughing. And then he started asking her questions. He wanted to know about living with Nick, about living with Leslie. Did she have curfews? Did they hit her? Were they ashamed?

"What are you talking about? They were never ashamed," Robin said hotly. "You're the only one who was ashamed."

"Oh, have it that way, then," he said.

"I'm back in school," she said proudly. "The same one."

"You're kidding!" he said, impressed. She felt his interest washing over her, and he launched into more questions. But all of them seemed to center on the past. Did she still wear those Mary Janes she used to wear, the ones that clicked on the floor so you always knew she was coming? Did she still carry her books clutched against her chest the way the junior-high-school kids did, to hide the fact that they didn't have much in the way of breasts yet? "Do you still sit in the front row and squint at the board? Do you still take your lunch in a brown paper bag?"

"It's different now," she said.

"Lord, I remember your curls bent over the microscope, the way you always were sucking on Lifesavers, telling me it was because of a sore throat so I wouldn't make you toss it into the wastebasket."

"That was a long time ago," she said, her voice flattening.

"You were so cute."

"You only like me when I'm a *girl*, don't you?" Robin said abruptly. "You only like me when I'm some kind of daughter, and then as soon as I stop, you don't even want to know me."

"That's not true—"

"Listen, I have to go," Robin said. "Don't call me again, all right? Just don't call me." She didn't wait for him to hang up. She gently replaced the receiver.

She was sitting on the front porch, just watching the stars spangling across the sky, when Leslie came home. She sat down beside her daughter. "Douglas called," Robin said.

"Oh?"

"I wish he hadn't," said Robin. "Now, I don't feel so good."

"Love's always a problem," Leslie said. She looked at Robin. "You still love him?"

Robin shifted. "Sometimes," she said. "When I think about how it was with him, when I remember being in that car, just driving across the country, and every five seconds he'd have to hold my hand." She looked at her hands. "No one ever loved me like that."

"Yes, they did," Leslie said.

"It's sad, isn't it, having to live without someone," Robin said.

"Yes, it is." Leslie touched Robin's hand.

"Would you ever get back together with Nick?" Robin asked.

"Would you with Douglas?" Leslie replied, and then she stood up, stretching. "Look at this night. Isn't it a beaut?" She bent to kiss Robin. "You smell good," she said.

Robin smiled, embarrassed.

"Is that my perfume?" Leslie asked.

"I'm eighteen—I thought I should wear something adult. Are you mad?"

"Baby, that's the first thing of mine you ever wanted. Douse yourself with it," Leslie said, and then she went inside, leaving Robin to sit out alone, dreaming at the stars, waiting for one to skyrocket across the night so she could wish upon it.

Leslie went to the kitchen for coffee, sitting down at the table while she waited for it to brew. She had never even liked coffee all that much, until Nick left her. Then she had drunk herself silly with it so she wouldn't sleep, so she wouldn't have to dream that she was still happy, that things were all right, that all she had to do was tilt her head and there would be her husband, smiling at her, reaching for a kiss.

She had even discovered these caffeine candies at the Rite Aid one day. "Chew a Cup of Coffee," the package said, and they came in three flavors—lime, mocha, and butterscotch. All three tasted medicinal, but she had gone through several packs a day, so jittery and hyped up that she would sew all night.

She had given the candies up when she became calmer, but she still wanted coffee all the time. She limited herself to just two cups—one in the morning, one in the evening. Otherwise she wouldn't be able to sleep, she'd be up all night, not wanting to sew, not wanting to watch TV, not wanting to do anything except the one thing she couldn't—dream in her bed.

Ah, but everything changed, everything worked itself right around. All those years when she was sure there must be some mistake, when she was sure the hospital had given her the wrong baby, because her baby wouldn't pull away from her, her baby would love her right from the start. Robin had seemed to belong to everyone but her. To her friend's family—what was that girl's name, the one with all the clothes? To that boy who had nearly killed them both. To Nick, and then—the deepest, widest hurt of all—to Dore. Leslie lifted herself up to get the coffee.

Her clients kept trying to fix her up. Why did people think one love could take the place of another? Hurt didn't end, any more than love ever did. You just tried to live with it as best you could. You watched it fade a little, but it was always there, always as much a part of you as your own heartbeat. Second helpings, she considered the men they described for her, trying to tempt her interest. Less-than-fresh second helpings.

It didn't matter. She didn't have to think about that now. Robin, her baby, was sitting outside right now, living right here, and the marvel of it was that she had come here on her own. She wasn't an adoring little girl—maybe she'd always be a little private, a little aloof—and maybe, too, Leslie would never, for the rest of her life, be able to look at her without seeing Nick. But she was here. All Leslie had to do was call her name and she would appear, smiling, just like any daughter in front of any mother. Just like normal.

For a long while Nick wouldn't touch anything in Robin's room. He couldn't bring himself to. He liked walking past her room and seeing her things still there, still in place, as if any moment she might be back. Sometimes he'd go inside and sit on her bed and think about her. He'd remember how it had been living with her and Leslie, and he missed that. Not the same way he missed Dore, but someplace different.

He went to work. He ate dinner with Jack sometimes, or with a neighbor down the street. He sat in the Lamplighter eating cold pizza, and he wrote Robin.

She wrote him back. She called. She was happy. She said she was back in school; she was even getting along with Leslie. It was so funny. He had been sure that as soon as she set foot in the house, the old problems would curl back around and eventually she'd come and live with him for good. He had carried that scenario around with him, because really, what other one did he have? Dore was gone, and Leslie's only connection with him was through Robin. But Robin's letters had dwindled, her calls grew less frequent, and then her last letter had said that she was thinking of going to summer school in Pittsburgh. As soon as he read that, he felt his heart being squeezed slowly shut.

He went up to clean her room, to put her things away. He sat down on her bed and he thought, well, at least he had done something right and good in his life, at least he had put a finish to the damage he had been doing to his daughter, and that was something, wasn't it?

He was lonely with her room so clean and bare. The house seemed newly empty, and he thought about getting a boarder to fill in the spaces. It didn't work out so well, though. He had one young girl who looked nothing like Robin but who still made him think he had his daughter back whenever he passed her room at night and heard the music going. In the end, the girl left after only one month, apologizing profusely, explaining that she wanted to live with her boyfriend because it would be rent-free. "Of course," Nick said, "I know," and he helped her carry her stereo system down to her boyfriend's car.

He didn't see Susan in the steam of the bathroom anymore. Now when he fumbled for a towel from the shower, he always thought he saw Robin, and he was sure he heard her in the creaks the house made at night. He had left her so many times, but he never thought she'd leave him, too.

He hadn't heard from her in three weeks and had just decided to call her when the phone rang, startling him. When he picked it up, there she was, asking if it would be all right if she spent her summer with him in Madison—if maybe she could even go to summer school there. "Leslie said she'd pay for it," she added. When he didn't answer, she said, "It's not all right?"

"Come," he said. "Your room's all ready for you and that itchy mutt of yours."

"My room," she said, delighted.

When he hung up the phone, he just sat there in the kitchen, resting both arms on the table, amazed that she was really coming back. Frozen, he was frozen. And then he suddenly remembered this game she had loved to play when she was a little girl. Red Light. He'd stand out in front of her, ten feet away on the tarry driveway, and he'd hide his eyes and turn his back to her. He'd call, "One . . . two . . . three . . ." and all the time she'd be moving toward him as fast as her legs would move her, and as soon as he barked out "Red light!"—as soon as he whipped around to try to catch her moving— she'd freeze in place, contorted. The whole game was her moving toward him in stops and starts, frozen in place half the time, and then when she reached him, she would squeal, "I have you! I have you!" and wouldn't let go, even when he swung her up in a playful arc, even when he gently set her down. The only way to pry open her fingers was to say yes, yes, they could play again, one more time, before they had to go in for dinner. They'd change places, and then he'd be the one moving toward her, he'd be the one paralyzed by her eyes.

It was night, the sky riddled with stars, a night so quiet you could imagine families in the houses in the neighborhood, you could hear the mothers calling their kids into supper, the fathers coming home from work. Slowly, he got up and he got the cleaning supplies from under the cabinets. He took everything upstairs to her room, to clean it, to put her things back into place, to make the room ready for her homecoming.